# Parenting Beliefs, Behaviors, and Parent–Child Relations

# Parenting Beliefs, Behaviors, and Parent–Child Relations

## A CROSS–CULTURAL PERSPECTIVE

EDITED BY

## Kenneth H. Rubin
## Ock Boon Chung

Psychology Press
New York • Hove

Published in 2006 by
Psychology Press
Taylor & Francis Group
711 Third Avenue
New York, NY 10017

Published in Great Britain by
Psychology Press
Taylor & Francis Group
27 Church Road
Hove, East Sussex BN3 2FA

First issued in paperback 2013

International Standard Book Number-10: 1-84169-438-X (Hardcover)
International Standard Book Number-13: 978-1-84169-438-2 (Hardcover)
International Standard Book Number-13: 978-0-415-65066-3 (Paperback)
Library of Congress Card Number 2004031082

### Library of Congress Cataloging-in-Publication Data

Parenting beliefs, behaviors, and parent-child relations : a cross-cultural perspective / edited by
  Kenneth H. Rubin & Ock Boon Chung.
      p. cm.
      Papers from a three day workshop sponsored by the International Society for the Study of
      Behavioural Development, held at Seoul National University, South Korea, June 2003.
    ISBN 1-84169-438-X (alk. paper)
    1. Parenting--Cross-cultural studies--Congresses. I. Rubin, Kenneth H. II. Chung, Ock Boon.

HQ755.8.P379128 2005
306.874--dc22                                                              2004031082

Taylor & Francis Group
is the Academic Division of Informa plc.

Visit the Taylor & Francis Web site at
http://www.taylorandfrancis.com

and the Psychology Press Web site at
http://www.psypress.com

# Contents

# Preface

The responsibilities of parents are probably too numerous to count. But among the many parenting responsibilities we can include such matters as having to think about developmental milestones and trajectories and having to contemplate appropriate and acceptable ways to help children reach these milestones in a normative fashion and at a normative pace. Parents must somehow translate their thoughts into action while at the same time ensuring that the relationships they are developing with their children are physically healthy and psychologically secure. For years, researchers have been studying parental thoughts, feelings, behaviors, and the relationships they form and maintain with their children. Much of this research has been focused directly on the parent. But researchers are also determined to demonstrate that parents' cognitions about children and child-rearing, parenting behaviors, and the quality of parent–child relationships actually contribute to the well- or ill-being of their offspring. In short, researchers the world over often find themselves in the business of demonstrating that parents matter.

The purpose of this book is to present a rather simple argument. Parents' thoughts about child-rearing and the ways in which they interact with children to achieve particular parenting or developmental goals are culturally determined.

Within any culture, children are shaped by the physical and social settings within which they live, culturally regulated customs and child-rearing practices, and culturally based belief systems. The bottom line is that the psychological "meaning" attributed to any given social behavior is, in large part, a function of the ecological niche within which it is produced. Clearly, it is the case that there are some cultural universals. All parents want their children to be healthy and to feel secure. However, "healthy," at least in the psychological sense of the term, can have different meanings from culture to culture. For example, in many Asian countries, a parental goal is to socialize a quiet, compliant, reserved child. Such a goal, if met, appears to ensure the acceptance of adults and peers in the child's social community. And yet, in North America and Southern Europe, such a goal, if met, would result in peer rejection and difficulty in the social world. Consequently, North American and Southern European parents appear to have as a parenting goal, the socialization of the potentially gregarious, outgoing child. In short, adaptation is culturally defined.

Put another way, if a given behavior is viewed as acceptable, then parents will attempt to encourage its development; if the behavior is perceived as maladaptive or abnormal, then parents (and significant others) will attempt to discourage its growth and development. Of course, the very means by which people go about encouraging or discouraging the given behavior may be culturally determined and defined. Thus, in some cultures, the response to an aggressive act may be to explain to the child why the behavior is unacceptable; in others, physical discipline may be the accepted norm; in yet others, aggression may be ignored or perhaps even reinforced.

All in all then, it would appear most sensible, for the international community of child development researchers, not to generalize to other cultures their own culture-specific theories of normal and abnormal development.

In an effort to shed light on the culture of parenting and on parenting from a cultural and cross-cultural perspective, a group of internationally esteemed scholars from Asia, Europe, and North America was invited to share and exchange information at a workshop sponsored by the *International Society for the Study of Behavioural Development*. The three-day meeting took place at Seoul National University, South Korea, in June, 2003. An audience of primarily Asian scholars interested in the study of parents and parenting was led in discussion by those scholars whose chapters appear in this volume.

The intellectually stimulating three-day meeting of scholars and the publication of this book would not have been possible without the financial support of the *International Society for the Study of Behavioural Development*, the Korea Research Foundation, the Korean Association of Child Studies, and Seoul National University. We gratefully acknowledge their assistance. Special thanks are also extended to those who devoted their precious time to the organizational matters required to bring together scientists from many countries.

We sincerely hope that you, the reader, find the contents of this volume sufficiently stimulating to join us in our quest to better understand parenting from a cultural and cross-cultural perspective.

**Kenneth H. Rubin**
College Park, Maryland

**Ock Boon Chung,**
Seoul, South Korea

# Contributors

**Marian J. Bakermans-Kranenburg,** Leiden University

**Marc H. Bornstein,** National Institute of Child Health and Human Development

**Charissa S. L. Cheah,** University of Maryland

**Xinyin Chen,** University of Western Ontario

**Ock Boon Chung,** Korea University

**Hyun Sim Doh,** Ewha Womans University

**Jacqueline J. Goodnow,** Macquarie University

**Sara Harkness,** University of Connecticut

**Paul Hastings,** Concordia University

**Sheryl A. Hemphill,** Center for Adolescent Health, Murdoch Children's Research Institute University of Melbourne

**Marinus H. Van IJzendoorn,** Leiden University

**Kwang-Woong Kim,** Sookmyung Women's University

**Alida LoCoco,** Università di Palermo

**Sung-Yun Park,** Ewha Womans University

**Kenneth H. Rubin,** University of Maryland

**Abraham Sagi-Schwartz,** University of Haifa

**Ann Sanson,** University of Melbourne

**Deepali Sharma,** Government Home Science College

**Charles M. Super,** University of Connecticut

**Gisela Trommsdorff,** University of Konstanz

**Suman Verma,** Government Home Science College

**Chong-Hee Yoon,** Dongduk Women's University

**Carla Zappulla,** Università di Palermo

# I

## Culture and Parenting

# 1

# The Place of "Culture and Parenting" in the Ecological Contextual Perspective on Developmental Science

MARC H. BORNSTEIN AND
CHARISSA S. L. CHEAH

## INTRODUCTION

Human beings do not grow up, and adults do not parent, in isolation, but in multiple contexts (Bornstein, 2002; Bronfenbrenner, 1999; Lerner, Rothbaum, Boulos, & Castellino, 2002). In this chapter, we discuss the several ecological contexts in which children develop and parents parent so that we can better understand how different contexts of development influence childhood and parenthood.

Figure 1.1 shows the main ecological settings in which child development and parenting take place. Parent–child relationships are at the heart of the ecological contextual view; however, parent–child relationships are themselves embedded in a mesosystem of broader contexts, such as the extended family, peers, school, and neighborhood. In turn, the family shapes and is shaped by the community of exosystem influences including the workplace and mass media in which it is embedded. In its turn, a macrosystem of values, laws, social class, and culture supports and encourages parenting cognitions and patterns of parent–child inter-action. Cultural prescriptions therefore shape and determine, to a great extent, the immediate contexts experienced by children, the short- and long-term goals parents have for their children, and the practices parents employ in attempting to meet those goals. In short, culture plays a major overarching role in shaping the ecology of parenting and childhood. This chapter is particularly concerned with the place of culture and parenting in the ecological contextual framework.

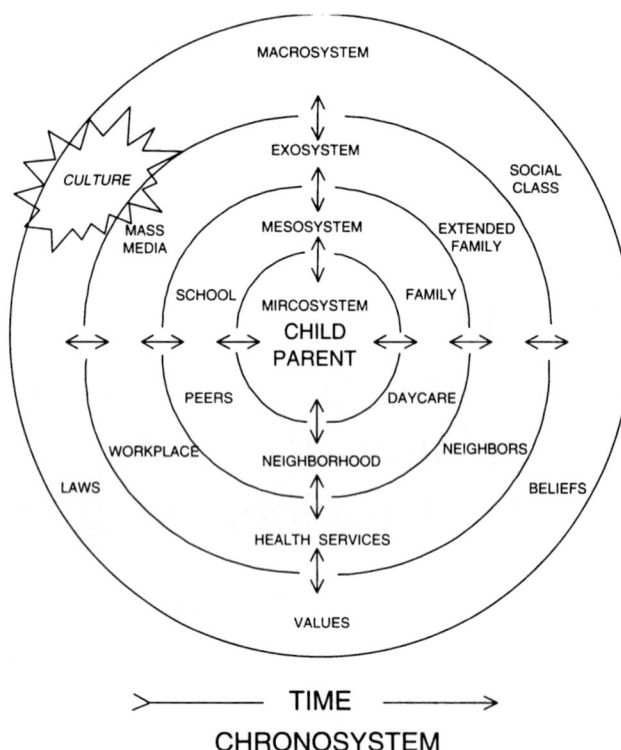

FIGURE 1.1    The contextual ecological view of development.

The child-rearing practices of one's own culture seem "natural," but some practices may actually be rather unusual in an absolute sense. Families take different forms; nuclear families represent only one of a variety of distinct social ecologies in which we find parents. Children in many cultures are tended to by a variety of nonparental care providers, whether in family day care, day care centers, villages, or fields. Situations like day care represent one of the ways in which people outside the family "parent" children in meaningful ways. Furthermore, most nations in the world are characterized by social heterogeneity; ethnic differences within countries equally color child-rearing beliefs and practices.

Parenting is at least partly culturally constructed. Some theory and research in the field of culture and parenting is concerned with how parenting expresses itself in the cultural *cum* developmental system, and other theory and research is concerned with why parenting differs across cultures. Although studies in culture and parenting have developed in several different disciplines, Harkness and Super (2002) identified a common set of assumptions underlying them.

First, studies of culture and parenting recognize the importance of settings for both children and parents. Normative cultural settings include the types of dwellings and household groups children and parents inhabit as well as the expected activities in which children and parents of different ages and sexes engage. The everyday settings in which parents and children find themselves define the parameters of their lived experiences, and those settings also embody important cultural meanings (Rogoff, 2003). Parents often choose their children's developmental settings and that process is continually renegotiated in response to the changing needs of parents themselves, children, and the environment.

Key to understanding cultural constructions of parenting and child development are, second, the activities that routinely take place within different settings. The cultural practices that define child care and child-rearing instantiate cultural themes that are important to parents, and they communicate and reinforce cultural messages.

Third, the cultural meanings inherent in both settings and activities appear to be characterized by a high level of thematicity, in that the same ideas or images (e.g., "independence" for American middle-class parents) are reexpressed on a variety of levels.

These ideas about culture and parenting have been formalized in the cultural and ecological framework of the "developmental niche" (Super & Harkness, 1986), a framework that helps to organize thinking about how the microenvironment of the child's daily life is culturally shaped. The developmental niche is conceptualized in terms of three subsystems, each of which relates centrally to parents. First are cultural variations in the physical and social settings of the child's life. The lives of children born into a group of nomadic hunter-gatherers, living in temporary homes, and spending each day in large multiage groups differ dramatically from the lives of children born into a modern Western culture, isolated at home with a single adult, and who may come into contact with a variety of individuals, few of whom are seen frequently or show much interest in the child's welfare. Second are culturally regulated customs and practices of parental childcare and child-rearing. Cultural differences in ideology influence such parenting factors as the frequency with which parents or unrelated adults care for the child, the extent to which the child is permitted freedom to explore, and whether the child's experiences are more nurturant or more restrictive, among other things.

Third is the psychology of children's caregivers. Cultural customary dimensions of parenting might include mother–child sleeping arrangements that result in very different expectations about such "norms" as sleeping through the night. These three subsystems

> . . . share the common function of mediating the individual's developmental experience within the larger culture. Regularities in the subsystems, as well as thematic continuities from one culturally defined developmental stage to the next, provide material from which the child abstracts the social, affective, and cognitive rules of the culture, much as the rules of grammar are abstracted from the regularities of the speech environment. The three components of the developmental niche form the cultural context of child development.

> (Super & Harkness, 1986, p. 552).

In this chapter, we discuss some main ideas concerned with culture and parenting. All societies prescribe certain characteristics that people are expected to possess and proscribe activities people must not engage in if they are to function adequately as members of their society. Some of these prescriptions and proscriptions might be universal across cultures, such as the requirement for parents (or specified parent surrogates) to nurture and protect children. Other standards and values might vary greatly from one cultural setting to another. In all societies, however, training children occurs, and social controls are in place, to ensure that children are "socialized"; that is, brought up in such a way that each new generation acquires prescribed patterns of beliefs and behaviors and avoids proscribed ones. When we consider culture and parenting jointly, we raise some enduring questions about each (Bornstein, 2001a). What is the nature and extent of variability in parenting? How do cultural factors relate to parenting beliefs and practices? What are the effects on children of different cultural approaches to parenting, both immediately and over the longer course of their development? To address these questions, we first set parenting in the context of the several forces that shape it.

## THE PLACE OF CULTURE AMONG DETERMINANTS OF PARENTING

A critical step on the path to fully understanding parenting is to evaluate the forces that shape it. The origins of variation in parental beliefs and behaviors are multivariate and extremely complex—Holden (1997) once identified more than 30 variables that have been found empirically to influence parenting—but certain factors seem to be of paramount importance; they may be arranged into classes of antecedents that accord with an ecological perspective (Belsky, 1984; Bornstein, 2002; Bronfenbrenner & Morris, 1998; Luster & Okagaki, 2005). They include biological processes and personality attributes of parents; actual or perceived characteristics of children; and contextual influences, including social situational factors, family background, socioeconomic status, and culture (Bornstein, 2002).

First, of course, forces within the parent shape parenting. Basic physiology is mobilized to support parenting (Corter & Fleming, 2002; Rosenblatt, 2002), and some parenting cognitions and activities initially arise around biological processes associated with pregnancy and parturition. Prenatal biological status—parental age, diet, and stress, as well as other factors such as contraction of disease, exposure to environmental toxins, and even anesthetics—also affects postnatal parenting. Furthermore, parenting reflects transient feelings and emotions as well as enduring personality traits (Vondra & Belsky, 2005).

Second, subtle as well as not-so-subtle characteristics of children influence parenting (see Hilldebrandt-Karraker & Coleman, 2005; Hodapp & Ly, 2005). So-called "child effects" may be of different kinds. Some are universal and common to all children; others will be unique to a particular child or situation. Lorenz (1935/1970) argued that universal physiognomic features of "babyishness" provoke adults to express nurturant reactions toward babies. Children's crying motivates adults to approach and soothe, and children's smiling encourages adults to stay near. Other structural characteristics of children affect parenting and the quality of parent–child interactions; child health status, gender, and age are three significant factors.

Biology, personality, and children constitute factors that influence parenting from the start. But societal factors condition and channel beliefs and behaviors of parents as well. Family structure, social class, and culture, for example, encourage diverse patterns of parenting perceptions and practices. Parents in different cultures receive many different kinds of guidance about how to rear children, whether in the form of formal sources, such as books of advice, or via informal sources, such as simply observing family examples. Advice is commonly accepted as basic truth within its own cultural context. Cultural variation in beliefs and behaviors is always impressive. As illustrations throughout this chapter attest, cross-cultural comparisons show that virtually all aspects of parenting children are informed by culture. A comparative investigation of expected developmental timetables in new mothers from Australia and Lebanon, for example, found that culture shaped mothers' expectations of children much more than other factors, such as experiences observing their own children, directly comparing them to other children, and receiving advice from friends and experts (Goodnow, Cashmore, Cotton, & Knight, 1984).

Culture influences when and how parents care for children, the extent to which parents permit children freedom to explore, how nurturant or restrictive parents are, which behaviors parents emphasize, and so forth (Benedict, 1938; Bornstein, 1991; Erikson, 1950). For example, Japan and the United States maintain reasonably similar levels of modernity and living standards, and both are child-centered societies, but the two differ dramatically in terms of history, beliefs, and child-rearing goals (e.g., Azuma, 1986; Bornstein, 1989). Japanese mothers expect early mastery of emotional maturity, self-control, and social courtesy in their offspring, whereas U.S. American mothers expect early mastery of verbal competence and self-actualization in theirs. American mothers promote autonomy and organize social interactions with their children so as to foster physical and verbal assertiveness and independence, and they promote children's interest in the external environment; by contrast, Japanese mothers organize social interactions so as to consolidate and strengthen closeness and dependency within the dyad, and they tend to indulge young children (see Befu, 1986; Bornstein, Azuma, Tamis-LeMonda, & Ogino, 1990; Bornstein, Tal, & Tamis-LeMonda, 1991; Bornstein, Toda, Azuma, Tamis-LeMonda, & Ogino, 1990; Doi, 1973; Kojima, 1986a, 1986b).

In a systems view, the development of a construct, structure, function, or process—like parenting—can be expected to be the product of interactions among multiple antecedents, including the environment and experience as well as genetics and biology. Parenting stands at the confluence of many complex tributaries of influence; some arise within the individual, whereas others have macrolevel determinants. Some reactions felt toward babies may be reflexive and universal, whereas others are idiosyncratic and vary with individual personality. By virtue of their temperament and the quality and contingency of their own responsiveness, children have a major impact on how parents parent and how parents perceive themselves as parents. In addition, however, culture looms large in shaping parenting as well.

Cultural ideology makes for meaningful differences in patterns of parenting beliefs and behaviors.

## WHY STUDY PARENTING ACROSS CULTURES

The scope of developmental science embraces both description and explanation of the nature of human behavior over the life span. Among the many perspectives from which to pursue these twin charges, the cross-cultural developmental method of comparison occupies a significant position because it encompasses the full spectrum of human variation across a worldwide context and over a life-span ontogeny. Many critics today point to culture-bound assumptions and limitations of prevailing Western psychologies. In actuality, three different cultural limitations have constrained the scope of psychological theory: a narrow participant database, a biased sampling of world cultures in its authorship, and a corresponding bias in the audience to which it is addressed (Serpell, 2000). Calls for more cross-cultural investigation echo increasingly strident critiques of the monocultural perspective (see Berry, Poortinga, Segall, & Dasen, 1992; Bornstein, 1980, 1991, 2001a; Kennedy, Scheirer, & Rogers, 1984; Tomlinson & Swartz, 2003). In response to such criticism, cultural context is achieving greater recognition in mainstream psychology, and most contemporary psychological investigators acknowledge that cross-cultural developmental inquiry is integral to understanding both substance and process in the field.

Description and explanation therefore constitute compelling reasons to undertake cross-cultural developmental comparisons. To discuss or reach conclusions about parenting outside a cross-cultural developmental framework can be short-sighted and wrong-headed. In practice, however, research has been only marginally cross-cultural or developmental in the sense of sampling adequately across place and across time. Most studies in the field compare only two cultures, the idea often being simply to incorporate "culture" as a variable in the experimental design. Yet cultures differ in many ways. By adopting pairwise comparison strategies, investigators run a risk of confounding variables over which they have no control or may even have no knowledge. In order to effect a comparative perspective, more than a single culture needs to be studied, and optimally more than two (Bornstein, 2002).

The history of investigation of child psychomotor development provides an illustrative case study of the pitfalls to which monocultural study is heir. On the basis of extensive and painstaking observations, Gesell constructed detailed cinematic atlases of what "normal" psychomotor development entails (see Bornstein, 2001b). Universal and culture-free concerns occupied Gesell, for he worked out of a maturationist theoretical framework, with very young infants, and on behaviors thought to be almost wholly under biological control. The regularity of motor development that he observed no doubt reinforced his beliefs. Gesell (Gesell & Amatruda, 1945) conceived psychomotor development to be ballistic and under unfolding genetic control. In fact, some data support a hypothesis of genetic differences or even prenatal influences among infants. Geber and Dean (1957a, 1957b), for example, found that nine-hour-old Ghandan neonates are significantly advanced in neuromuscular standing; and Tanner (1970) found that African neonates are advanced beyond Western European neonates in skeletal maturation and ossification at birth. Although Gesell's tests, and those of other developmentalists of the same ilk (e.g., Bayley, 1969, 1970; Griffiths, 1954), were continuously refined, infant testing did not reach beyond the confines of the Gesell Institute in New Haven, Connecticut, and beyond the middle-class European American society that it served until the 1940s.

The results of cross-cultural surveys among native peoples in America, in Bali, and in Africa, challenged Gesell's conclusions and undermined Gesell's assumptions. These studies showed that babies from different cultures deviated from the accepted "norms" for American middle-class society with respect to both the stages and the timing of motor development in the first years. Hopi infants begin to walk alone late (Dennis & Dennis, 1940); Balinese infants follow a different series of stages on their way to walking (Mead & MacGregor, 1951); and Ghandan, and Wolof infants tend to be more advanced in motor development than U.S. age norms would predict (Ainsworth, 1967; Geber, 1956, 1958; Lusk & Lewis, 1972; Werner, 1972). In the absence of a "generalized precocity" among infants, Super was led to study Kipsigis mothers and their parenting practices: he found that over 80 percent deliberately taught their infants to sit, stand, and walk. Rebelsky (1967, 1972) found that Dutch infants, who are stimulated less than American infants, scored lower than American infants on scales of psychomotor development. Similarly, Bovet, Dasen, and Inhelder (1974) accounted for sensorimotor retardation in Baoulé (Ivory Coast) infants relative to French babies by the fact that the African babies tend to be carried on their mothers' backs. Pertinently, Geber (1958) and Super (1976) found that African infants (Ghanda and Kipsigis, respectively) reared in the manner of European babies lose the advantage that their traditionally reared, genetically similar compatriots maintained.

Cross-cultural developmental data demonstrate that psychomotor differences among infants must reflect in some substantial degree the influence of parents' child-rearing practices and that those practices vary with culture. In retrospect, the norms of psychomotor development that Gesell strived to canonize on biological bases must be viewed as plastic (within limits) to culture and parenting.

Many reasons justify cross-cultural developmental research (Bornstein, 1991, 1995; M. Cole, 2005; Harkness & Super, 2002). First, people are always curious about development in foreign cultures, and anthropologists, sociologists, and psychologists have long sought to compare and contrast parenting children of different ages from different regions of the world (e.g., Bornstein, 1991; Bronfenbrenner, 1970; Erikson, 1950; French, 2002; Kessen, 1975; LeVine, 2003; Montagu, 1974; Munroe & Munroe, 1975; Werner, 1972). Insofar as cultural developmental descriptions of parenting attempt to encompass the widest spectrum of human variation, they are also the most comprehensive in science. They are vital to delimiting the full range of human experience, and in this sense they are also critical to establishing realistic and valid developmental norms. Psychological science has long been concerned with description in the service of defining normality and identifying abnormality. Yet "normal" for many phenomena is a relative and situation-specific concept. Before the advent of cross-cultural study, the relativity of normal was acknowledged in psychological and developmental science to only a small degree. The study of parenting across cultures provides a check against the uncritical adoption of such an ethnocentric world view and the implications of such a view. Perhaps because the first developmental scientists were Western, because they established the subject matter, and because they trained others (even non-Westerners), our acceptance of Western norms has often been too willing and ready. Needless to say, awareness of alternative modes of development sharpens our perceptions and enhances our understanding of the nature of culture, our own as well as others'.

Second, the examination of other cultures uniquely facilitates the quest to understand forces at work in parenting by exposing variables that may be influential but "invisible" from a monocultural perspective. The rationale for submitting parenting in different cultures to psychological study derives from the extraordinary and unique power cross-cultural comparisons furnish parenting science. Cross-cultural developmental study helps to explain the origins and contingent developmental course of the widest possible variety of constructs, structures, functions, or processes in parenting. This type of analysis also helps to distinguish those phenomena that emerge and evolve in a culture-dependent fashion from those that transcend or are independent of culture. Crossing cultures can aid uniquely in the quest to understand *what* forces contribute to parenting and *how* those forces contribute to its course and outcome. In essence, then, culturally sensitive study occasions an unconfounding of variables thought to influence development, but that might be compromised by monocultural investigation. In a related way, designs of studies of parenting that cross cultures can provide natural tests of specific hypotheses or special circumstances that surround development, and are critical to exploring cultural uniformity versus diversity of psychological constructs, structures, functions, and processes.

A third reason motivating cross-cultural parenting study is interpretation. Understanding an activity and its meaning often depends on examining that activity in the context of culture (Bornstein, 1995). A given parenting activity can have the same meaning in different cultures, just as one parenting activity can have different meanings in different cultures. Conversely, different parenting activities can have similar or different meanings depending on culture. Culture is a prime context for determining relations between activity and meaning. The cross-cultural perspective provides social-scientific analysis with unique and extraordinary power to unravel meaning and the association of meaning with action (e.g., Bronfenbrenner, 1970; Erikson, 1950; Kessen, 1975; LeVine, 2003; Montagu, 1974; Munroe & Munroe, 1975; Werner, 1972; Whiting & Whiting, 1960).

Anthropology sensitized psychology to culture and to the limitations that loom over monocultural science. Can a psychological phenomenon be understood apart from its cultural context? Writing in the *Handbook of Research Methods in Child Development*, Whiting and Whiting (1960, p. 933) observed that:

> If children are studied within the confines of a single culture, many events are taken
> as natural, obvious, or a part of human nature and are therefore not reported and

not considered as variables. It is only when it is discovered that other peoples do not follow these practices that have been attributed to human nature that they are adopted as legitimate variables.

The Whitings (1960, p. 933) further observed that "even when individual variation . . . within western society suggests the presence of an important variable, the range of variation is often very small in contrast with its range in the societies of the world at large." Thus, anthropological inquiry offers information about where variables in a particular society stand in relation to the range, helping psychology (and that society) to determine their position in the world spectrum.

The service that a cross-cultural perspective can provide for researchers in parenting and child development is to encourage them to take a systematic look at contextual parameters that vary within and across cultures and that are often restricted and/or confounded in the settings and samples they more often choose to study. For example, one of the reasons why the effects of day care have constituted such a controversial and heavily researched topic is that nonparental care was believed by influential Europeans and North Americans in the mid-twentieth century to be unnatural—to represent a break with traditional child-care practices—even though, historically, aristocratic and affluent Europeans and North Americans had long depended on wet nurses, nannies, and governesses to care for their children. The existence of such powerful ideological beliefs under-scores the importance of identifying cultural factors that shape the social ecology of childhood. There are many societies in which both nonmaternal care practices and maternal employment are normative; citizens of these societies might be amazed to find that there exist cultures in which mothers are expected to devote themselves extensively or exclusively to child care (Lamb & Sternberg, 1992).

## THEORY AND METHODOLOGY IN CULTURE AND PARENTING

### Multiculture Multiage Multimethod Parenting Science

Some would argue that the description of a phenomenon, say parenting, mea-sured in a given way at a given age in a given sample serves developmental science adequately. Alternatively, others adopt the view that, to comprehend a phenom-enon in a deeper sense, we need to understand various perspectives and dimen-sions of the phenomenon (*multimethod*); we need to understand how those perspectives and dimensions present and develop across various ages or stages in the life course (*multiage*); and we need to understand how those different perspectives and dimensions at different developmental periods manifest them-selves in different contexts (*multiculture*). First, it is generally acknowledged that no single approach to measuring a phenomenon is best, that no one representa-tion of a phenomenon trumps all others. Historically, assessment selection in developmental science has been guided by tradition, tractability, goal, or conve-nience and was dominated by single methods of data collection. Researchers today advocate applying multiple assessments from multiple perspectives/reporters in multiple contexts and employing converging operations concentrated on the same phenomenon.

Similarly, second, developmental scientists are interested in aspects of phenomena that implicate time and growth. Certainly descriptions of parenting at a given child age or stage serve important functions, but comparative longitudinal or cross-sectional designs are critical to an ontogenetic field of study and are the mainstay of the field's unique contribution to human knowledge. Developmental research is concerned with the continuity or discontinuity of group average performance across time, the stability or instability of individual variation about the average across time, and the predictive validity of individual variation at one time for individual variation at a later time.

Lastly, contemporary researchers see development in an ecological framework, with the parent and child developing in nested contexts, and one context that is increasingly recognized as vital to development is culture. Cross-cultural research explores and explains cultural similarities and differences (Bornstein, 1980; van der Vijver & Leung, 1997). Cross-cultural developmental research was historically conducted by scientists usually investigating a single-culture extension of their intracultural research. Even these initial forays, however, demonstrated that cultural variation must be "part and parcel" of developmental study. Notable limitations imposed by monocultural investigation of a phenomenon include a narrow generalization about its nature and scope and restricted understanding of its origins and ontogeny. It is advantageous, therefore, to developmental science to explore its phenomena in multiple cultural settings.

## A Multiculture Multiage Multimethod Study

In a parenting study illustrative of this comprehensive approach, Bornstein and colleagues (1992) examined multiple dimensions of maternal speech (affect-salient and different kinds of information-salient speech) to children of two ages (5 and 13 months) in four countries (Argentina, France, Japan, United States) to probe how dimensions of maternal speech, child age, and cultural variation might influence what mothers say to their babies. One of the principal ways children become cultural beings is through mother–infant communication.

**Multimethod.** One approach of developmental psycholinguistics to the analysis of maternal speech to children has been to evaluate its functional aspects, for example, to contrast categories of speech where the mother's intent is social interaction and emotional exchange from categories of speech directed toward the infant's discovering the environment. Bornstein and colleagues (1992) coded maternal speech in terms of the primary function of each maternal utterance: (1) affect-salient speech, which is expressive, generally nonpropositional, idiomatic, or meaningless, that is, statements that include greetings, recitations, onomatopoeia, endearments, and the like, and (2) information-salient speech, which consists of generally propositional direct statements, questions, and reports about the infant, mother, or environment.

**Multiage.** As children grow over the first year, maternal speech and action patterns shift from feeling-oriented and self-marking to object-oriented and environment-marking in ways that are consistent with infants' increasing interest in their surroundings. By the middle of the infant's first year, "conversations" with mothers take on many mature characteristics, such as turn taking, but infants are still almost exclusively preverbal and noncomprehending. By the start of the second year, infants comprehend considerable amounts of speech they hear, and many are even themselves beginning to talk. For this reason, the investigators analyzed speech in mothers at two ages, first when the children were 5 months old and then again when the children were 13 months old.

**Multiculture.** Finally, the investigators evaluated maternal speech to children in four different cultural settings: Argentina, France, Japan, and the United States. There were several reasons why they chose to study Porteños, Parisians, Tokyo people, and New Yorkers. On the one hand, considerable differences existed among the four samples in terms of history, beliefs, and values concerned with child-rearing. This quartet of cultures also contrasted three Western societies and one Eastern society. The locales and samples are roughly comparable in terms of sociodemographics, however, such as modernity, level of industrialization, urbanity, per capita income, education, and standard of living; in all four, family organization is nuclear and the mother is normally the primary caregiver in the family setting. Thus, the particular cultural comparison assembled directly contrasted cultural conditions of child-rearing and disentangled them (to the degree possible) from economic and educational, urban–rural, modern–traditional, as well as ecological and climatic factors.

**Findings.** Maternal language to infants and toddlers contained affect-salient as well as information-salient topics. The consistency and face validity of findings resulting from the cross-cultural application of the speech categorization scheme gave evidence of its generalizability in culturally contrasting settings. It is likely that mothers everywhere intend to share feelings and contribute to emotional exchanges via their affect-salient speech to babies, just as they wish to impart or confirm cognitive information that is referential of children's perceptual experiences.

Mothers spoke more frequently to their 13-month-olds than to their 5-month-olds. Notably, predicted age effects emerged for affect- and information-salient speech, but with nearly one-third more affect and more than twice as much information. Argentine, French, Japanese, and U.S. American mothers favored affect over information in speaking to their 5-month-olds and information over affect in speaking to their 13-month-olds. Over the second half of the first year of life, mothers appear to expect that their infants need to be directed more, expect that their infants know more or will perhaps better comprehend their questions, and expect that they can and should give their infants more information about the infants themselves, their mothers, and the environment. During this period, infants themselves are also, of course, beginning to talk, a fact that presumably encourages mothers to speak to them more in an increasingly adult-oriented conversational manner.

Finally, growth patterns of maternal speech varied by method and age in inter-action with culture. For example, Japanese mothers used the most affect-salient speech, whereas mothers from the three Western cultures favored information-salient speech and more often used grammatically complete utterances in speaking to their babies, that is, speech more characteristic of adult–adult conversation. These mothers were apparently more interested in supporting individual expres-sion and imparting information to their children from an early age.

Method, age, and cultural similarities speak to the universality of maternal speech to infants, provoked perhaps by infants' common psychological status; dif-ferences in the speech mothers choose to emphasize may reflect the expression of cultural preferences. Mothers showed certain similarities across method, age, and culture, and so these findings point to universality of certain processes related to mother–child speech. Exceptions to these generalities, and variations in the speech of mothers in these four cultures project more specific cultural beliefs and values. Sampling different cultures showed that parenting in different cultures functions similarly and differently. The simultaneous evaluation of multiple methods, ages, and cultures adds information over and above the study of any one alone. There are manifest advantages to assessing developmental phenomena with two or more con-verging measures at two or more developmental periods (longitudinally or cross-sectionally) in two or more different cultures. Such designs promote confidence in the reliability of assessments, permit strong developmental inferences, and rule out both monocultural bias and oversimplified cultural contrasts.

Still multiculture, multiage, multimethod science begs many questions. His-torically, even multiculture, multiage, multimethod studies have been only mar-ginally multiculture, multiage, or multimethod. Research has usually involved the comparison of two cultures or two ages or two methods. By adopting pairwise comparisons, however, investigators have run a risk of confounding variables. For researchers to assume that a target culture, age, or method lies toward the opposite pole from some other culture, age, or method on a unitary dimension, and that the two are otherwise equivalent, may be to assume in error; cultures, ages, and methods are complex entities that differ from one another in many ways. The larger the number of methods, ages, or cultures studied, the more compelling is the conclusion that observed findings can be validly attributed to the theoretical dimension of interest.

# CULTURE AND PARENTING

## What Is Culture?

Culture is considered by some to reflect a complex of variables, a set of separable (if related) contextual factors, and by others to constitute a more abstract entity of learned meanings and shared information transmitted from one generation to the next through social interaction. The concept of culture is frequently used as a means of understanding relations between physical and social environments on the one hand and individual psychological structures on the other (Adamopoulos

& Lonner, 2001). Every psychological construct, structure, function, and process has cultural continuo or overtones. Cultures (and subcultures) consist of distinctive patterns as well as norms, ideas, values, and assumptions about life that are shared by the people in a given society and that guide and regulate specific behaviors and inculcate valued competencies. Geertz (1973, p. 44) interpreted culture ". . . as a set of control mechanisms—plans, recipes, rules, instructions . . . —for the governing of behavior." Culture is not a static entity, however; it is rather a dynamic system that is constantly in the process of reconstruction and renegotiation in the context of individual lives (see M. Cole, 2005).

Central to every concept of culture is the expectation that different peoples possess different beliefs and behave in different ways with respect to their parenting. It is a particular and continuing task of parents and other caregivers to enculturate children, that is, to prepare them for socially accepted physical, economic, and psychological situations that are characteristic of the culture in which they are to survive and thrive (Benedict, 1938; LeVine, 2003). Actively or passively, to a greater or lesser degree, intentionally or unwittingly parents pass their "culture" on to their offspring. Parenting is a principal reason why individuals in different cultures are who they are and often differ so from one another. What are the chief processes of enculturation? As culture is organized information, parenting consists of mechanisms for transmitting that information, and childhood comprises the processing of that information. Both parent and child "select, edit, and refashion" cultural information. So, minimally, enculturation involves bidirectional processes in which adult and child play active roles.

Not yet well worked out, therefore, are functional and theoretical connections between culture and parenting. How do components of culture relate to parenting attitudes and actions? Much more work needs to be accomplished linking parenting to culture, just as more work needs to link culture to parenting. The result will be a greater understanding of the processes and contents of parents' particular competencies and roles as members of a culture.

## What Is Parenting?

It has been said that parents "create" persons because mothers and fathers and significant others in the child's life influence the development of children in many ways. Direct effects are most obvious. Biological parents contribute directly to the genetic makeup of their children, and parents and others directly shape children's experiences. Parents and others also influence children indirectly by virtue of each partner's influence on the other and their associations with larger social networks (Bornstein & Sawyer, 2005).

**Mothers, Fathers, and Significant Others.** Different cultures distribute caregiving responsibilities in different ways. In some, the mother is the principal caregiver; for others, multiple caregiving models apply. In many places, babies and toddlers spend much or even most of their time with significant others, including siblings, nonparental relatives, or nonfamilial caregivers.

In the minds of many observers, mothers are unique, the role of mother universal, and motherhood is unequivocally principal to development. Various categories of parenting, such as nurturance, social interaction, and didactics, may be distributed across various members of the culture; however, the ultimate responsibility for young children within the context of the nuclear or extended family usually, if not universally, falls to the mother. Indeed, to this day, many societies place the strongest emphasis on the mother–child relationship. Mothers therefore normally play the principal part in child development (Barnard & Solchany, 2002), even if historically fathers' social and legal claims and responsibilities on children were preeminent (French, 2002). Cross-cultural surveys attest to the primacy of biological mothers' caregiving (e.g., Leiderman, Tulkin, & Rosenfeld, 1977). On average, mothers spend between 65 and 80 percent more time than fathers do in direct one-to-one interaction with young children (Parke, Dennis, Flyr, Morris, Leidy, & Schofield, 2005), and mothers spend more time with babies than do fathers whether in the United States, the United Kingdom, Australia, or France and Belgium. Mothers also interact with and take care of babies and toddlers more than fathers (e.g., Belsky, Gilstrap, & Rovine, 1984). Fathers may withdraw from their children when they are unhappily married; mothers typically do not.

Fathers are neither inept nor uninterested in child caregiving, however. Fathers interact with and care for their children, frequently in ways that are distinctly different from those of mothers (Parke, 2002). Western industrialized nations have witnessed relative increases in the amount of time fathers spend with their children; in reality, however, fathers typically assume little or no responsibility for child care and rearing, and fathers are primarily helpers (see Cabrera, Tamis-LeMonda, Bradley, Hofferth, & Lamb, 2000). Mothers and fathers interact with and care for children in complementary ways; that is, they tend to divide the labors of caregiving and engage children emphasizing different types of interactions (Parke, 2002). In research involving both traditional families (Belsky et al., 1984) and traditional and nontraditional (father primary caregiver) families (Lamb, Frodi, Frodi, & Hwang, 1982), parental gender is found to exert a greater influence in these respects than, say, parental role or employment status: mothers are more likely to kiss, hug, talk to, smile at, tend to, and hold children than fathers, regardless of degree of involvement in caregiving. In general, mothers are associated with caregiving, whereas fathers are identified with playful interactions (Parke, 2002).

**Direct and Indirect Effects of Parenting.**   Mothers and fathers contribute directly to the nature and development of their children by passing on some of their biological characteristics. Modern behavior genetics argues that a host of different characteristics of offspring—height and weight, intelligence, and personality—reflect inheritance in at least some degree (e.g., Plomin, 1999). However, the strength or expression of the contribution of genetic inheritance for a particular characteristic depends on the environmental or cultural "niche" in which the child is reared.

At the same time, all prominent theories of psychology and development put experience in the world as either the principal source of individual growth or as a major contributing component (Dixon & Lerner, 1999; Wachs, 2000). Thus, evidence for heritability effects neither negates nor diminishes equally compelling evidence for the direct effects of parent-provided experiences (Collins, Maccoby, Steinberg, Hetherington, & Bornstein, 2000). To cite the most obvious example, genes contribute to making siblings alike, but (as we all recognize) siblings are normally very different from one another, and it is widely held that parental difference in treatment of siblings within the same family and home setting (the "nonshared environment") contributes to making them distinctive individuals (Dunn & Plomin, 1991; Stoolmiller, 1999; Turkheimer & Waldron, 2000).

Empirical research attests to the short- and long-term influences of parent-provided experiences in child development. Children do not and cannot grow up as solitary individuals; parenting constitutes the initial and all-encompassing ecology of child development. Parents influence child development both by their beliefs and by their behaviors. In this respect, similarities as well as differences in mothers' and fathers' attitudes and actions affect the nature and course of child development, and they do so according to different mechanisms and following different models. Even features of the parent-outfitted physical environment influence child development directly (e.g., Wachs & Chan, 1986). Culture perfuses all of these. In the natural course of things, the two sorts of direct effects are confounded: the parents who endow the child genetically also structure their child's world and experiences. Indirect effects are more subtle and less noticeable than direct effects, but perhaps no less meaningful. One type of indirect effect is marital support and communication (Cowan & Cowan, 1992). Effective co-parenting bodes well for child development (McHale, Khazan, Rotman, DeCourcey, & McConnell, 2002), and mothers who report supportive relationships with "secondary parents" (spouses/partners or grandparents) are more competent and sensitively responsive to their children than are women lacking such relationships (Grych, 2002). Both direct and indirect effects vary by culture.

Not only do children normally experience multiple formative relationships, but so too do their mothers and fathers. As a result, parents influence children not only by virtue of interactions with them (direct effects) but also by virtue of each party's influence on others (indirect effects). Because students of childhood have come to recognize multiple social influences on child development—maternal, paternal, and other—they have come to appreciate that many influences are indirectly mediated through complex paths and networks. Parke et al. (2005) suggest that many paternal influences on child development, for example, are indirectly mediated through the father's impact on the mother. In other words, even if the mother has the major direct influence on child development in a "traditional family" (in which the mother stays at home to care for and socialize her children and the father is a breadwinner), the father may have important indirect influences.

To understand fully the effects of family climate on child–parent relationships and other aspects of child development requires multiple types of data representing multiple levels of analysis. Information about parents' attitudes, values, perceptions, and beliefs helps to explain when and why parents behave as they do.

Likewise, observations of parenting behaviors in multiple caregiving situations are required to tell the full scope of how parents behave.

**Mechanisms of Parenting.**   Parents' beliefs and behaviors influence children and child development via different paths. A common assumption in parenting is that the overall level of parental involvement or stimulation affects the child's overall level of development (see Maccoby & Martin, 1983). An illustration of this simple model suggests that the expression of language in children is determined (at least to some degree) by the language children hear (Hart & Risley, 1992, 1995). Increasing evidence suggests, however, that analysis of more sophisticated mechanisms needs to be brought to bear to explain parenting effects (Collins et al., 2000).

First, the *specificity principle* states that specific parent-provided experiences at specific times exert specific effects over specific aspects of child development in specific ways (Bornstein, 2002). Obviously, cultural experiences are specific. Second, the *transaction principle* recognizes that the characteristics of an individual shape her or his experiences and, reciprocally, that experiences shape the characteristics of the individual through time (Sameroff, 1983). Biological endowment and experience mutually influence development from birth onward, and each life force affects the other as development proceeds to unfold through the lifespan (Lerner, 2002).

By virtue of their unique characteristics and propensities (state of arousal, perceptual awareness, cognitive status, emotional expressiveness, and individuality of temperament) children actively contribute, through their interactions with their parents, toward producing their own development (Lerner, 2002). Children influence which experiences they will be exposed to and how they interpret those experiences, and so determine the ways those experiences will affect them (Scarr & McCartney, 1983). Child and parent bring distinctive characteristics to, and each is believed to change as a result of, every interaction; both then enter the next round of interaction as different individuals. Vygotsky (1978) contended that, as a central feature of this transactional perspective, the more advanced or expert partner (the parent) raises the level of performance or competence of the less advanced or expert partner (the child), and the "dynamic systems perspective" posits that reciprocity between parent and child specifically facilitates higher-level forms of interaction (Thelen & Smith, 1998). In essence, transactional, goodness-of-fit models best explain much of child development.

Parents influence their children directly via their genes, beliefs, and behaviors as well as indirectly via their influences on one another and the multiple contexts they choose for their children. Out of the dynamic range and complexity of individual activities that constitute parenting children, major domains of parent–child interaction have been distinguished; they include nurturing, interacting socially, stimulating cognitively, provisioning the environment, and speaking to children (Bornstein, 2002). The attitudes parents hold about their children and the activities they engage in are each meaningful to development. As noted above, mothers typically take more responsibility for and engage in more child caregiving than do fathers, but fathers play complementary and important roles.

Parent-provided experiences affect children via different mechanisms of action, but tend to follow principles of specificity and transaction. Concern with the impact of stress, supportiveness, and other relationships is also intrinsic to ecological and contextual approaches to the study of parenting and development (Dixon & Lerner, 1999). Advocates of the contextual approach also caution that relationships, like individuals, change over time. As the dynamics of the family change (e.g., with the birth of other children), changes in relationships between the two parents, and between each parent and the child, can be expected to change (Bornstein & Sawyer, 2005).

## CULTURE AND PARENTING: BELIEFS AND PRACTICES

How to care for children, how to rear them, and how to apprentice them into the culture are, as Benedict (1938) observed, perennial concerns of parents in every society. Ancient Greek lawgivers and philosophers gave special attention to the education of children, just as we do today. Today, extensive efforts are being made to understand the impact of culture on parenting and child development. It is still the case, however, that much of what is known about parenting and child development derives from observations of middle- SES (socioeconomic status) families living in modern industrialized and Western countries, particularly the United States and Western Europe. That is rapidly changing, however (Bornstein, 1991; Harkness & Super, 2002).

Cross-cultural comparisons show that virtually all aspects of parenting children, whether beliefs or practices, are shaped by cultural habits. Ethnotheories represent homogenizing influences on parents within a group. Cultures provide their members with implicit or explicit models for child-rearing. They include when and how to care for children, what child characteristics are desirable, which parenting practices are accepted or expected, as well as cultural orientations toward family versus work, maternal employment, and child care. Culture influences some parenting patterns and practices (and, in turn, child development) through such persuasive factors as what parents expect of children, when and how parents care for children, and which behaviors parents appreciate and emphasize. Parents are influenced by conventionalized images of what is and what ought to constitute childhood and child care, and so they seek to implement an agenda derived from culture-specific concepts.

In reality, the parent–child dyad is embedded in a nexus of multiple contexts and environments (Figure 1.1), and each contributes in critical ways to promote and support parenting and developing characteristics in children. Culture is a crucial decider in this contextual view of parenting. In consequence, adults in different cultures adopt some similar, as well as some different, approaches to parenting, and insofar as some psychological characteristics arise early in life and the nature of parent–child interaction is at least one important influence on individual development, cultural variation in the parent–child coconstruction of parenthood and childhood is a significant topic of study.

## Parental Cultural Beliefs

Parents' beliefs—their ideas, knowledge, values, goals, and attitudes—hold a consistently popular place in the study of parent–child relationships (e.g., Goodnow, 2002; Holden & Buck, 2002; Sigel & McGillicuddy-De Lisi, 2002). Parental beliefs are conceived to serve many functions; they may generate and shape parental behaviors, mediate the effectiveness of parenting practices, or help to organize parenting (Darling & Steinberg, 1993; Maccoby & Martin, 1983; Teti & Candelaria, 2002), and, in a larger sense, they may contribute to the "continuity of culture" by helping to define culture and the transmission of cultural information across generations. Thus, how parents see themselves vis-à-vis their children generally can lead to their expressing one or another kind of affect, thinking, or behavior in child-rearing. How parents construe childhood in general functions in the same way. How parents see their own children has its specific consequences too. In investigating and understanding child-rearing beliefs, we may come to better understand how and why parents behave in the ways they do as well as what consequences their beliefs hold.

Cultures help to "construct" children by shaping parental beliefs about child-rearing and attributions about the developmental capacities of children, which in turn influence parents' actions (Bornstein, 1991; M. Cole, 2005; McGillicuddy-De Lisi & Subramanian, 1996). Significantly, parents in different cultures harbor different beliefs about their own parenting as well as children (e.g., Bornstein, 2001a; Bornstein et al., 1998; Goodnow, 2002). Parents then act on culturally defined beliefs as much or more than on what their senses tell them about their children. Parents in Samoa reportedly think of young children as having an angry and willful character, and, independent of what children might actually say, parents consensually report that their children's first word is *tae*, Samoan for "shit." Parents who believe that they can or cannot affect their children's temperament, intelligence, and so forth tend to modify their parenting accordingly.

Harwood and colleagues (Harwood, Schölmerich, & Schulze, 2000; Harwood, Schölmerich, Ventura-Cook, Schulze, & Wilson, 1996) compared long-range socialization goals held by Puerto Rican mothers with those of European American mothers. In general, they found that the European American mothers talked most about goals for their children related to "self-maximization" (development of one's talents, self-confidence, and independence) in contrast to the Puerto Rican mothers, who spoke most about "proper demeanor" (including respectfulness and the appropriate performance of role obligations). Also, Puerto Rican mothers encouraged instrumental independence as necessary for meeting societal independence, whereas European American mothers emphasized independence as important for emotional autonomy.

Cheah and Rubin (2003) compared Mainland Chinese and European American mothers on their beliefs regarding preschoolers' social skills and found that the Mainland Chinese mothers' beliefs reflected traditional Chinese ideologies and values in meaningful ways. Chinese mothers provided more socially conventional reasons for why sharing, helping others, and controlling negative emotions were important social skills for young children, reflecting the significant role of the collective in determining child behavior. In contrast, European American mothers focused on the same skills as important because they were developmentally feasible and appropriate for their child. In line with Confucian beliefs about the importance of the proper environment and training in rearing children, Chinese mothers also made more external causal attributions for why children acquired these skills, and they endorsed higher proportions of training and education strategies than European American mothers, who provided more internal causal reasons and focused on modeling strategies.

When the same questions were posed to mothers in South Korea, which is also traditionally a Confucian-based culture but has undergone considerable political, economic, and social change in the past 60 years, Korean mothers suggested more developmental reasons for the importance of social skills (similar to their European American counterparts), perhaps reflecting the influence of more "Westernized" views on child development (Park & Cheah, 2005; Ju & Chung, 2000). However, South Korean mothers were more influenced than their Mainland Chinese counterparts by gender-role expectations in that these social skills were thought of as more compulsory for girls, but less compulsory for boys. This finding supports previous research indicating that South Korean parents hold more traditional gender-role attitudes than their Chinese counterparts (Arnold & Kuo, 1984; Han, 1999; Sagara & Kang, 1998). Although both modeling and direct teaching are traditional ideas of training and socialization in Korean families, Korean mothers endorsed modeling strategies rather than direct teaching, again indicative of the growing Western influence on contemporary South Korean mothers' child-rearing ideas.

In a comparative study of parent beliefs in seven countries (Argentina, Belgium, France, Israel, Italy, Japan, and the United States), mothers evaluated their competence, satisfaction, investment, and role balance in parenting and attributed their successes and failures in parenting to ability, effort, mood, task difficulty, or child behavior (Bornstein et al., 1998). Systematic country differences for both self-evaluations and attributions emerged that were interpretable in terms of cultural proclivities and emphases. For example, Argentine mothers rated themselves relatively low in parental competence and satisfaction and blamed parenting failures on lack of ability. Their insecurity about mothering appeared to be consistent with the relative lack of support, particularly the help and advice about child-rearing provided to Argentine mothers. By contrast, Belgian mothers rated themselves as relatively satisfied with their parenting, which might be expected in light of the strong child-care support provided to parents in Belgium (e.g., in terms of periodicals, consultancies, home visits, health-care information workshops, and parenting demonstration sessions).

Notable cultural differences in parenting beliefs appear to persist even among parents born and reared in one culture but who then move and live in another culture with different child-rearing norms. Bornstein and Cote (2001; Cote & Bornstein, 2000, 2001) studied Japanese American and South American families who had moved from their home countries to live in the United States. Japanese and South American immigrant mothers' parenting cognitions (attributions and self-perceptions) were compared to those of mothers in their respective countries of origin (Japan and Argentina, respectively) and to European American mothers in the United States. Generally, South American immigrant mothers' parenting cognitions more closely resembled those of mothers in the United States, whereas Japanese immigrant mothers' cognitions tended to be similar to those of Japanese mothers or intermediate between Japanese and U.S. mothers. Such findings provide insight into the nature of parenting cognitions generally and those of immigrant mothers specifically, and therefore the parenting climate in which immigrant children are reared.

## Parental Cultural Practices

Perhaps more salient in the phenomenology of the child are parents' practices, the actual experiences parents provide. Most of children's worldly experiences stem directly from interactions they have within the family. The contents of parent–child interactions are dynamic, varied, and largely discretionary in human beings. Nonetheless, a small number of domains of parenting interactions have been identified as a common "core" of parental care (Bornstein, 2002; LeVine, 2003). Moreover, there is initially asymmetry in parent and child contributions to interactions and control: postinfancy, children play more active and anticipatory roles in interaction, whereas initial responsibility for adaptation in child development lies more unambiguously with parents (Barnard & Solchany, 2002).

Parents' ethnotheories are thought to play a powerful role in shaping parental practices. Differences in cultural ideology make for subtle, but potentially meaningful, differences in patterns of parent–child interaction. Harwood, Miller, and Irizarry (1995) found that European American mothers underscore the importance of values such as independence, assertiveness, and creativity when asked to describe an ideal child, whereas Latin American mothers emphasize the importance of obedience and respect for others. These differences related to the mothers' actual behavior. European American mothers used suggestions (rather than commands) and other indirect means of structuring their children's behavior, and Puerto Rican mothers used more direct means of structuring, such as commands, physical positioning, restraints, and direct attempts to command their children's attention. European American mothers fostered independence in their children; for example, in naturalistic mother–child interactions during feeding, European American mothers encouraged their children to feed themselves at eight months of age. In contrast, Latina mothers held their children closely on their laps during mealtimes and took control of feeding them meals from start to finish. These observations are consistent with reports that emphasize the "interdependent/sociocentric" orientation of Latino families as opposed to the "individual/independent" orientation of European American families.

The distinction between interdependent/sociocentric versus individual/independent cultural child-rearing ideologies on parenting behavior is also illustrated in studies of Japanese and American mothers and their five-month-olds (Bornstein et al., 1991; Bornstein, Azuma, et al., 1990; Bornstein, Toda, et al., 1990). American mothers respond more to their children's orienting to the environment relative to their children's social orienting, whereas Japanese mothers respond more to their children's social than environmental orienting. When responding to their children, Japanese mothers tend to direct their children's attention to themselves, whereas American mothers tend to direct their children's attention away from themselves and to the environment. Viewing their own findings in the context of earlier research (Befu, 1986; Hess et al., 1986; Kojima, 1986a, 1986b), Bornstein and his colleagues (1990, p. 290) concluded:

> Mothers in these two cultures . . . follow different rules of interaction with their children. In general, Japanese mothers are believed to organize their interactions so as to consolidate interdependence and strengthen the mother–child bond, whereas American mothers are believed to organize their interactions so as to foster physical and verbal independence in their children.

Distinctive child-rearing practices are not limited to comparisons between European American and non-European American families; substantial differences in parenting practices toward children can be found between preindustrial, non-Western "small-scale" cultures. In their study of the nomadic hunter-gatherer Aka and the Ngandu farming cultures in central Africa, Hewlett, Lamb, Shannon, Leyendecker, & Scholmerich (1998) observed that three- to four-month-old Aka children experienced a more "proximal" relationship with their caregivers (i.e., they were more likely to be held and fed) than were same-age Ngandu children, who were more likely than Aka children to be left alone, fuss, smile, vocalize, and play. The Aka and Ngandu cultures have similarly high levels of child mortality, equivalently hazardous living conditions, equally healthy children, and comparable maternal workloads, and thus these sociodemographic factors do not explain differences in parenting practices of the two cultures. Hewlett et al. speculated that Aka parents stayed closer to their children because of their frequent moves from one location to the next in search of food. Aka parents are always less familiar with their home surroundings than are Ngandu parents, who live a comparatively sedentary existence, and thus Aka parents may feel more inclined to stay in closer proximity to their children to better protect them in unfamiliar environments.

Parents' beliefs presumably relate to parents' behaviors and in turn to children's development. To explore this chain, P. Cole and Tamang (1998) contrasted Chhetri–Brahmin and Tamang parents and children in Nepal. They hypothesized that cultural differences in the two groups, related to religious traditions of Hindu versus Tibetan Buddhism, would manifest themselves in parents' socialization practices and their children's emotional sensitivities. Chhetri–Brahmin life emphasizes self-awareness and discipline; in contrast, Tamang is more egalitarian, emphasizing the importance of maintaining a calm and peaceful mind. Interviews with mothers showed cultural differences in their preferred socialization practices; Chhetri–Brahmin mothers reported that they tended to teach their children about emotional displays, whereas Tamang mothers maintained that children learn on their own. Tamang mothers favored cajoling and comforting a young child who expressed anger toward them; Chhetri–Brahmin mothers favored reprimanding. These ethnotheories were further reflected in children's early understanding of "masking" emotions. Differences in the children's choice of masking in hypothetical challenge situations were dramatic: 40 to 70 percent of the Chhetri–Brahmin children reported masking, whereas virtually no Tamang children did. The Cole–Tamang study focuses on a progression of ideas, from cultural belief systems to parental beliefs regarding the socialization of children to parents' child-rearing practices to the ideas and actions of children themselves.

One significant theme in cultural approaches to parenting turns on the question of culture-specific versus culture-universal parenting activities. Some authors find that certain aspects of parenting recur across cultures, even very different ones. This observation naturally raises the question, "Why?" Parents, even from different cultures, must show some similarities in interacting with their children. All must nurture and promote the physical growth of children if their children are to survive (Bornstein, 2002; LeVine, 2003). Whether converging patterns in mothers reflect factors indigenous to children and their biology, biological bases of caregiving, the historical convergence of parenting styles, the fact that economic or ecological factors are shared, or the increasing prevalence of a monolithic child-rearing pattern as fostered through migration or dissemination via mass media is difficult, if not impossible, to determine. Recent times have witnessed a worldwide pattern of change toward some homogeneity, promoted by urbanization, modernization, mass media, and Westernization, that cumulatively contributes to breaking down traditional cultural patterns. In the end, different peoples (presumably) wish to promote similar general competencies in their young. Some do so in qualitatively and quantitatively similar ways.

By contrast, some authors focus on behaviors of parents that are culturally unique and specifically contextualized. Unsurprisingly, the arguments marshalled by culture-specifists are of the same kind as those invoked by culture-universalists. Certain culturally consistent biological factors in children, such as constitutionally based characteristics of temperament, could promote parental attitudes and/or activities that vary systematically across cultures. Adults in different cultures could parent differently because of their own biological characteristics, for example, differential threshold sensitivities or attention to child signals. Finally, ecological or economic conditions specific to a given cultural setting might promote parental beliefs and activities indigenous to that culture, ones evolved differentially to optimize adjustment and adaptation in offspring to the circumstances of the local situation. Culture-specific patterns of child-rearing can always be expected to be adapted to a specific society's settings and needs (Lerner, 2002).

In this context, one challenge in the study of culture and parenting is how parents' responses to individual differences among children are culturally shaped (Bornstein, 1995). The work of Chen, Rubin, and their colleagues (Chen et al., 1998) in China and Canada with respect to children's behavioral inhibition, parental responses to this behavioral constellation, and children's development is illustrative. They found that Chinese children tend to be more inhibited than Canadian children, but mothers in the two cultures respond to inhibition differently: Chinese mothers of inhibited children harbor more warm and accepting attitudes, whereas Canadian mothers of inhibited children tend to be more punitive. In school, Chinese children who were shy achieved academically and their teachers and peers rated them more positively; by contrast, shy Canadian children did worse in general (Chen, Rubin, Li, & Li, 1999; Chen, Rubin, & Li, 1995). As Rubin (1998, p. 612) noted:

> Given that the majority of the world's inhabitants do not reside in culturally "Westernized" countries, the cross-cultural work on behavioral inhibition bears careful note. From the example of a single individual characteristic, social inhibition, one can begin to understand the significance of culture in determining the "meanings" of social and emotional behavior and development at all levels of social complexity. Clearly, child development is influenced by multiple factors. Within any culture, children are shaped by the physical and social settings within which they live, culturally regulated customs and child-rearing practices, and culturally based belief systems (Harkness & Super, 2002). The bottom line is that the psychological "meaning" attributed to any given social behavior is, in large part, a function of the ecological niche within which it is produced. If a given behavior is viewed as acceptable, then parents (and significant others) will attempt to encourage its development; if the behavior is perceived as maladaptive or abnormal, then parents (and significant others) will attempt to discourage its growth and development. . . . All in all, then, it would appear most sensible for the international community of child development researchers not to generalize to other cultures their own culture-specific theories of normal and abnormal development.

## CONCLUSIONS

Parenting a child is a "24/7" job, whether by the parent her- or himself or by a surrogate caregiver who is on call. That is because the young human child is totally dependent on parents for survival. In a given year, and worldwide, each day approximately three-quarters of a million adults experience the joys and heartaches as well as the challenges and rewards of becoming new parents. Children have many of the same biological needs and must meet and succeed at many of the same developmental tasks and challenges, and their parents have many of the same responsibilities to guide children to survival and adaptation to their physical and social environment and culture. Notably, parents everywhere appear highly motivated to carry out these tasks. Parents constitute the "final common pathway" to early childhood oversight and caregiving. For this reason, many theorists have asserted that the family generally, and the parent–child relationship specifically, constitute the effective crucible for the early (and perhaps eventual) development of the individual and continuity of the culture.

Theoreticians have also contended that, in greater aggregations, parent–child interactions equally well subserve evolving aspects of cultural style. The family is shaped by its cultural context, just as the family shapes its culture. Every culture promotes unique ways of adapting to the stringencies of its ecology and environment and has developed traditions and parental ethnotheories to achieve its common goals of child-rearing. As a consequence, parenting children can vary dramatically across cultures. The cultural contexts of parenthood and childhood are therefore of increasing interest to developmental science.

A major task of developmental science is to explain how contexts and settings help to shape children's development (Bradley, 2002; Bronfenbrenner & Morris, 1998). Yet, after approximately a century of developmental study, with considerable attention paid to children and their parents, still too little is known about the behaviors and activities, life circumstances, and experiences, of children or their parents in non-American, non-European cultural conditions. The vast majority of the literature in parenting and developmental science, and consequently our understanding, still derives from studies conducted in Western industrialized and developed nations, and where there are exceptions precious little standardization has been brought to bear on comparative examinations of even the most basic psychological constructs, structures, functions, or processes.

In turn, a major task of developmental theory is to explain how culture-specific forces help to shape children's development. Parenting researchers, like all social scientists, need to recognize the subtleties, complexities, and unique qualities that manifestly reflect the richness of each culture they study, while simultaneously trying to determine and understand the similarities in beliefs and behaviors that equally and clearly exist across cultures. The challenge that confronts cross-cultural developmental scientists of parenting is to understand and represent these similarities and differences in and across groups in order to transcend simplistic dichotomous group comparisons.

The long-standing issues of developmental science are as follows. What are the universals of child development and child care in our species? How do children participate in and shape the environments of child development? How do parents parent and organize the effective environment of childhood? What are the contributions of culture to parenting, childhood, and parent–child relationships? No study of a single society (even comparison with populations previously studied) can answer these broad questions. It is possible, however, to learn lessons from different societies that may shed light on these questions and perhaps lead to their more meaningful reformulation for future research. The parental perspective provides the social and cultural context that affects those responsible for organizing child care; the child perspective provides an indispensable basis for assessing the impact of caregiving and social exposure on behavioral development; and, the cultural perspective tells us about the ideals and practices of the society and how they are instantiated.

Cultural ideology shapes child care patterns and child development. It is important also to keep in mind the cultural relativity of much of our thinking and knowledge about children, because it may set limits on the generalizability of our findings. We cannot fathom parenthood or childhood fully unless we know more about the multiple ecologies in which parents parent and children develop. Cultural variation in patterns of child-rearing exert important influences on the ways in which children are reared and what may be expected of them as they grow up. These variations merit study because they illustrate the limits of what we know about development, because they serve to highlight the narrow perspective researchers often bring to their studies, and because they identify the importance of factors that are often discounted or overlooked completely.

Studies of culture and parenting have developed from individual ethnographic reports to multicultural, multivariate, multiage studies that occupy an important position in developmental science. Nonetheless, researchers in this area have concerned themselves with a small number of central issues (see Harkness & Super, 2002). First is the question of cultural variation and universality in parenting. Here our knowledge base has grown considerably, even if it is still skewed. Second is the quest for causal explanations of cultural variation in parenting. Explanatory models range from global theories of contrasting value orientations to discrete analyses of how individual parents enculturate their children. The third major issue is the communicative function of cultural parenting practices to children. Approaches that consist of the close analysis of parental behavior can be combined with cultural psychologies concerned with meaning. Fourth are analyses of the short- and long-term developmental effects of culturally constituted parenting cognitions and practices.

In order to understand the place of culture and parenting in developmental science, we need to collect more detailed and systematic data on cultural cognitions, practices, and the settings of parenting and child development. This call challenges research because it requires combining strategies traditionally associated with different disciplines. Further complicating the issue is the fact that culture is recreated and reconstituted across the lifespans of individuals. All are requisite to the ultimate goal, however, of better understanding how parents in a variety of cultural contexts come to think and behave the way they do.

## ACKNOWLEDGMENTS

This chapter summarizes selected aspects of our research, and portions of the text have appeared in previous scientific publications cited in the references. We thank C. Varron for assistance. Address correspondence to: Marc H. Bornstein, Child and Family Research, National Institute of Child Health and Human Development, National Institutes of Health, Suite 8030, 6705 Rockledge Drive, Bethesda, MD 20892-7971, U.S.A. E-mail: marc_h_bornstein@nih.gov.

## REFERENCES

Adamopoulos, J., & Lonner, W. J. (2001). Culture and psychology at a crossroad: Historical perspective and theoretical analysis. In D. Matsumoto (Ed.), *The handbook of culture and psychology* (pp. 11–34). Oxford: Oxford University Press.

Ainsworth, M. (1967). *Infancy in Uganda*. Baltimore, MD: Johns Hopkins University Press.

Arnold, F., & Kuo, E. C. Y. (1984). The value of daughters and sons: A comparative study on the gender preference of parents. *Journal of Comparative Family Studies, 15*, 299–318.

Azuma, H. (1986). Why study child development in Japan? In H. Stevenson, H. Azuma, & K. Hakuta (Eds.), *Child development and education in Japan* (pp. 3–12). New York: W. H. Freeman.

Barnard, K. E., & Solchany, J. E. (2002). Mothering. In M. H. Bornstein (Ed.), *Handbook of parenting: Vol. 3. Status and social conditions of parenting* (2nd ed., pp. 3–25). Mahwah, NJ: Erlbaum.

Bayley, N. (1969). *Bayley scales of infant development*. New York: Psychological Corporation.

Bayley, N. (1970). Development of mental abilities. In P. Mussen (Ed.), *Carmichael's manual of child psychology* (Vol. 1, pp. 1163–1209). New York: Wiley.

Befu, H. (1986). Social and cultural background for child development in Japan and the United States. In H. W. Stevenson, H. Azuma, & K. Hakuta (Eds.), *Child development and education in Japan* (pp. 13–27). San Francisco: W. H. Freeman.

Belsky, J. (1984). The determinants of parenting: A process model. *Child Development, 55*, 83–96.

Belsky, J., Gilstrap, B., & Rovine, M. (1984). The Pennsylvania infant and family development project, I: Stability and change in mother-infant and father-infant interaction in a family setting at one, three, and nine months. *Child Development, 55*, 692–705.

Benedict, R. (1938). Continuities and discontinuities in cultural conditioning. *Psychiatry, 1*, 161–167.

Berry, J. W., Poortinga, Y. H., Segall, M. H., & Dasen, P. R. (1992). *Cross-cultural psychology: Research and application*. Cambridge: Cambridge University Press.

Bornstein, M. H. (1980). Cross-cultural developmental psychology. In M. H. Bornstein (Ed.), *Comparative methods in psychology* (pp. 231–281). Hillsdale, NJ: Erlbaum.

Bornstein, M. H. (1989). Cross-cultural developmental comparisons: The case of Japanese-American infant and mother activities and interactions. What we know, what we need to know, and why we need to know. *Developmental Review, 9*, 171–204.

Bornstein, M. H. (1991). Approaches to parenting in culture. In M. H. Bornstein (Ed.), *Cultural approaches to parenting* (pp. 3–19). Hillsdale, NJ: Erlbaum.

Bornstein, M. H. (1995). Form and function: Implications for studies of culture and human development. *Culture & Psychology, 1*, 123–137.

Bornstein, M. H. (2001a). Some questions for a science of "culture and parenting" (... but certainly not all). *International Society for the Study of Behavioural Development Newsletter, 1*, 1–4.

Bornstein, M. H. (2001b). *Arnold Lucius Gesell. [Arnold Lucius Gesell]*. Sozialp%odiatrie: Kinder- und jugendheilkunde/Social Pediatrics.

Bornstein, M. H. (2002). Parenting infants. In M. H. Bornstein (Ed.), *Handbook of parenting: Vol. 1. Children and parenting* (2nd ed., pp. 3–43). Mahwah, NJ: Erlbaum.

Bornstein, M. H., Azuma, H., Tamis-LeMonda, C. S., & Ogino, M. (1990). Mother and infant activity and interaction in Japan and in the United States: I. A comparative macroanalysis of naturalistic exchanges. *International Journal of Behavioral Development, 13*, 267–287.

Bornstein, M. H., & Cote, L. R. (2001). Mother-infant interaction and acculturation I: Behavioral comparisons in Japanese American and South American families. *International Journal of Behavioral Development, 25*, 549–563.

Bornstein, M. H., Haynes, O. M., Azuma, H., Galperin, C., Maital, S., Ogino, M., Painter, K., Pascual, L., Pêcheux, M.-G., Rahn, C., Toda, S., Venuti, P., Vyt, A., & Wright, B. (1998). A cross-national study of self-evaluations and attributions in parenting: Argentina, Belgium, France, Israel, Italy, Japan, and the United States. *Developmental Psychology, 34*, 662–676.

Bornstein, M. H., & Sawyer, J. (2005). Family systems. In K. McCartney & D. Phillips (Eds.), *Blackwell handbook on early childhood development*. Malden, MA: Blackwell.

Bornstein, M. H., Tal, J., Rahn, C., Galperín, C. Z., Pêcheux, M.-G., Lamour, M., Azuma, H., Toda, S., Ogino, M., & Tamis-LeMonda, C. S. (1992). Functional analysis of the contents of maternal speech to infants of 5 and 13 months in four cultures: Argentina, France, Japan, and the United States. *Developmental Psychology, 28*, 593–603.

Bornstein, M. H., Tal, J., & Tamis-LeMonda, C. S. (1991). Parenting in cross-cultural perspective: The United States, France, and Japan. In M. H. Bornstein (Ed.), *Cultural approaches to parenting* (pp. 69–90). Hillsdale, NJ: Lawrence Erlbaum Associates.

Bornstein, M. H., Toda, S., Azuma, H., Tamis-LeMonda, C. S., & Ogino, M. (1990). Mother and infant activity and interaction in Japan and in the United States: II. A comparative microanalysis of naturalistic exchanges focused on the organization of infant attention. *International Journal of Behavioral Development, 13,* 289–308.

Bovet, M. C., Dasen, P. R., & Inhelder, B. (1974). Etapes de l'intelligence sensori-mortice chez l'enfant Baoulé. *Archives de Psychologie, 41,* 363–386.

Bradley, R. H. (2002). Environment and parenting. In M. H. Bornstein (Ed.), *Handbook of parenting, Vol 2: Biology and ecology of parenting* (pp. 235–261). Mahwah, NJ: Erlbaum.

Bronfenbrenner, U. (1970). *Two worlds of childhood.* New York: Russell Sage Foundation.

Bronfenbrenner, U. (1999). Environments in developmental perspective: Theoretical and operational models. In S. L. Friedman & T. D. Wachs (Eds.), *Measuring environment across the lifespan: Emerging methods and concepts* (pp. 3–28). Washington, DC: American Psychological Association.

Bronfenbrenner, U., & Morris, P. A. (1998). The ecology of developmental processes. In R. M. Lerner (Ed.), W. Damon (Series Ed.), *Handbook of child psychology: Vol. 1. Theoretical models of human development* (5th ed., pp. 993–1028). New York: Wiley.

Cabrera, N. J., Tamis-LeMonda, C. S., Bradley, R. H., Hofferth, S., & Lamb, M. E. (2000). Fatherhood in the twenty-first century. *Child Development, 71,* 127–136.

Cheah, C. S. L., & Rubin, K. H. (2003). European American and Mainland Chinese mothers' socialization beliefs regarding preschoolers' social skills. *Parenting: Science and Practice, 3,* 1–22.

Chen, X., Hastings, P. D., Rubin, K. H., Chen, H., Cen, G., & Stewart, S. L. (1998). Child-rearing attitudes and behavioral inhibition in Chinese and Canadian toddlers: A cross-cultural study. *Developmental Psychology, 34,* 677–686.

Chen, X., Rubin, K. H., Li, B., & Li, D. (1999). Adolescent outcomes of social functioning in Chinese children. *International Journal of Behavioral Development, 23,* 199–223.

Chen, X., Rubin, K. H., & Li, Z. (1995). Social functioning and adjustment in Chinese children: A longitudinal study. *Developmental Psychology, 31,* 531–539.

Cole, M. (2005). Culture in development. In M. H. Bornstein & M. E. Lamb (Eds.), *Developmental psychology: An advanced textbook* (5th ed.), Mahwah, NJ: Erlbaum.

Cole, P. M., & Tamang, B. L. (1998). Nepali children's ideas about emotional displays in hypothetical challenges. *Developmental Psychology, 34,* 640–646.

Collins, W. A., Maccoby, E. E., Steinberg, L., Hetherington, E. M., & Bornstein, M. H. (2000). Contemporary research on parenting: The case for nature and nurture. *American Psychologist, 55,* 218–232.

Corter, C. M., & Fleming, A. S. (2002). Psychobiology of maternal behavior in human beings. In M. H. Bornstein (Ed.), *Handbook of parenting: Vol. 2. Biology and Ecology of Parenting* (2nd ed., pp. 141–181). Mahwah, NJ: Erlbaum.

Cote, L. R., & Bornstein, M. H. (2000). Social and didactic parenting behaviors and beliefs among Japanese American and South American mothers of infants. *Infancy, 1,* 363–374.

Cote, L. R., & Bornstein, M. H. (2001). Mother–infant interaction and acculturation II: Behavioral coherence and correspondence in Japanese American and South American families. *International Journal of Behavioral Development, 25,* 564–576.

Cowan, C. P., & Cowan, P. A. (1992). *When partners become parents.* New York: Basic.

Darling, N., & Steinberg, L. (1993). Parenting style as context: An integrative model. *Psychological Bulletin, 113*, 487–496.

Dennis, W., & Dennis, M. G. (1940). The effect of cradling practices upon the onset of walking in Hopi children. *Journal of Genetic Psychology, 56*, 77–86.

Dixon, R. A., & Lerner, R. M. (1999). History of systems in developmental psychology. In M. H. Bornstein & M. E. Lamb (Eds.), *Developmental psychology: An advanced textbook* (4th ed., pp. 313–373). Mahwah, NJ: Erlbaum.

Doi, T. (1973). [*The anatomy of dependence*] (J. Bester, trans.). Tokyo: Kodansha International.

Dunn, J., & Plomin, R. (1991). *Separate lives: Why siblings are so different*. New York: Basic.

Erikson, E. H. (1950). *Childhood and society*. New York: Norton.

French, V. (2002). History of parenting: The ancient Mediterranean world. In M. H. Bornstein (Ed.), *Handbook of parenting: Vol. 2. Biology and ecology of parenting* (2nd ed., pp. 345–376). Mahwah, NJ: Erlbaum.

Geber, M. (1956). Developpement psychomoteur de l'enfant africain.*Courrier, 6*, 17–28.

Geber, M. (1958). The psychomotor development of African children in the first year, and the influence of maternal behavior. *Journal of Social Psychology, 47*, 185–195.

Geber, M., & Dean, R. F. A. (1957a). Gesell tests on African children. *Pediatrics, 20*, 1055–1065.

Geber, M., & Dean, R. F. A. (1957b). The state of development of newborn African children. *Lancet, 272*, 1216–1219.

Geertz, C. (1973). *Interpretation of cultures*. New York: Basic.

Gesell, A. L. (1946). The ontogenesis of infant behavior. In L. Carmichael (Ed.), *Manual of child psychology*. New York: Wiley.

Gesell, A. L., & Armatruda, C. S. (1945). *The embryology of behavior: The beginnings of the human mind*. New York: Harper.

Goodnow, J. J. (2002). Parents' knowledge and expectations: Using what we know. In M. H. Bornstein (Ed.), *Handbook of parenting: Vol. 3. Status and Social Conditions of Parenting* (2d ed., pp. 439–460). Mahwah, NJ: Erlbaum.

Goodnow, J. J., Cashmore, R., Cotton, S., & Knight, R. (1984). Mothers' developmental timetables in two cultural groups. *International Journal of Psychology, 19*, 193–205.

Griffiths, R. (1954). *The abilities of babies*. New York: McGraw-Hill.

Grych, J. H. (2002). Marital relationships and parenting. In M. H. Bornstein (Ed.), *Handbook of parenting: Vol. 4. Applied Parenting* (2nd ed., pp. 203–225). Mahwah, NJ: Erlbaum.

Han, N. (1999). *Understanding of contemporary Korean family*. Seoul: Ilji-sa (in Korean).

Harkness, S., & Super, C. M. (1996). *Parents' cultural belief systems: Their origins, expressions, and consequences*. New York: Guilford.

Harkness, S., & Super, C. M. (2002). Culture and parenting. In M. H. Bornstein (Ed.), *Handbook of parenting: Vol. 2. Biology and ecology of parenting* (2nd ed., pp. 253–280). Mahwah, NJ: Erlbaum.

Hart, B., & Risley, T. R. (1992). *The social world of children learning to talk*. Baltimore, MD: Brookes.

Hart, B., & Risley, T. R. (1995). *Meaningful differences in the everyday experience of young American children*. Baltimore, MD: Brookes.

Harwood, R. L., Miller, J. G., & Irizarry, N. L. (1995). *Culture and attachment: Perceptions of the child in context*. New York: Guilford.

Harwood, R. L., Schölmerich, A., & Schulze, P. A. (2000). Homogeneity and heterogeneity in cultural belief systems. In S. Harkness & C. Raeff (Eds.), *Variability in the social construction of the child* (pp. 41–57). *New directions for child and adolescent development*, No. 87. San Francisco: Jossey–Bass.

Harwood, R. L., Schölmerich, A., Ventura-Cook, E., Schulze, P. A., & Wilson, S. P. (1996). Culture and class influences on Anglo and Puerto Rican mothers' beliefs regarding long-term socialization goals and child behavior. *Child Development, 67*, 2446–2461.

Hess, R. D., Azuma, H., Kashiwagi, K., Dickson, W. P., Nagano, S., Holloway, S., Miyake, K., Price, G., Hatano, G., & McDevitt, T. (1986). Family influences on school readiness and achievement in Japan and the United States: An overview of a longitudinal study. In H. W. Stevenson, H. Azuma, & H. Hakuta (Eds.), *Child development and education in Japan* (pp. 147–166). New York: W. H. Freeman.

Hewlett, B. S., Lamb, M. E., Shannon, D., Leyendecker, B., & Scholmerich, A. (1998). Culture and early infancy among central African foragers and farmers. *Developmental Psychology, 334*, 653–661.

Hilldebrandt-Karraker, K., & Coleman, P. K. (2005). The effects of child characteristics on parenting. In T. Luster & L. Okagaki (Eds.), *Parenting: An ecological perspective* (2nd ed.). Mahwah, NJ: Erlbaum.

Hodapp, R. M., & Ly, T. M. (2005). Parenting children with developmental disabilities. In T. Luster & L. Okagaki (Eds.), *Parenting: An ecological perspective* (2nd ed.). Mahwah, NJ: Erlbaum.

Holden, G. W. (1997). *Parents and the dynamics of child rearing.* New York: Perseus.

Holden, G. W., & Buck, M. J. (2002). Parental attitudes toward child-rearing. In M. H. Bornstein (Ed.), *Handbook of parenting: Vol. 3. Status and social conditions of parenting* (2nd ed., pp. 537–562). Mahwah, NJ: Erlbaum.

Ju, D.-B., & Chung, I.-H. (2000). The effect of maternal employment on schoolchildren's educational aspirations in Korea. *Journal of Research in Childhood Education, 15*, 1–20.

Kennedy, S., Scheirer, J., & Rogers, A. (1984). The price of success: Our monocultural science. *American Psychologist, 39*, 996–997.

Kessen, W. (1975). *Child care in China.* New Haven: Yale University Press.

Kojima, H. (1986a). Child-rearing concepts as a belief-value system of the society and the individual. In H. Stevenson, H. Azuma, & K. Hakuta (Eds.), *Child development and education in Japan* (pp. 39–54). New York: W. H. Freeman.

Kojima, H. (1986b). Japanese concepts of child development from the mid-17th to mid-19th century. *International Journal of Behavioral Development, 9*, 315–329.

Lamb, M. E., Frodi, A. M., Frodi, M., & Hwang, C.-P. (1982). Characteristics of maternal and paternal behavior in traditional and nontraditional Swedish families. *International Journal of Behavioral Development, 5*, 131–141.

Lamb, M. E., & Sternberg, K. J. (1992). Sociocultural perspectives on nonparental child-care. In M. E. Lamb, K. J. Sternberg, C. P. Hwang, & A. Broberg (Eds.) *Childcare in context: Cross-cultural perspectives.* Hillsdale, NJ: Erlbaum.

Leiderman, P. H., Tulkin, S. R., & Rosenfeld, A. (Eds.) (1977). *Culture and infancy: Variations in the human experience.* New York: Academic.

Lerner, R. M. (Ed.). (2002). *Concepts and theories of human development.* Mahwah, NJ: Lawrence Erlbaum Associates.

Lerner, R. M., Rothbaum, F., Boulos, S., & Castellino, D. R. (2002). Developmental systems perspective on parenting. In M. H. Bornstein (Ed.), *Handbook of parenting: Vol. 2. Biology and ecology of parenting* (2nd ed., pp. 285–309). Mahwah, NJ: Erlbaum.

LeVine, R. A. (2003). *Childhood socialization: Comparative studies of parenting, learning and educational change*. Hong Kong: University of Hong Kong.

Lorenz, K. (1935/1970). *Studies in animal and human behavior* (R. Martin, Trans.). London: Methuen.

Lusk, D., & Lewis, M. (1972). Mother-infant interaction and infant developing among the Wolof of Senegal. *Human Development, 15*, 58–69.

Luster, T., & Okagaki, L. (Eds.). (2005). *Parenting: An ecological perspective* (2d ed.). Mahwah, NJ: Erlbaum.

Maccoby, E. E., & Martin, J. A. (1983). Socialization in the context of the family: Parent-child interaction. In M. Hetherington (Ed.), *Handbook of child psychology* (Vol. 10, pp. 1–103). New York: Wiley.

McGillicuddy-De Lisi, A. V., & Subramanian, S. (1996). How do children develop knowledge? Beliefs of Tanzanian and American mothers. In S. Harkness & C. M. Super (Eds.), *Parents' cultural belief systems: Their origins, expressions, and consequences* (pp. 143–168). New York: Guilford.

McHale, J., Khazan, I., Rotman, T., DeCourcey, W., & McConnell, M. (2002). Co-parenting in diverse family systems. In M. H. Bornstein (Ed.), *Handbook of parenting: Vol. 3. Status and social conditions of parenting* (2nd ed., pp. 75–107). Mahwah, NJ: Erlbaum.

Mead, M., & MacGregor, F. C. (1951). *Growth and culture*. New York: Putnam's Sons.

Montagu, A. (Ed.). (1974). *Culture and human development: Insights into growing human*. Englewood Cliffs, NJ: Prentice-Hall.

Munroe, R. L., & Munroe, R. H. (1975). *Cross-cultural human development*. Monterey, CA: Brooks/Cole.

Park, S.-Y., & Cheah, C. S. L. (2005). Korean mothers' proactive socialization beliefs regarding preschoolers' social skills. *International Journal of Behavioral Development, 29*, 24–34.

Parke, R. D. (2002). Fathers and families. In M. H. Bornstein (Ed.), *Handbook of parenting: Vol. 3. Status and social conditions of parenting* (2nd ed., pp. 27–73). Mahwah, NJ: Erlbaum.

Parke, R. D., Dennis, J., Flyr, M. L., Morris, K. L., Leidy, M. S., & Schofield, T. J. (2005). Fathers: Cultural and ecological perspectives. In T. Luster & L. Okagaki (Eds.), *Parenting: An ecological perspective* (2nd ed.). Mahwah, NJ: Erlbaum.

Plomin, R. (1999). Behavioral genetics. In M. Bennett (Ed.), *Developmental psychology: Achievements and prospects* (pp. 231–252). Philadelphia: Psychology Press/Taylor & Francis.

Rebelsky, F. (1967). Infancy in two cultures. *Nederlands Tijdschrift voor de Psychologie, 22*, 379–385.

Rebelsky, F. G. (1972). First discussant's comments: Cross-cultural studies of mother–infant interaction. *Human Development, 15*, 128–130.

Rogoff, B. (Ed.). (2003). *The cultural nature of human development*. New York: Oxford University Press.

Rosenblatt, J. S. (2002). Hormonal basis of parenting in mammals. In M. H. Bornstein (Ed.), *Handbook of parenting: Vol. 2. Biology and ecology of parenting* (2nd ed., pp. 31–60). Mahwah, NJ: Erlbaum.

Rubin, K. H. (1998). Social and emotional development from a cultural perspective. *Developmental Psychology, 34*, 611–615.

Sagara, J. & Kang, R. H. (1998). Parents' effects on children's gender-role attitudes: A comparison between Japan and Korea. *Psychologia, 41*, 189–198.

Sameroff, A. J. (1983). Developmental systems: Contexts and evolution. In W. Kessen (Ed.), P. H. Mussen (Series Ed.), *Handbook of child psychology: Vol. 1. History, theory, and methods* (pp. 237–294). New York: Wiley.

Scarr, S., & McCartney, K. (1983). How people make their own environments: A theory of genotype-environment effects. *Child Development, 54*, 424–435.

Serpell, R. (2000). Intelligence and culture. In R. J. Sternberg (Ed.), *Handbook of intelligence* (pp. 549–577). New York: Cambridge University Press.

Sigel, I. E., & McGillicuddy-De Lisi, A. V. (2002). Parental beliefs and cognitions: The dynamic belief systems model. In M. H. Bornstein (Ed.), *Handbook of parenting: Vol. 3. Status and social conditions of parenting* (2nd ed., pp. 485–508). Mahwah, NJ: Erlbaum.

Stoolmiller, M. (1999). Implications of the restricted range of family environments for estimates of heritability and nonshared environment in behavior-genetic adoption studies. *Psychological Bulletin, 125*, 392–409.

Super, C. (1976). Environmental effects on motor development: The case of "African infant precocity." *Developmental Medicine and Child Neurology, 18*, 561–567.

Super, C. M., & Harkness, S. (1986). The developmental niche: A conceptualization at the interface of child and culture. *International Journal of Behavioral Development, 9*, 545–569.

Tanner, J. M. (1970). Physical growth. In P. Mussen (Ed.), *Carmichael's manual of child psychology* (Vol. 1, pp. 77–155). New York: Wiley.

Teti, D. M., & Candelaria, M. (2002). Parenting competence. In M. H. Bornstein (Ed.), *Handbook of parenting: Vol. 4. Applied parenting* (2nd ed., pp. 149–180). Mahwah, NJ: Erlbaum.

Thelen, E., & Smith, L. B. (1998). Dynamic systems theories. In R. M. Lerner (Ed.), W. Damon (Series Ed.), *Handbook of child psychology: Vol. 1. Theoretical models of human development* (5th ed., pp. 563–634). New York: Wiley.

Tomlinson, M., & Swartz, L. (2003). Imbalances in the knowledge about infancy: The divide between rich and poor countries. *Infant Mental Health Journal, 24*, 547–556.

Turkheimer, E., & Waldron, M. (2000). Nonshared environment: A theoretical, methodological, and quantitative review. *Psychological Bulletin, 126*, 78–108.

van de Vijver, F. J. R., & Leung, K. (1997). Methods and data analysis of comparative research. In J. W. Berry, Y. H. Poortinga, & J. Pandey (Eds.), *Handbook of cross-cultural psychology: Vol. 1. Theory and method* (2nd ed., pp. 257–300). Needham Heights, MA: Allyn & Bacon.

Vondra, B., & Belsky, J. (2005). Developmental origins of parenting: Personality and relationship factors. In T. Luster & L. Okagaki (Eds.), *Parenting: An ecological perspective* (2nd ed.). Mahwah, NJ: Erlbaum.

Vygotsky, L. (1978). *Mind in society.* Cambridge, MA: Harvard University Press.

Wachs, T. D. (2000). *Necessary but not sufficient: The respective roles of single and multiple influences on individual development.* Washington, DC: American Psychological Association.

Wachs, T. D., & Chan, A. (1986). Specificity of environmental action, as seen in environmental correlates of infants' communication performance. *Child Development, 57*, 1464–1474.

Werner, E. E. (1972). Infants around the world: Cross-cultural studies of psychomotor development from birth to two years. *Journal of Cross-Cultural Psychology, 3*, 111–134.

Whiting, J. W. M., & Whiting, B. B. (1960). Contributions of anthropology to the methods of studying child rearing. In P. Mussen (Ed.), *Handbook research methods in child development* (pp. 918–944). New York: Wiley.

# 2

# Cultural Perspectives and Parents' Views of Parenting and Development: Research Directions

## JACQUELINE J. GOODNOW

## INTRODUCTION

One of the goals of this volume is the encouragement of research on culture and parenting. This chapter asks: If you were considering research in this area, what might guide your choice of topic and method? The several chapters provide examples of a variety of choices of topics and methods. I mention some further examples. My main purpose, however, is to step back a little, highlighting questions that many of us have come to see as needed only after becoming immersed in various studies.

The material is in several sections. Each takes for granted that choices of topic and of method are interwoven. Each also starts from a cultural perspective, from an awareness of the fact that we are always members of cultural groups and that both development and parenting need to be seen from that point of view.

The opening pair of sections takes up some large questions that arise at the start of any culturally oriented research. The first asks: *Are cross-cultural comparisons the only way forward*? We may, I suggest, also consider making comparisons within a culture (across subgroups, across historical times, or across generations). Without direct attempts at any comparisons, we may also concentrate on some particular aspects of one culture, including attempts to understand the culture we often see as not needing to be studied: our own.

The second asks: *Why do you want to know? How are others likely to view your interest*? The starting point for researchers may be the wish to add to our conceptual understanding of an issue. It may also be the wish to provide a more informed basis to policy or practice. The starting point (theory, policy, or practice) can make a difference in the kinds of topics we consider. From any starting point, however, it is important to consider in advance how what we propose will be interpreted by the people with whom we wish to work. What are they likely to see as our purpose and to regard as worth doing?

The next three sections assume that we have decided to focus on some specific aspects of parenting. The first of these asks: *Why consider parents' ideas?* That is a major focus for this volume. It has also been a topic of increasing interest over the last 20 years or so. I shall add, however, some arguments for also considering parents' practices, and some proposals for ways of bringing parents' ideas to the surface.

The next question takes the form: *What shall be the focus—the content or the quality of parents' ideas?* Content refers, for example, to parents' ideas about the ages at which children develop various skills, about why they differ from one another, or what is needed for them to do well at school. Quality refers to aspects such as the extent to which ideas are widely shared in a group or—within an individual—are open to change. Content has so far received the lion's share of attention. I argue, however, for increased attention also to aspects of quality.

The last section is headed: *Choosing aspects of parenting: The implications of "parenting in context."* In essence, it takes up questions that follow from regarding parenting as involving more than the face-to-face interactions of parents and their children. Cultural perspectives draw our attention instead to parenting as taking place both within families and within neighborhoods or communities, as not a private activity, as a matter of economics, and as a lifelong activity.

In each section, the examples I use come from a mixture of research by others and research in which I have been involved, with an inevitable bias toward the latter. The several chapters of this book provide additional examples, directions, and bases for the choices we make of topics and of methods. So also does a special issue of the journal *Human Development* (2002, 45 (4)) devoted to the question of how we can study cultural aspects of development. There are times, however, when the sharpest reminders to me of the need to consider various questions about topics and methods come from my own experiences and my own shifts in understanding.

With that much introduction, let me turn to the first issue, the place of cross-cultural methods.

## CROSS-CULTURAL COMPARISONS: ARE THEY THE ONLY WAY FORWARD?

I place this question first because cross-cultural comparisons are often considered as the only way forward if one adopts a cultural perspective. This type of method is certainly one with a long history and one with many examples available. This volume contains several. Others may be seen in a recent issue of a journal for which one of the contributors to this book, Marc Bornstein, is the editor: *Journal of Parenting: Science and Practice*, 2002, 2 (3).

This method is often informative. It has as well the advantage of clearly building on research elsewhere and of being able to capitalize on team efforts. For some time, it was also regarded as the only way of asking whether some behaviors, some developmental sequences, or some ways of thinking are "universal." Part of that thinking was also the assumption that any culture other than the one from which the original data came might serve the purpose. The choice could then easily be made on the basis of convenience.

There are still occasions when we need to turn to other cultures in order to be reminded that the assumptions we make about the "natural" course of development, the "necessary" nature of various conditions, or the "true signs" of successful development are culture-bound. We need to learn that there are other ways of looking after babies or children, other ways of encouraging children to be reasonable members of a family or a group, other ways of schooling, and of defining outcomes such as competence. We also need to learn that these other ways do not end in the disasters to which we expect them to lead.

Why then not stop with this one method? Part of the answer is that this method alone will not always tell us what gives rise to diversity or how particular conditions might be related to particular effects: particular skills, styles, or values. Why is it, for example, that parents in some cultural groups use shaming or teasing more often than parents in other groups do? Tell their children particular kinds of stories? Are more accepting of children sleeping with parents or living with other relatives? How also do we account for the fact that, within any cultural group, there is diversity as well as some degree of similarity?

With questions such as these in mind, we may well turn to comparisons within a culture. We may turn to comparisons across subgroups. The interesting comparisons might be, for example, children with different kinds of schooling or different kinds of experience. They might also be parents with different kinds of employment or different approaches to child-rearing.

The interesting comparisons might also be comparisons across cohorts. Within a culture, we might compare a current time with a previous time, choosing periods where there has been a shift in the social conditions. That second type of comparison is less well known than the first. Let me offer two examples. One is work in Germany on developmental patterns before and after the end of the Berlin Wall, before and after the unification of the two countries. Silbereisen and his colleagues have been making that kind of comparison in relation especially to the ages at which young people make the transitional step of moving away from their parents' home (Silbereisen, Schwartz, & Rinker, 1996).

The second example is the replication of an earlier study on what parents saw as "the value of children." The earlier study was carried out in the 1980s in nine countries by Hoffman and her colleagues, with parents asked to describe "the good things about having children compared with not having children at all" (Hoffman, 1988, p. 109). (Nowadays we might want to phrase that request a little differently). Since that time, however, the labor value of children has often decreased, and the talk is more often—at least in some countries—about the cost of children.

It is then of major interest to discover that Trommsdorff and her colleagues (see chapter by Trommsdorff herein) have repeated that study and that we can look forward to the results soon being available. The study in itself, however, is an example of a method seldom used: one that combines both comparisons across cultures and across cohorts.

Let me broaden the scope still further. Culturally informed perspectives may encourage us to stay within one culture and one group within that, putting our effort into a fuller understanding of some particular viewpoints or some particular practices. Now, in a sense, we are going "down" rather than "across," the essence of what is often referred to as "cultural psychology" rather than "cross-cultural psychology."

### Within a Culture: Working Toward a Deeper Understanding

For an example of this method, I use a series of studies in which I have been involved. They have the advantage of beginning with a cross-cultural comparison, then going down rather than across, and finally returning to a cross-cultural comparison with a new understanding and a change in questions.

The topic in this case concerns the views of parents and children about children carrying out some household tasks, either regularly or on a request basis. The series began with some comments made in the course of comparing two groups of mothers in Australia. These were Anglos (born in the country and native English speakers), and Lebanese-Australian (Lebanese-born but resident in Australia). The research focus was mothers' developmental timetables, the ages at which mothers expected children to display various kinds of competence. One of the questions asked was when children might be expected to have some small but regular jobs around the house, when they might, for example, help set a table, clear a table, hang up some of their clothes, or feed an animal such as a cat. Most of the Anglo mothers saw this as a very sensible question. They also thought it important that children from about the ages of five or six made some contribution to household tasks, with these progressing by age. In contrast, the Lebanese-born mothers thought the question was absurd. They were also quick to offer several reasons for not expecting this kind of behavior from a child. The jobs belonged to the mother. The mother did not need the help. The children were too young (they were not, however, too young to mind still younger children). Daughters would do enough of this kind of work when they got married.

Those comments led me to take a second look at my own unquestioned assumption that of course children should be involved in some way in the work of the household. I began looking for what was expected in several other countries. I also began to look for evidence that involvement in the work of the house had the assumed beneficial effects in the form of "developing character" or "learning about responsibility" (there was very little). The real problem, I came to realize, was that I did not understand why children's contributions mattered so much to Anglo mothers (including myself). There was no point, I felt, in making any further cultural comparisons until I knew more about the meanings of children's tasks within the Anglo group.

With several colleagues, I then came to ask why children's contributions to household tasks were so important to most Anglo mothers, which contributions they saw as more important than others, the extent to which tasks could be moved from one family member to another, what happened if the work was not done, and the place of money in relation to children's contributions (Goodnow, 1996, and Goodnow, in press, provide accounts of much of this work and its implications). In the process, I came to see involvement in the work of a household as a way in which parents introduced children to distinctions among relationships. Making these contributions is one way in which children learn the meaning of being "a family": a unit in which people both receive and contribute. It is as well a way of introducing children to distinctions among relationships (e.g., "mothers" are not "maids" and "the house" is not "a hotel"). In a linked lesson, it also introduces children to recognizing what you should do yourself and what you can ask someone else to do, together with who can be asked and for what reasons.

With the meanings for Anglos better understood, I came to see the possible movement of tasks as part of the definition of family and as relevant to families over the lifespan. Jeanette Lawrence and I, for example, have been using questions about the moveability of various forms of work to explore family members' ideas about the care of elderly parents (Goodnow, Lawrence, Ryan, Karantzas, & King, 2002; Lawrence, Goodnow, Woods, & Karantzas, 2002). What are the parts of caring that can be moved from one family member to another, or to help from outside the family? What are the contributions that should never be passed to someone else, that you should never cease making?

In time also, moves back into cross-cultural comparisons have been made. Now, however, these moves had a more specific focus. Both have been made by a colleague who worked with the Anglo groups (Jennifer Bowes) and has now gathered other colleagues in collaborative work. One move had to do with the place of money in several groups (Bowes, Flanagan, & Taylor, 2000). Could children ever be paid for the work they did? This comparison cut across several countries, comparing those with an essentially socialist ethos with those from an essentially capitalist ethos. Another study looked more to the nature of negotiations within a family. It asked about the extent to which children can negotiate or acceptably decline requests for carrying out a household task, and the bases on which they can do so. Can they, for example, offer bases such as "I didn't make that mess" or "I need to do my homework"? Among Anglo families in Australia, both bases are accepted as grounds for negotiation (not necessarily accepted, but tolerated). Among families in Beijing, only the second kind of negotiation—the first is rejected—is acceptable (Bowes, Chen, Qing San, & Yuan, 2004).

In effect, it is feasible to move back and forth between both approaches: cross-cultural and within a culture. We do not need to choose the one and reject the other. We do, however, need to ask when one approach, or a blend of both, is needed.

## What Does Any Particular Group Especially Offer?

It is temptingly easy to choose to work with a particular culture on the basis of convenience. The ideal, however, is to choose on the basis of there being something available that is especially needed.

Australia, for example, contained at one point some regions that did not yet have television. Some had only the government-sponsored programs. Some had both the government-sponsored and the commercial stations. Here then were conditions that would not be easy to find elsewhere, offering a particular opportunity to study the effect of television on children's use of time and their perceptions of other parts of Australia and other countries.

A second possibility is that a particular place or a particular group presents contrasting values, practices, or effects. Here, for example, is a country where children are expected to sleep alone (own bed, own room) from an early age. Here, in contrast, is another where such "aloneness" is regarded as very strange, as in fact close to neglect or abuse. Given that comparison, we can ask both about how such differences arise or are justified. We can also ask about possible effects on children's preferences, not only when it comes to sleeping, but also in the case of other social activities. Are these also in group rather than solo form? How do others perceive a child's wish to play alone?

The moral in both cases is the same. One needs to ask what any particular place or people or time offers and what specific developmental questions these opportunities might allow one to explore.

## Asking: Why Do You Want to Know? How Will Your Interest Be Interpreted?

At this point, I wish to introduce two sources that influence what we choose to work on and how we proceed. The two sources are sometimes combined. They can, however, lead to different questions or different lines of research.

One of these sources is primarily theoretical. We become aware, for example, of a possible alternative to a basic proposal in someone's theory, of behavior that our current theories would find difficult to account for, or of an unquestioned assumption that may not apply outside our own group.

The other source is primarily related to action or policy. Here, for example, is a group that we wish to work with, give advice to, or persuade to change in their behaviors or their concepts. We start with recognition of there being some differences between this group and our own. In the "old days," researchers were tempted to work from gross descriptions of these differences and gross explanations. These "others," for example, were simply described as "less advanced." The accounts of their being different were also simplistic. They were attributed to "others" being less "modern," less "Western," "disadvantaged," "poor," or "living in unstimulating environments." Now we recognize that such descriptions are both ethnocentric and too gross to be useful. We would do better, for example, to start by asking about the ideas that various groups of people bring to particular situations. What ideas do they already hold, for instance, about schooling, medical problems, the needs of young children, or the influence and responsibilities of parents? We need to understand their ideas, their values, and the meanings they attach to particular ways of thinking or acting.

Let me briefly describe two examples of those beginning points. I take both from my own experience.

The example for starting from a primarily theoretical question is a study in Hong Kong, carried out at a time when Hong Kong offered a special opportunity. Here were children who were not in formal schooling (the schools could not keep pace with the rush of incomers). The children, however, were not rural and their parents valued schooling. Here then was an opportunity to ask: Do Piaget's stages reflect school sequences? Does the big shift from ages 5 to 7 and again around ages 12 to 14 reflect the changes in schooling that typically occur at these times?

For an example of starting more from an interest in action or policy, I go back to the comparison of Anglo-Australian with Lebanese-Australian mothers. That work started with a request from a school facing an ethnic mixture of children at the start of school. Some were seen as ready for school; others were felt not to be ready. Most of the "not ready" came from families where the parents were Lebanese-born. The school had sent home numerous letters, in Arabic, asking the mothers to make sure that the children acquired some "minimal" skills before starting school, skills, for example, such as tying shoelaces or buttoning coats. The request that came to me was phrased as follows. Why are these families not following our advice?

Our first guess was that there could be a difference in when the two sets of mothers—Lebanese and Anglo—thought children were able to do a variety of things. That turned out to be often the case. There was also a difference, however, in the skills mothers thought their children needed to acquire. Knowing how to tie their shoelaces was definitely not a priority for the Lebanese-born mothers. They were, in fact, puzzled as to why this was such a preoccupation on the part of the school. There was as well a difference in what was defined as a parent's responsibility and a school's responsibility. To make headway with the issue of preparations for starting school, the school needed to take all those factors into account. Their letters were being read. The requests simply did not make sense.

Let me now step back from those specific examples and make two general points. The first is that theoretically oriented questions need not be of the kind that asks if the same forms of development will occur under different conditions. The starting point can also be the sense of a gap or a lack of fit. Here, for example, is "a homeless phenomenon," a behavior or a point of view that is not accounted for easily by our current theories. We become aware, for example, that our own current theories say little about the importance of honor or face, that they have difficulty accounting for parents' shaming or teasing their children and regarding these as essential for the development of character. The low degree of attention currently given to spiritual or religious accounts or forms of development is, as Hudley, Haight, and Miller (2003) point out, a prime example of what can be centrally important for many cultural groups but has currently little place in secular "Western" accounts of development.

The second point is that we do not have to choose between starting from a theoretical or an action-oriented problem. Both starting points are feasible and can lead to cultural explorations. The two starting points, however, may highlight different research questions. A concern with action, for example, brings up especially questions about change and about advice, information, or education (Goodnow, 2002). Now we need to explore which ideas are more versus less easy to change. We also need to consider the nature of change. Who is most likely to be listened to, for example? What is regarded as a reasonable request? What happens to the advice we give? Why is some or all of it ignored? What happens if some of our advice is accepted? (The consequences can be destabilizing.) What do we know in general about the ways in which ideas change or about the fate of advice? Questions of that kind do have theoretical significance. They are more likely to be asked, however, if we start with the action-oriented goal of facilitating change and with a culturally informed view of difficulties and misunderstandings.

## How Is What We Propose Likely to Be Interpreted by Others?

I have suggested so far that we ask ourselves what our reasons are for undertaking any particular piece of research. One of the salutary lessons learned from cultural research is that we would also do well to consider how what we do is regarded by the people with whom we hope to work. We often say to children, for example, that the tasks we present are a test or a game. Those words, however, have very different meanings for children of different ages and different backgrounds. The questions we ask of parents can also be interpreted in many ways. At the least, for example, we have all learned that the tasks we give to children can be interpreted by mothers as assessing the child's or the mother's competence.

For an example of needing to consider interpretations, I draw again from my own experience. I had, without difficulty, used several Piagetian tasks with children in Hong Kong, both schooled and unschooled. With a few exceptions (within the schooled group), these children took quite readily to the tasks. They gave some thought to what they were asked and, when asked why they gave a particular answer to a problem, happily went through their reasons. In my naïveté at the time, I did not anticipate great difficulty when I tried the same tasks with African-American children in some "poor" schools. These children, however, quickly made it clear that they were present only because they had been told to do so. They found the tasks uninteresting. Asked why they gave a particular answer, they interpreted the question as meaning the first one was unsatisfactory, so they switched to the opposite answer.

I threw the data out, feeling that it was "unreliable" and "meant nothing." It was only later that I realized that it meant a great deal. It meant that the tasks and I were irrelevant to these children's lives. If I wanted to know anything about what they could do, I would need to start by knowing more about their lives and their valued skills. It meant also that I should give more serious thought to the assumptions we bring to all the tasks and questions that we present to children or to parents, to the efforts we are asking them to make, and to what they regard as the interesting things to talk about or to assess. That is an issue to which I have continued to return (e.g., Goodnow and Collins, 1990). It is one we all too readily forget, especially when people cooperate with us out of courtesy but with their own understanding and their own assessment of what we are asking.

# CHOOSING A RESEARCH TOPIC: THE NATURE OF PARENTS' IDEAS

Choosing a research topic involves moving toward an increasingly specific question, asking all the time why the choice goes in one direction rather than another. I take as an example the study of parents' ideas about parenting and development, a topic of interest in several of the chapters in this volume and of interest to me for some time. Why choose such a topic? The most general reason is that meanings matter as well as behaviors. The actions by children or professionals that parents observe may be interpreted by them in more than one way. The actions they take may reflect a variety of goals or intentions.

What do cultural perspectives add to that general argument? To start with, they add considerable strength to the argument that meanings matter. Behaviors that seem the same across cultural groups, it is pointed out, may differ in their meanings from one group to another. Behaviors that seem "strange" to an outsider can become comprehensible once we know what they mean to the people within a culture. In effect, the second reason is that meanings make "strange" behaviors comprehensible.

A third reason often offered is that the ideas people hold may lead to the actions they take. If we change the ideas people hold, we might then change their behaviors.

At this point, culturally informed perspectives put up a large warning sign: Be careful! They also add some new ways of considering actions and the links between ideas and actions. To bring those out, let me introduce the concept of cultural practices.

## The Nature of Cultural Practices

This concept starts with the recognition that actions or behaviors differ from each other. Some parental actions, for example, have qualities that give them the form of "cultural practices." To take one summary definition, these are "actions that are repeated, shared with others in a social group, and invested with normative expectations and with meanings or significances that go beyond the immediate goals of the action" (Miller & Goodnow, 1995, p. 7). The ways in which people dress, the forms of speech they use to others, arrangements for where children sleep, divisions of parenting between mothers and fathers, the care that older children provide for younger children, distinctions between what occurs in public or in private: all of these may have the quality of cultural practices.

Why are practices interesting? Cultural perspectives urge us to consider four possibilities when it comes to ideas and actions.

- Actions with the quality of practices may be so taken for granted that reasons for them are difficult to put into words. They are, in many ways, not examined or reflected upon.
- Changing the stated reasons may not alter the practices. People may learn, for example, to say that children should be treated equally without regard to whether they are sons or daughters, or that fathers should share in the care of children, but continue to act differentially. They may be genuine and sincere in the way their views are changed, but the behaviors could still have a life of their own.
- Ideas may emerge from practices, rather than the other way round. As parents or as children, for example, we are drawn into ongoing practices and the ideas we hold are then constructed around those. To use one often-quoted phrase, the first step in the development of gender schemas is one of "doing gender" (West & Zimmerman, 1987). Parents may also begin parenting (or new phases of parenting) with relatively unformed ideas that are quickly shaped by the established, taken-for-granted practices they encounter and in which they take part.
- Practices may offer a very useful step toward unraveling the ideas that people hold. It may be far easier, for example, to begin talking about the way things are done than to ask a question about an abstract concept. To take a concrete example, we found it best, when exploring the ideas that mothers held about children's contributions to the work of a family, to walk through the child's day asking exactly what a child did at various times, starting from the time of waking up, and then building our questions about any tasks on the basis of those sequences. Starting with a general question about a child's work gave us essentially stereotyped replies.

## How Shall We Bring Parents' Ideas to the Surface?

It is sometimes feasible to ask people directly about the ideas they hold. We might ask, for example, how important certain kinds of skills or certain personal qualities are to parents, what kinds of occupations they would like their children to have, whether they think children learn better by example or by direct instruction, or when they think it is too early or too late to offer advice or information.

One difficulty, however, is that asking such direct questions, especially in a series and in an interview format, may not be meaningful to our informants (Miller, Wang, Sandel, & Cho, 2002, is an excellent source that details this difficulty and some ways of overcoming it; see also Miller, Hengst, & Wang, in press). Another difficulty, even when people are accustomed to direct questions and to an interview format, is that some of the ideas that are most central to our thinking are not easily put into words. These ideas may, in fact, be so much taken for granted and so bound up in routine ways of acting that we have never needed to come up with a reason for doing them. I, for example, had never given thought to why my children should make some contribution to the work of a household. They "just owed something to the house." Within limits, they could choose what they contributed. Tasks such as setting the table or washing the dishes (in the days before dishwashers), however, were simply "children's jobs" except in special circumstances, and negotiations were seldom about "why" this might be so.

We may then need a variety of ways to bring parents' ideas to the surface. We may start from the words parents use, the stories they tell about their children or to their children, their everyday routines, their description of times when they felt happy or less than happy about the way things were going, or their comments on other parents' ways of doing things. To return to the example of children's jobs, for example, it helped—once we had a sense of what mothers and children did—to ask mothers if they would ever do things in some other way, choosing an approach we thought they would reject, and then ask why not. It helped as well to describe some of what other mothers had reported. We began, for example, to ask what mothers said to their children if their jobs were not done. We then added some comments from other mothers. For example: "Some mothers tell us that they say things like 'I'm not your servant' or 'the maid didn't come today.' Do you have any favorite sayings like that? " That question brought us a great deal more information.

Such approaches may take a variety of forms (cf. Miller et al., 2003). Let me select two that illustrate ways of starting from apparently simple behaviors and working toward the meanings that they hold.

One of these approaches uses as a base the stories that parents tell to or about their children, stories that bring out the extent to which parents see their goal as one of raising a child's confidence and self-esteem or of shaping the extent to which a child acquires "correct" behaviors (e.g., Miller, Fung, & Mintz, 1996).

The other comes from some work by Thorne (personal communication, July 2003). Part of her research on the nature of parenting within several cultural groups in Oakland (California) consisted of exploring the nature of invitations and of "who plays with whom": behaviors embodying ideas about the place and relevance of family and friends. (Thorne, in press, has also used the way school lunches are organized as an everyday practice that brings out the way differences in practices are negotiated.)

As those examples suggest, I see great benefit in drawing methods and concepts from several areas of theory and research. These may range, for example, from the psychology of social cognition to anthropologists' approaches to cultural models and cultural practices. They may cover methods described as quantitative, qualitative, or ethnographic. Especially for the study of parents' ideas, I propose, we need to be eclectic. One approach often highlights what another misses. One method may be better suited to research at a particular point than others. The critical task is to ask when, and for what questions, one method or some mixture of methods meets our purposes better than others.

## FOR THE STUDY OF PARENTS' IDEAS: FOCUS ON CONTENT OR ON QUALITY?

Suppose you have decided to work on the ideas people hold. You now have a choice among three large topics. These have to do with the nature of parents' ideas, their sources, and their consequences. The three are interrelated and I have an interest in all three. To ask effectively about sources and consequences, however, we first need useful ways of describing the nature of the ideas held. I then give priority to that area, but without suggesting that this is the only question that matters.

Deciding to work on parents' ideas, however, is not the end of one's choices. The next decision is whether to concentrate on an aspect of content, an aspect of quality, or some concentration on both. The distinction is not always an obvious one, but it is important.

We are exploring *content* when we ask what parents' ideas are about: when we ask about the goals parents hope to achieve, the means they see as best to use, the sequence that development takes, or the ways in which they can tell if all is going well. Research on parents' ideas covers a wide range of such questions. For example:

- What do you think children are like?
- How do they change as they grow older?
- Are they very much like one another or are there large individual differences?
- How early can you see the kinds of personality they are likely to have, or how intelligent they are?

In contrast, *quality* refers to some particular characteristics of the ideas people hold. We are exploring the quality of ideas, for example, when we ask about the extent to which one idea is consistent with another, the extent to which ideas are shared across generations or among parents in a given cultural group, the degree of conviction or commitment attached to an idea, or the ease with which an idea shifts in the face of a change in information or experience.

Does the distinction matter? One reason for making it is that aspects of content and quality may vary in their consequences. To take one example, consider the quality of being shared with others: an integral part of approaches to parents' ideas in terms of ethnotheories, cultural models, folk theories, or social representations. The quality of being shared has some specific consequences. When people share a common view, for example, they can communicate more easily with each other. They feel more at ease with each other. They feel "understood." And, if you hold ideas like theirs, they tend to think that you are also a sensible person.

A second reason is that the quality of ideas may be what distinguishes one person from another, even when the content of their ideas is the same. To use an example from D'Andrade (1992) and Strauss (1992), most people may consider that we should all help the poor. For some, however, that idea may be held without conviction. It leads to no action. For others, that idea may guide action when a choice arises. For still others, it may initiate action: it is held with a level of conviction or commitment that gives rise to a search for ways to put it into action.

## Focusing on the Quality of Parents' Ideas

Questions about the content of parents' ideas are the ones that most readily come to mind. Questions about quality, however, are often of particular interest. To make that point clearer, let me choose two qualities. The first has to do with the extent to which parents' ideas are shared with other parents. The second has to do with variations among people (among parents or between generations) in the degree of importance attached to various values or goals. There are other qualities we might consider. We might ask, for example, about the extent to which ideas that are "different" are approved, tolerated, or regarded as dangerous or, looking more within the individual, about the extent to which ideas are consistent with each other, are reflected upon, or rise quickly to the surface (are "highly accessible"). The two qualities chosen, however, provide a base for bringing out how cultural perspectives may inform the ways in which we consider parents' ideas. Both also suggest directions for further research.

**Parents' Ideas as Shared With Others.**  I set aside here interest in the extent to which ideas are shared among members of a family: between a mother and a father, for example, or between parents and children. The focus instead is on the extent to which ideas are shared with others in the community or culture.

What do cultural perspectives suggest on this score? The major analysis comes from Romney and his colleagues (e.g., Romney, Weller, & Batchelder, 1986). That analysis points to differences among individuals in the extent to which the views held are close to those that are modal in the group or are at some distance from the center. Interestingly, that position affects the way in which individuals are regarded by others. Those closest to the center, for example, are likely to be seen by others as especially trustworthy. In a sense, here are our "solid citizens."

Surprisingly, there are relatively few studies of parenting that study this quality. One that stands out for me, and that offers a possible basis for further research, is a study by Deal, Halvorson, and Wampler (1989). In that study, the children of parents whose views on parenting were most like those of other parents tended to be regarded by people outside the family as well-adjusted. How that kind of effect comes about remains to be determined. Another is a study by Dawber and Kuczynski (1997). Parents who expected other parents to hold values similar to their own were likely to feel confident in their judgments and to treat other people's children in ways similar to the ways they treated their own.

We could well take those studies further. As Kuczynski (1997) points out, we have a great deal yet to learn about parents' views of the degree of conformity that others see as unimportant, will tolerate, or will condemn. We also have much to learn about children's perceptions of parents' holding shared or "different" views. When, for example, do children see parents' holding modal views as quaint or old-fashioned? When do they see a parent's difference from other parents as an amusing eccentricity, a positive quality, or as weird?

## Variations in the Importance Attached to Various Values or Goals.

Both differentiate among the ideas that people hold in terms of the quality of commitment. To repeat an earlier example, there may be a great deal of consensus within a culture on views such as "everyone should help the poor," or "everyone can be whatever they want to be, if they try hard enough." Some people, however, may hold those views at the level of a cliché. Others may hold them at a level of commitment that will guide action when a choice or a demand arises or initiate actions in line with the view held (D'Andrade, 1992; Strauss, 1992).

How is that kind of view relevant to the study of parents' ideas? It has three ramifications. It alters our view of differences among parents or between generations. It is also relevant to questions about change. Let me add some reasons for being interested in each of those implications.

The first implication is that *differences among people or between generations may take the form of similar content but different degrees of importance.* When we compare one set of views with another, we may find that the list of valued goals or approved methods is the same. What varies, however, is the position on the list. What is high on one may be less high on another. What is valued in one culture is not then simply absent in another. The difference may lie instead in the relative value attached.

As a specific example, and one that provides a useful base for further research, I take studies by Fuligni and his colleagues (Fuligni, 2001; Fuligni, Tseng, & Lam, 1999). Fuligni is interested in several groups in the United States—groups varying in cultural heritage—and in the relative degrees of importance attached to various goals and family obligations. The reports focus on the views of adolescents, but they could be considered also in relation to parents. Here is Fuligni's own summary of some of these results.

> As compared to their peers from European backgrounds, Chinese, Filipino, Mexican, and Central and South American youths believe that they should spend more time doing things such as taking care of their siblings, helping out around the house, assisting their parents at work and in official tasks (such as dealing with government offices), and spending time with the family.
>
> (Fuligni, 2001, p. 62).

These activities are not devalued by those with European backgrounds. The amount of time and effort they warrant, however (their position on the list in comparison with, say, time spent in leisure or with peers), is simply lower.

A further difference, Fuligni continues, is the perception of school achievement as an obligation to parents. Asian and Latin-American adolescents often attach a high degree of importance to success in education not for themselves but as a family obligation. Again, that view of education is not unknown among European-American teenagers. Who wishes to disappoint their parents? The level of importance attached to this aspect of education, however, is less than it is among teenagers from Asian and Latin-American families.

A similar type of analysis can also be brought to bear on cross-generation differences. A lack of consensus is often viewed as a "disagreement," with the implication that this is likely to be a cause for disappointment or conflict. The difference in viewpoints, however, may be on a topic that is of little importance to parents. Parents may even view a difference in a positive light, seeing it as a sign that their children are moving forward rather than being constrained by the views of an older generation (Goodnow, 1994).

Considering variations in importance can also be helpful when it comes to *understanding aspects of change and flexibility in parents' ideas.* Let me anchor that kind of possibility in a specific area. This concerns the ideas parents hold about money in relation to the household tasks that children do. Suppose, for example, that a child is reluctant to do the household jobs that he or she is expected to do. For some Anglo-Australian parents, that kind of circumstance makes no difference to the view they hold about money. Money and household contributions should never be associated with each other. Children should con-tribute work because "they live here," or because "they are part of the family." In effect, the level of importance attached to this way of proceeding remains steady. For other parents, a child's reluctance weakened their attachment to the view that money and children's work should not go together. In the words of one, "If that's what it takes to get them started or keep them involved, then OK." They still felt that money and work should not go together but that goal now moved down the list in the face of competition with the goal of involving the child in some form of work.

With those kinds of comments in mind, we began to change the kinds of question we asked. We came, for example, to ask—about money and about other aspects of work—whether doing things in a particular way would be regarded by a parent as "no problem," "not my first choice," "only as a last resort," or "never—out of the question." The "purists" about money, you may wish to note (the "never" group) were very much a minority in this Anglo-Australian sample (Goodnow & Warton, 1992). The majority did not attach a fixed level of importance to a particular way of proceeding. Instead, they met changing circumstances by shifting the position of various items in their list of hoped-for outcomes.

I have since kept an eye open in the literature for other examples of parents changing the level of attachment to a particular view, either about goals or about methods. The analysis I draw attention to is one by Rodman (1963). The difference between parents of varying income with regard to goals such as children's levels of education, he argued, is in the degree of "value-stretch." Both groups list a child's education as an important goal. In the face of difficulty, however, low-income parents are more likely to compromise or to lower their hopes rather than hold to their original goals and redouble their efforts. Why that might be the case is an open question. So also is the possibility that value-stretch might apply more to some other values among middle-income parents. Degrees of stretch, however—together with what parents see as a "bottom line"—are aspects of parents' ideas that call for more attention than they have so far.

## NEW QUESTIONS: SEEING PARENTING FROM A CULTURAL PERSPECTIVE

One of the major ways in which culturally informed perspectives influence our thinking and our decisions is by *changing our concepts of parenting*. They do so in a variety of ways. Here, for example, is a short list, starting with the familiar phrase, "parenting occurs in context."

- *Parenting occurs in several contexts.* It occurs in a family context: a context usually of siblings and often that of another parent, another interested adult, or a larger and more extended family. It occurs also in a context of neighborhoods or communities and, on a larger scale, a cultural/economic/historical context.
- *Parenting is not a private activity.* At the very least, others in the family provide an audience. The audience extends also to all those who observe what happens and may feel that they have the right to judge, to comment, or to take over.
- *Parenting is a lifelong activity.* It is one that extends well beyond the years of childhood.
- *Parenting is a matter of economics.* Decisions about whether to have children, how many to have, and at what time, for example, are increasingly influenced by questions of cost as well as by religious advice or by assessments of the pleasures of children.

Each of those views of parenting corrects a bias often found in Western research on parenting. Each also opens new questions about parents' ideas. To make them concrete, let me take the first three proposals in the list, breaking the first one into two parts (family and social contexts).

**Parenting Takes Place in a Family Context.**   Given its emphasis on social groups, cultural perspectives might seem to have less to say about the exploration of interactions and ideas within the family. They contain, however, an emphasis on the family as a unit that tends to be forgotten when we focus on parent–child dyads and on parents' perceptions of individual differences among their children (differences, for example, in temperament rather than the differences in birth order that are emphasized by labels or names such as "first son" or "girl with an older brother").

Interest in families as units has sometimes surfaced in the form of whole cultures being described as either "individualist" or "collectivist" in orientation, with the latter giving more value, for example, to "the good of the family" than to "the good of the individual." More subtly, it has also surfaced in the form of regarding people as being "individualist" in some situations and "collectivist" in others. Cultures then differ in the situations in which they emphasize or talk about the good of the family, the good of the community, or the good of the individual.

To what do cultural perspectives of that kind alert us? For me, they have had the effect of alerting me to occasions when parents within a supposedly individualist culture use terms such as "the family" or when they justify their actions with statements such as "Because we're a family" or "You don't do things like that in a family." Statements of that kind were certainly one reason for my interest in children's household tasks in an Anglo-Australian group. Here were actions that parents often commented on as needing to be taken because "We're a family." Some put the reasons for tasks in more individualist terms (e.g., "It develops character"). The more frequent reasons, however, were in terms of children learning that "We're a family."

It seems reasonable to assume that parents in all cultures teach children about the implications of "being a family": the obligations and entitlements it involves, for example, and the behaviors seen as a violation of being "one of the family." The challenge is to find ways of exploring the nature of that teaching and the ways in which parents, in any cultural group, introduce children into concepts of family and into distinctions between "family" and "not family."

## Parenting Takes Place in Neighborhoods and Communities.

Developmental psychology, to provide a rough summary, has often shown an interest in parent–child pairs or dyads. We have learned a great deal, for example, about who initiates interactions between mother and baby, about the ways in which parents draw distinctions among their children as individuals, and about the effects of matches or mismatches in temperament. Bit by bit, we have added other people to the dyad. We have come, for example, to take an increasing interest in the effects of the mother–father relationship, in the place of siblings, in the place of grandparents, and in the way one family relationship affects others. Family psychology (especially "family systems" theory) has added a further interest in the way several relationships are intertwined, with particular attention to the way stability is regained after change. Within a "system," for example, stability can be regained by people coming to stand in for each other, by tasks being moved around, or by alliances being formed or reshaped.

Now we are being asked to consider as well contexts and conditions outside the family. Where does that added consideration lead? To start with, it can lead to a search for ways of distinguishing one neighborhood context from another. We might, for example, differentiate among them in terms of the levels of "toxicity" or violence that family members encounter (e.g., Garborino, Kostelny, & Barry, 1997), the resources and opportunities that a community may offer (e.g., Weisner, 2002), or the way spaces, activities, and parental time are arranged for children of various ages (e.g., Harkness & Super, 1995).

In less ecological fashion, we might also now consider parents' and children's perceptions of their neighborhood. We are encouraged, for example, to ask about the way parents view their neighborhoods (its dangers and its possibilities), about the skills they see themselves as able to bring to bear, about the ways in which they can best prepare their children to make the most of their neighborhood or avoid the worst of it. When parents anticipate a critically evaluative audience, for example, they may see it as important to teach a child a great deal about the public "presentation of self." When they anticipate an indifferent or hostile world (one that threatens to undermine their efforts), they may see it as important to "cocoon" a child from outside influences or to "pre-arm" them for difficult events (Goodnow, 1997).

Suggestions of that kind, I need to underline, do not imply that developmental psychology ignores the way parents prepare their children for life beyond the family. The work of Rogoff and her colleagues, for example (work that also starts from a cultural perspective) is built around a view of parents as assisting children to participate in joint activities with adults (e.g., Rogoff, 2002). I am proposing, however, that we now broaden the forms of anticipatory parental work that we consider, with an eye particularly to the views that parents hold about the worlds their children are likely to encounter and the qualities or the armor they are likely to need.

### Parenting Is Not a Private Activity.

What do cultural perspectives add on this score? I see them as first helping to correct a bias in the way we often think about parenting. We are often slow, I suggest, to recognize the extent to which the notion of parenting as private is an illusion. Other people always evaluate and comment, but perhaps not face to face. "The law" can also always "interfere," with control ranging from compulsory schooling to constraints over forms of discipline.

Cultural perspectives also encourage us to ask about the nature of the distinctions that people draw between what is regarded as public and what is regarded as private. All cultures make a distinction. They differ, however, in what they place in the public or private categories. In Western societies with an "Anglo" or "European" heritage, for example, people often regard as private many aspects of parenting that other cultures would regard as less so. Many, for example, consider that breast-feeding should always be a private activity. Many also regard as private, sexual activity (affectionate or abusive in type) and, perhaps, discussions of money.

Cultural perspectives encourage us also to ask: Does "private" mean "not in front of the child" or "not for discussion outside the family?" People engaged in discussions with parents often find themselves faced with differences on this score. In many groups formed to give advice on family planning to mothers from immigrant groups in Australia, for example, Anglo instructors find it difficult to proceed when the mothers bring children with them.

A third suggestion stems again from my recurring interest in the nature and fate of advice. Once parenting is recognized as not a private activity, questions quickly arise about differences in who is seen as able to give what advice, and when advice, however helpful, is regarded as interference. Within Australia, for example, to stay within an Anglo world, one of the biggest debates has been around official reluctance to interfere in domestic disputes or in the sanctity of the home. This definition of what is "private" has often been a major handicap in the recognition and treatment of abuse, both of children and of adults. The definitions are changing. Both the changes and the variations across groups, however, alert us to the need to know more about what parents regard as appropriate areas of silence or family matters only, and about the distinctions they draw between helpful advice and interference.

A fourth and last suggestion has to do with the need to explore what child behaviors parents see as reflecting on the quality of a child's parenting or on a family's reputation. It is not uncommon for parents to feel embarrassed by the actions of their children. The degree to which embarrassment is felt, however, and the particular behaviors that give rise to a sense of embarrassment or dishonor, are matters that we do not yet fully understand.

**Parenting Is a Long-Term, Lifespan Activity.**  This is the last aspect of parenting that I choose as an area where a cultural perspective can alter the way we look at the nature of parenting and the research questions we ask. Western families, Margaret Mead once proposed, often tend to regard themselves as "launching pads" (Mead, cited in Wolfenstein, 1955). Children are expected to move out of the family and to establish relationships with people to whom they are not related. That kind of expectation seems to be mirrored in our research emphasis on topics such as the development of independence and autonomy in children and on the way parents encourage and help their children to develop friendships with unrelated others. It may also contribute to the conviction that parents' interactions with very young children are the most important interactions to consider. Overall, we seem, Ryff and Seltzer (1996) comment, to focus on relationships between parents and children up to the end of adolescence and then take the subject up again only when parents are elderly and in possible need of care.

What do cultural perspectives add here? They remind us that in many cultural groups family ties are expected to become deeper rather than weaker over time. With that view of the future, parents are likely to see it as important to encourage kinship ties and family obligations. They are also likely to hold quite different expectations about patterns of contact during a child's adulthood. Those differential views of involvement over time may apply also to young adults. To take a further comment from Fuligni (2001, p. 62), "Asian and Latin American teenagers . . . tend to believe that . . . obligations to their families exist through their lives; they do not diminish as the youths themselves become adults." That view seems also to resist Americanization: "Even adolescents from American-born Asian and Latin American families endorse such a belief more strongly than their European American peers do" (Fuligni, 2001, p. 62).

Cultural perspectives also suggest that we might well explore ideas about parenting in relation to time. At the moment, for example, we know relatively little about when parents regard their work as done, their influence as largely over, or their advice as no longer appropriate. Exploring those aspects of parents' ideas would round out our understanding of the ways in which parents, and probably their children, view the nature of parenting.

One last suggestion: once we begin to see parenting as a lifelong activity, we are more likely to ask what is expected of parents and children toward the end of parents' lives. That question is often taken up in terms of the extent to which parents, in various cultures, are expected to plan to be self-supporting in late life, or can anticipate being supported or helped by their children. It can also be taken up in terms of the extent to which the distribution of parents' goods or assets is linked to the extent to which children provide care for their parents. We know already that patterns such as these vary across cultures. Most of the work, however, is linked to studies focused on aging or on changes in social mores and the distribution of wealth. We know far less about the ways in which the expectations of later-life arrangements alter the ways in which parents treat children at a younger age. We know little also about the extent to which parents regard arrangements in the later phases of the family cycle as a continuation or a revival of parenting tasks faced earlier (e.g., the tasks of maintaining family harmony or of avoiding any appearance of favoritism). Cultural perspectives remind us that the kinds of sharp divides that developmental psychology often places between earlier and later phases of the family cycle and the individual life cycle may well be artificial.

## A FINAL COMMENT

Throughout this chapter, I have taken the viewpoint of someone considering how to combine an interest in culture with the study of development and parenting. What might be done differently if we start from the recognition that all parenting and all development occur within a cultural setting? What new questions, what new groups of people, or new methods might now be considered?

   With that possible position in mind, I have begun by first trying to undo any assumption that the first and only thing to do is to compare people from different cultural groups, a task that may as well seem to call for a discouraging search for at least one group that is exotically different from the cultures we know best. I have instead proposed that cross-cultural comparisons are only one of a collection of methods we might use, directed toward only one of many questions we might ask. I have, as an alternate approach, set the goal as one of bringing a culturally oriented or culturally informed perspective to all aspects of development or parenting. With that in mind, I have proceeded through a series of questions, each oriented toward choices of topic and method and each building on the view. That series, I hope, brings with it a view of development and parenting that rounds out and enriches the views we already hold and the research questions we already ask.

## ACKNOWLEDGMENTS

This chapter was based on a paper given at an ISSBD Workshop, Seoul, Korea, 2003, on the topic: Parental Beliefs, Parenting, and Child Development From Cross-Cultural Perspectives.

   My debts are several. Thanks are due especially to colleagues in several Universities with whom these ideas have been discussed, to Peggy Miller for her timely provision of especially relevant material, to participants in the ISSBD workshop at Seoul who gave the first version of this chapter a constructive hearing, and to Macquarie University for research support.

# REFERENCES

Bowes, J. M., Chen, M.-J., Qing San, L., & Yuan, L. (2004). Reasoning and negotiation about child responsibility in urban Chinese families: Reports from mothers, fathers, and children. *International Journal of Behavioral Development, 28,* 48–58.

Bowes, J. M., Flanagan, C. A., & Taylor, A. J. (2000). Adolescents' ideas about individual and social responsibility in relation to children's household work: International comparisons. *International Journal of Behavioral Development, 25,* 60–68.

D'Andrade, R. G. (1992). Schemas and motivations. In R. G. D'Andrade & C. Strauss (Eds.), *Human motives and cultural models* (pp. 23–44). Cambridge, UK: Cambridge University Press.

Dawber, T., & Kuczynski, L. (1997). The question of ownness: Parent-child interactions in the context of the relationship. Manuscript, Department of Family Studies, University of Guelph.

Deal, J. E., Halvorson, C. F., & Wampler, K. F. (1979). Parental agreement on child-rearing orientations: Relations to parental, marital and child characteristics. *Child Development, 60,* 1025–1034.

Fuligni, A. J. (2001). Family obligation and academic motivation of adolescents from Asian, Latin American, and European backgrounds. In A. J. Fuligni (Ed.), *Family obligation and assistance during adolescence: Contextual variations and developmental implications* (pp. 61–76). San Francisco: Jossey-Bass.

Fuligni, A. J., Tseng, V., & Lam, M. (1999). Attitudes toward family obligations among American adolescents from Asian, Latin American, and European backgrounds. *Child Development, 70,* 1030–1044.

Garborino, J., Kostelny, K., & Barry, F. (1997). Value transmission in an ecological context: The high-risk neighborhood, In J. E. Grusec & L. Kuczynski (Eds.), *Parenting and children's internalization of values* (pp. 307–333). New York: Wiley.

Goodnow, J. J. (1994). Acceptable disagreement across generations. In J. Smetana (Ed.), *Beliefs about parenting: Origins and developmental implications* (pp. 51–64). San Francisco: Jossey-Bass.

Goodnow, J. J. (1996). From household practices to parents' ideas about work and interpersonal relationships. In S. Harkness & C. Super (Eds.), *Parents' cultural belief systems* (pp. 313–344). New York: Guilford.

Goodnow, J. J. (1997). Parenting and the "transmission" and "internalization" of values: From social-cultural perspectives to within-family analyses. In J. E. Grusec & L. Kuczynski (Eds.), *Handbook of parenting and the transmission of values* (pp. 333–361). New York: Wiley.

Goodnow, J. J. (2002). Parents' knowledge and expectations: Using what we know. In M. H. Bornstein (Ed.), *Handbook of parenting* (2nd ed., Vol. 3, pp. 439–436)). Mahwah, NJ: Erlbaum.

Goodnow, J. J. (in press). Contexts, diversity, pathways: Linking and extending with a view to theory and practice. In C. R. Cooper, C. García Coll, T. Bartko, H. Davis, & C. Chatman (Eds.), *Hills of gold: Rethinking diversity and contexts as resources for children's developmental pathways.* New York: Oxford University Press.

Goodnow, J. J. (in press). Fiske's model of orientations to social life: The domain of work in households. In N. Haslam (Ed.), *Relational models theory: Advances and prospects.* Mahwah, NJ: Erlbaum.

Goodnow, J. J., Lawrence, J. A., Ryan, J. K., Karantzas, G., & King, K. (2002). Extending studies of collaborative cognition by way of caregiving situations. *International Journal of Behavioral Development, 26,* 16–25.

Goodnow, J. J., & Collins, W.A. (1990). Development according to parents: The nature, sources, and consequences of parents' ideas. Hillsdale, NJ: Erlbaum.

Goodnow, J. J., & Warton, P. M. (1992). Contexts and cognitions: Taking a pluralist view. In P. Light & G. Butterworth (Eds.), *Context and cognition* (pp. 85–112). London: Harvester Wheatsheaf.

Harkness, S., & Super, C. M. (1995). Culture and parenting. In M. Bornstein (Ed.), *Handbook of parenting* (pp. 211–234). Hillsdale, NJ: Erlbaum.

Hoffman, L. W. (1988). Cross-cultural differences in child-rearing goals. In R. A. LeVine, P. M. Miller, & M. M. West (Eds.), Parental behavior in diverse societies. San Francisco: Jossey-Bass.

Hudley, E. V. P., Haight, W., & Miller, P. J. (2003) *"Raise up a child": Human development in an African–American family.* Chicago: Lyceum.

Kuczynski, L. (1997). Models of conformity and resistance in socialization theory. In J. E. Grusec & L. Kuczynski (Eds.), *Handbook of parenting and the transmission of values* (pp. 227–258). New York: Wiley.

Lawrence, J. A., Goodnow, J. J., Woods, K., & Karantzas, G. (2002). Distributing caregiving tasks among family members: The place of gender and availability. *Journal of Family Psychology, 16,* 493–569.

Miller, P. J., Fung, H., & Mintz, J. (1996). Self-construction through narrative practices: A Chinese and American comparison of socialization. *Ethos, 24,* 1–44.

Miller, P. J., & Goodnow, J. J. (1995).Cultural practices: Toward an integration of culture and development. In J. J. Goodnow, P. J. Miller, & F. Kessel (Eds.), *Cultural practices as contexts for development* (pp. 5–16). San Francisco: Jossey-Bass.

Miller, P. J., Hengst, J. A., & Wang, S.-H. (2003). Ethnographic methods: Applications from developmental cultural psychology. In P. Camic, J. Rhodes, & L. Yardley (Eds.), *Qualitative research in psychology: Expanding perspectives in methodology and design.* (pp. 219–242). Washington, DC: American Psychological Association.

Miller, P. J., Wang, S.-H., Sandel, T., & Cho, G. E. (2002). European American and Taiwanese mothers' beliefs about self-esteem fit into their local folk theories about parenting. *Journal of Parenting: Science and Practice, 2,* 209–240.

Rodman, H. (1963). The lower-class value stretch. *Social Forces, 42,* 205–215.

Romney, A. K., Weller, S. C., & Batchelder, W. H. (1986). Culture as consensus: A theory of culture and informant accuracy. *American Anthropologist, 88,* 313–332.

Rogoff, B. (2003). *The cultural nature of human development.* New York: Oxford University Press.

Ryff, C. D., & Seltzer, M. M. (1996). *The parental experience in mid-life.* Chicago: University of Chicago Press.

Silbereisen, R. K., Schwartz, B., & Rinker, B. (1996). The timing of psychosocial transitions in adolescence: Commonalities and differences in unified Germany. In J. Youniss (Ed.), *After the wall: Family adaptation in East and West Germany* (pp. 23–38). San Francisco: Jossey-Bass.

Strauss, C. (1992) Models and motives. In R. G. D'Andrade & C. Strauss (Eds.), *Human motives and cultural models* (pp. 1–20). Cambridge, UK: Cambridge University Press.

Thorne, B. (in press). Unpacking school lunchtime: Structures, practices, and the negotiation of differences. In C. R. Cooper, C. García Coll, T. Bartko, H. Davis, & C. Chatman (Eds.), *Hills of gold: Rethinking diversity and contexts as resources for children's developmental pathways).* New York: Oxford University Press.

Weisner, T. (2002). Ecocultural pathways, family values, and parenting. *Journal of Parenting: Science and Practice, 2,* 325–334.

West, C., & Zimmerman, D. (1987). Doing gender. *Gender and Society, 1987,* 125–151.

Wolfenstein, M. (1955). French parents take their children to the park. In M. Mead & M. Wolfenstein (Eds.), *Childhood in contemporary culture* (pp. 99–117). Chicago: University of Chicago Press.

# II

*Cultural Perspectives on Parents' Beliefs About Childhood, Parenting, and Parent–Child Relationships*

# 3

# Themes and Variations: Parental Ethnotheories in Western Cultures

## SARA HARKNESS AND CHARLES M. SUPER

## INTRODUCTION

From an Asian perspective, all Western cultures may look more or less alike. Indeed, many Westerners believe that there are no real cultural differences among societies in Europe, the United States, and other parts of the European diaspora. Much cross-cultural research has been based on this assumption: it is not hard to find comparative studies of societies in Africa, Latin America, the Pacific, and Asia, but there is very little cross-cultural research comparing various Western cultures to each other. The lack of such studies is all the more striking given that cultural differences among European groups in social and emotional behavior have been the subject of frequent literary comment. Nash, for example, offered his observations of English and Italian passengers disembarking from ships at an Australian port:

> "I had occasion twice in one week to meet passengers from ships at the ocean terminal in Sydney. One ship was the *Southern Cross*, from Southampton, and the other was the *Galileo Galilei* from Milan. In the one case the dockside was crowded with a throng of people, babies, and grandparents, laughing, weeping, shouting. Men embraced and kissed; women shrieked and rushed into passionate greetings. There was tumultuous confusion. From the other ship the passengers passed sedately down the gangplank, in orderly groups; there were waves of hands and smiles, polite handshakes and impassive greetings such as "how nice to see you again."

> (Nash, 1970, p. 428).

The issue of cultural variability among Western societies is particularly relevant when we consider ideas and practices of parenting, since inasmuch as families bear the fundamental responsibility of producing the next generation of citizens who will need to work together across cultural boundaries in an increasingly complex world. In addition, cross-cultural research within a larger category such as "the West" offers the possibility of discovering both universals and differences; the themes and variations that make each culture seem recognizable yet different.

In this chapter, we offer some observations on research with parents and children in several Western countries, focusing on the process of discovery of parental ethnotheories and their instantiation in parenting practices. The approach described here is an elaboration of the "developmental niche," a theoretical framework proposed by Super and Harkness for understanding the interface between child and culture (Super & Harkness, 1997; Harkness & Super, 1993). In the developmental niche framework, the culturally constructed environment of the child is conceptualized as consisting of three components or subsystems: (1) the physical and social settings in which the child lives; (2) culturally regulated customs of child care and childbearing; and (3) the psychology of the caretakers, including parents and others such as teachers or child care providers (Super & Harkness, 1997). The three components operate together as a system, although each is functionally embedded in aspects of the larger culture. It follows from this principle that parental ethnotheories, as an aspect of the third component of the developmental niche, can be accessed and studied through the other two components of the niche as well as directly.

### Parental Ethnotheories: What Are They?

Culture and parenting has long been a topic of interest to anthropologists (Harkness & Super, 2001), but it has only recently come to the fore in psychological research and thinking (Bornstein, 1991; Goodnow & Collins, 1990; Sigel, McGillicuddy-DeLisi, & Goodnow, 1992). Our approach draws from both disciplines, and has evolved to an increasing emphasis on the importance of parents' cultural belief systems, or parental ethnotheories, as the nexus through which elements of the larger culture are filtered, and as an important source of parenting practices and the organization of daily life for children and families (Axia, Prior, & Carelli, 1992; Eliasz, 1990; Harkness & Super, 1996; Palacios & Moreno, 1996; Welles-Nyström, 1996).

Parental ethnotheories are cultural models that parents hold regarding children, families, and themselves as parents. The term "cultural model," drawn from cognitive anthropology, indicates an organized set of ideas that are shared by members of a cultural group (D'Andrade & Strauss, 1992; Quinn & Holland, 1987). Like other cultural models related to the self, parental ethnotheories are often implicit, taken-for-granted ideas about the "natural" or "right" way to think or act, and they have strong motivational properties for parents. It is this characteristic—the relationship between ideas and goals for action—that ties parental ethnotheories to the other two components of the developmental niche.

## International Collaborative Studies of Parental Ethnotheories and Practices

Recent research by our international collaborative team has been organized by this conceptualization, as we will illustrate here with findings from research through the International Study of Parents, Children and Schools (ISPCS), the International Baby Study (IBS), and earlier studies of Dutch and U.S. parents. The ISPCS—a collaborative effort in seven countries with core funding provided by the Spencer Foundation—investigates parents' and teachers' cultural belief systems, practices at home and at school that instantiate these beliefs, and the normative issues that children encounter in the transition from home to school. The lead investigators include Giovanna Axia (University of Padua, Italy), Andrzej Eliasz (Advanced School of Social Psychology and Polish Academy of Sciences, Warsaw, Poland), Jesus Palacios (University of Seville), Barbara Welles-Nyström (University of Stockholm, Sweden), as well as the late Harry McGurk, who was at the time of data collection the director of the Australian Institute of Family Studies. Sara Harkness and Charles Super (now at the University of Connecticut, United States) have been the lead investigators for the Dutch and American research in addition to coordinating the overall project.

In each cultural site, we recruited a sample of 60 families with target children divided evenly into five age groups balanced for birth order and sex: 6 months, 18 months, 3 years, 4.5 years, and 7 to 8 years. The sample families, recruited mostly through community networks, were broadly middle-class, with one or both parents employed and no major health problems; most of them were nuclear families with both parents present in the home; and parents in each sample were all native-born to that culture. Using a combination of psychological and ethnographic methods, we collected parallel data in each sample on parents' and teachers' ideas, on many aspects of child and family life, and on child temperament. The sample and methods for the ISPCS were elaborated from earlier research on American parents' ethnotheories of child development, funded by the National Science Foundation, and a comparative study of Dutch parents, funded by the Spencer Foundation (Harkness & Super, 1992; Harkness & Super, 1993). The ISPCS, in turn, provided a foundation for the International Baby Study.

## Parental Ethnotheories in the Developmental Niche

Parental ethnotheories are difficult to see directly, but they are intricately related to the other components of the developmental niche; thus, gaining understanding of parental ethnotheories is best achieved through use of multiple methods. In our research, we have used several methods in combination in order to achieve convergent validity (Campbell & Fiske, 1959). This is particularly important because of the implicit nature of many parental ethnotheories, which may not even be readily accessible to members of the culture themselves. In addition, the study of parental ethnotheories requires a comparative cross-cultural perspective in order to make apparent the patterns of belief and practice that are both shared and culture-specific, and which may easily escape notice in a flat, monocultural perspective.

## Settings of Daily Life in the Family

Observation of how children's environments of daily life are actually organized can provide a starting point for both researchers and parents to reflect on the meanings that shape parental strategies of care. In the studies mentioned above, parents themselves have been ethnographic observers through keeping "parental diaries" of their children's daily routines over the course of several days. These diaries can be used to generate a narrative account of the child's day, as in the following examples from the American and Dutch studies (adapted from (Harkness, 1998).

It's 7:30 a.m., and Jane, a 3-year-old girl living with her family in a suburb of Boston, gets up to have breakfast with her mother and little brother. Daddy has already left for work, but her mother, a part-time social worker, has planned a special day to make the most of her time at home with the children. After breakfast, they all pile into the car and drive into town where, after dropping the little brother at his babysitter's, they meet another mother and her 3-year-old at a theater to watch a performance of *Pinocchio*. After the show, the two mothers and daughters go to McDonald's for lunch; then they part company and Jane goes with her mother to do some shopping. After picking up Jane's little brother, it's home again, where Jane plays by herself in the backyard while her mother does housework. In mid-afternoon, Jane is taken by her mother to a swimming lesson at the town pool (her little brother comes along in the car and watches with her mother). After coming home at the end of the afternoon, Jane watches *Sesame Street* on TV, then eats her supper in her parents' bedroom while her mother folds laundry. Daddy gets home at 7:30, in time to read Jane a story and tuck her into bed at 8:15.

On the other side of the Atlantic Ocean, in the Dutch town of "Bloemenheim," another little three-year-old girl has also gotten up. Marja's day begins with a shower with Daddy at 7:00 a.m., followed by breakfast with mother, father, older sister (aged 7) and brother (aged 5). At 8:15, it's time for Marja's older sister to leave for school. It's just a 5-minute bike ride away, but today Mother will take the car rather than haul the other two children along on her bike, as Marja's brother is staying home with a cold. When they get back home, Marja plays at counting pennies in her piggy bank in the family room, and then goes out to ride her bike in the child-safe streets of the neighborhood. The morning ends, and it's time to go back to school to pick up Marja's big sister, along with a neighbor child who will spend the afternoon at their home. After lunch with mother, siblings, and the neighbor child, Marja is taken by her mother to the "Children's Playroom," a nursery school where 3-year-olds go for a couple of hours twice a week to get used to being in a group outside the home. Mother comes back at 3:00 to pick Marja up and then get her sister at school . . . then it's time for a snack of juice and a cookie at home. By 4:00, Marja is outside riding her bike around with other children in the neighborhood. At 5:30, Daddy arrives home on his bike from his job as a chemist at a nearby factory, and the children play together in the family room while the parents prepare dinner. At 6:00 the family sits down to eat together . . . then Daddy gets Marja ready for bed. By 6:50, Marja is tucked in and off to sleep.

These narratives of two middle-class children's days, based on their mothers' diaries, tell stories richly laden with cultural meanings. In each place, the child's daily routines—an aspect of the physical and social settings—are structured to help the child become a competent member of her culture, but there are systematic similarities and differences between them. Both Jane and Marja spend their days in the company of their mothers and siblings, engaged in activities designed for their enjoyment and development. Unlike 3-year-old girls in non-Western cultures such as those of Africa, neither Jane nor Marja is expected to take responsibility for helping with household tasks such as food preparation or the care of a younger sibling. In this regard, Jane's and Marja's days are organized by similar themes. There are variations too, however: whereas Jane's mother takes her to two special events away from home, Marja's day is spent entirely in the familiar settings of home, neighborhood, and pre-school. Whereas Marja has three meals and a snack in the company of her family, Jane's family has no meals together. Although both girls have bedtime routines with their fathers, Marja's bedtime is almost an hour and a half earlier than Jane's.

## Customs and Practices of Parenting

Reflection on the structure of children's daily life, as recorded in parental diaries, can lead to the discovery of culturally regulated customs of care, the second subsystem of the developmental niche. As we have explained elsewhere, customs in this sense are behavioral sequences or arrangements of care that are so well integrated into the culture that they seem to require no justification; they appear to be self-evident, common-sense solutions to everyday problems (Super & Harkness, 1997), although parents and other caregivers generally find it easy to identify and talk about them. Implicit in the daily routines of Jane and Marja are different parental ethnotheories about what kinds of activities or experiences are most important in these formative years. We focus here on two of these ethnotheories as expressed in interviews with U.S. and Dutch parents; both have to do with the ways that parents think about using time with their children.

**"Special Time" and Family Time.**  Two contrasting themes were evident in the interviews: the idea of "special time" (or "quality time") as expressed by American parents, and the theme of "family time" as described by the Dutch parents. One American couple, parents of a 3-year-old girl and her toddler sister, were particularly expressive in talking about the importance of special time with their children. In the following interview excerpt, they describe what special time means to them, and how it helps both them and their children.

Father:  Well, I think it is [important]. Quality time, whatever, whatever they want to use. I think it's important. I think kids need to start connecting with each parent in some way. At this point I don't think it matters necessarily which parent, but I think if each parent can give a certain amount of time to each kid, I think it's important.

Interviewer:  Why?

Father:  Well, maybe just in getting to know the parent better, sooner. Does that make sense? I don't know, because it seems like when I got to know my parents, it was through a period of accretion kind of thing, over a number of years. And it wasn't—I mean I had special time for my father and he would coach a baseball team, but it wasn't necessarily that one-to-one kind. I think it's—it makes—I think it makes parents stop and think about what they're doing here. What the purpose is for this whole thing. Maybe that's too much. I don't know. I just think it slows things down a little bit. It puts things a little bit more in perspective.

Interviewer:  Marianne, what are your thoughts on special time?

Mother:  Well, I just think from—well first of all, I think that any time that we can spend with them, even if it's time where we're sitting there watching the same TV show as they are, I think that is their thing that they love the best of all. We're sharing something with them. I think that it happens less than it should. You think you're spending time with them when you're kind of in the same room, but on the phone or making dinner or something, but it's not really the same as just putting down whatever you're doing and just kind of being with them at their level.

Father:  But you do that. You allow them to participate in like making cookies.

Mother:  Well, that's different though. That's kind of involving them in something that I'm doing. But I mean really just doing something for their own sake. Cookies aren't going to be made out of it. Know what I mean? Nothing is going to get produced. It's just kind of time spent with them.

Interviewer:  I mean, I think that's a very interesting distinction. Why is it important to have it that way rather than kind of incorporating them into some of your tasks and routines, do you think?

Mother:  I haven't really thought about it that much, but maybe something about timing and something about being able to go at their pace and kind of let them take the lead.

Interviewer:  Let me put it this way. What do you think that does for kids that's different from having them help you cook in the kitchen or something?

Mother:  I don't know. Something about you're interested in something that they're doing, is really important for them. It's important for their growth. Then they believe that what they're doing is important. I mean even when we were outside with them tonight and they just—we were just kind of swinging them—that was a big thing for them.

These parents went on to describe another family in which the mother would routinely take a whole day to spend "special time" with one or the other of her children; like many of the American parents in our study, that family found it easiest to focus exclusively on the needs and developmental capacities of one child at a time. The couple quoted here, in contrast, describe activities involving the whole family but their focus on the needs of the child (rather than a product such as cookies) puts these activities in the category of "special time."

In contrast, the Dutch families we interviewed, when asked about the idea of special time with their children, tended to give rather relaxed commentaries about how it was enjoyable to do something with just one child occasionally. When talking about family time together, however, the Dutch parents had more to say, and they tended to wax eloquent about the importance of such customs as family dinners. For example, the parents of a 6-month-old girl (Sietske) talked about making sure that the baby was right with them at the dinner table every night.

Father: If I leave at quarter of seven in the morning then I hear something, but if I come home and for example they're again in bed, now I really don't like that.

Mother: Ya, it's really the only time that he is often home . . . often in the evening either I have to go out or he has to go out again . . . so at six o'clock we are all three always home.

Father: And after that, Sietske goes to bed.

Mother: Ya, she went to bed at eight or seven, so really it is a short time.

Father: It was really just an hour, an hour and a half that I saw her, and then you can also put her in the playpen and you go eat, but no, we sit her here. Then she is close by . . . that is important.

Mother: In the beginning it was not so nice, because she had a terrible "screaming hour" at six o'clock, so no, that really was not nice. But now that is over, luckily.

Interviewer: But did you sit her here at the table in spite of that?

Father: Yes, certainly—or on our laps here.

Looking toward the future when the baby was a bit older, the parents explained the importance of having dinner together as a family.

Father: Because you want to hear about each other. I am curious, how did things go for Sietske today, and that is important, you're away during the day and you don't think about it, but when you come home you really do think about it, and ya. . . . I think that it is out of curiosity, wanting to see . . . it's so new and it goes fast. Development goes very fast, and if I . . . I notice that a little while ago I was very busy and then I couldn't put her to bed at night or I had to pay less attention to her, then I thought that she recognizes me less or she is less involved with me. And I think that therefore that hour at least is very important. [(And what about dinner in particular?)] Now, why dinner time . . . Now dinner is functional, it has to take place, and so if you sit outside or you sit here, or if you watch TV or read a book or a newspaper, but at dinner you are busy with eating, and then, that is really a resting point in the day. We eat also . . . we take a long time over dinner. We . . . it seems cozier, and that, not just quickly in between things, no—really sit and sit with everyone there together. So I think that dinner is very important for that reason. It has to happen, and during dinner you can pay attention to each other.

The contrast in emphasis on "special time" versus family time in the American and Dutch interviews is evident not only in *how* parents talk about each theme, but also in *how much* they talked about them. A comparison of the frequency of comments about each cultural theme showed that the Dutch parents talked three times as often as the American parents about family time, whereas the pattern was reversed in relation to "special time."

**Management of Sleep.**   As in the interview excerpt quoted above, many of the Dutch parents we interviewed seem to show a fine-tuned awareness of the allocation of time during the day, and in particular the importance of regularity and rest. These parents both comment on how the structure of their own days leaves open only limited time for being with their daughter, and thus note the importance of using this time for dinner as a "restpoint" and time that the family can be together—even though the baby was at first colicky at that hour! As we have described elsewhere (Super, et al., 1996), this reasoning fits well with a Dutch ethnotheory that, like the American construct of "special/quality time," actually has a name: the "3 R's" of child-rearing, which in Dutch are expressed as *rust* (rest), *regelmaat* (regularity), and *reinheid* (cleanliness). With the last of these easily taken care of by the daily bath, parents focused a great deal of care and attention on providing adequate rest or sleep in a regularly scheduled day, with the goal of bringing up children who would be calm, cheerful, and self-regulated. These ideas were particularly evident in the ways that the Dutch parents, in contrast to American parents, talked about the regulation of infant sleep. Whereas the American parents described their child's sleep patterns as innate and developmentally driven, the Dutch parents hardly mentioned these ideas and instead spoke frequently about the importance of a regular sleep schedule, which they saw as fundamental to healthy growth and development. It is noteworthy that the Dutch ethnotheory of infant sleep, and the caretaking practices that they described to foster it, apparently were more successful in averting children's sleep "problems," at least from the parents' perspective: these Dutch parents hardly mentioned having any problems getting their children to follow the desired schedule. In contrast, the American parents spoke frequently about their struggles to deal with babies and young children whose innate temperaments and developmental patterns militated against easy management at night. As one couple recounted of their 1-year-old son:

Mother:       He wakes up a couple of times a night, [did it] right from the start. I kept waiting for him to start sleeping through the night. Ever since he was born, he was up most of the night as a brand-new baby, and then he was up like four times a night, going to bed at 7:30 and he'd be up at 11:00 and he'd be up at 1:00, 3:00, 5:00. So the doctor said to let him cry. That was effective when we could stand it, but both of us—it drives us crazy. He could cry for 45 minutes. There were nights when he would not cry, but scream and shriek for 45 minutes.

Father:      I know that you should just wait it out, but it's 3:00 in the morning and you know you've got to get up at 6:15.

Mother:      And to know that he would go right back to sleep like that [snaps fingers] in our bed.

Father:      It's a tough call.

Mother:      Now usually he wakes up around 4:30 and he's hanging on to the headboard, jumping up and down. So finally at 5:00 I get up.

Interviewer:  What do you do with him?

Father:      We both have different strategies. She'll put him in the walker down here and I generally put him in the playpen and try to keep him somewhat entertained, either by the TV or he loves the stereo. He loves music. If he's crying and he sees me going for the stereo, he'll stop crying and start to laugh, in anticipation of the music. Even when he was a tiny baby, one night at 3:30 we discovered a particular song that would calm him down.

Mother:      It was a psalm. We wondered if it was some divine intervention.

The key to the Dutch parents' success in achieving a good night's sleep for both their child and themselves seems to lie in the second component of the "three R's" ethnotheory: regularity. Many parents stressed the importance of a regular schedule, including a set time for both meals and bed. As one mother of an 18-month-old explained: "To bed on time, because they really need rest to grow, and regularity is very important when they are so little. If she gets too little rest, she is very fussy." A mother of a 6-month-old commented, "We are very strict about going to bed—at 6:30, upstairs."

The results of the different customs related to rest and regularity were evident in the children's actual daily routines as recorded by their parents in parent diaries: at six months of age, the Dutch children were getting on average 2 hours more sleep per 24-hour day; the difference narrowed with age but was still evident when the children were 4.5 years old. Moreover, observations of the 6-month-old Dutch babies showed statistically reliable differences from an American sample in general state of arousal and related behavior: during observations, the Dutch babies were more often in a state of "quiet alert," in contrast to the American babies who were more frequently in an "active alert" state. The higher state of arousal of the American babies corresponded to differences in their mothers' behavior: the American mothers touched and talked to their babies more than the Dutch mothers did (Super, et al., 1996).

## A MODEL OF PARENTAL ETHNOTHEORIES, PRACTICES, AND OUTCOMES

Settings and customs of children's lives are relatively easy to access through methods such as observation, parents' record-keeping, and focused interviews. These subsystems of the developmental niche can thus provide a basis for exploring parental ethnotheories more directly. In our recent international collaborative research, however, we have given this third subsystem of the developmental niche a privileged status in relation to the other two subsystems, in order to gain a greater understanding of the power of cultural ideas as they contribute to the ways that parents organize their children's settings of daily life, the customs that are instantiated within these settings, and their developmental outcomes (Harkness & Super, 1992). From this perspective, the Dutch and American parents' beliefs and practices related to infant sleep, and the actual outcomes in infant sleep patterns and awake behavior, can be seen as parts of a system of ideas, practices, and developmental or family outcomes. A theoretical model of this system entails a hierarchy of ideas, with the most general, implicit ideas about the nature of the child, parenting, and the family at the top. Below this triad, we find ideas about specific domains, such as infant sleep or parent–child relationships. These ideas are closely tied to ideas about appropriate practices, and also imagined child or family outcomes. Ideas are translated into action in this model, although mediated by intervening factors such as child characteristics, situational characteristics that may be influenced by aspects of the larger culture, and competing cultural models and their related practices. The final results can be seen in actual parental practices or behaviors, and actual child and family outcomes.

Using this model is helpful for understanding the connections between parental ethnotheories and practices related to infant sleep, as shown in Figure 3.1. As we have seen, the Dutch ethnotheory of the importance of rest and a regular schedule contrasts with the American cultural concept of infant sleep as determined almost entirely by age and individual child characteristics. The official "three R's" of Dutch child-rearing provide a clear set of guidelines for Dutch parents by mandating a regular bedtime as well as keeping the child's waking environment calmer and less stimulating. It is interesting to note that the "3 R's" were long formalized in advice routinely given to parents through the Dutch national infant health care clinics. The advice reported by the American parents quoted above also comes from an "expert" source: the pediatrician. Note further, however, that this advice is given to solve a problem that the Dutch parents rarely reported, namely, unwanted night waking. The American parents, in contrast to the Dutch parents, feel confused because they do not have a clear sense of what practice will be both consistent with their ethnotheory of infant sleep, and do the job of getting the baby to sleep through the night.

Another contrast appears at the next stage of the model: whereas the Dutch parents emphasized the importance of rest and regularity for the child's growth and mood regulation, the American parents focused on the sequelae of interrupted infant sleep for themselves rather than for the child; the assumption seems to have been that children essentially regulate their own sleep needs, and that

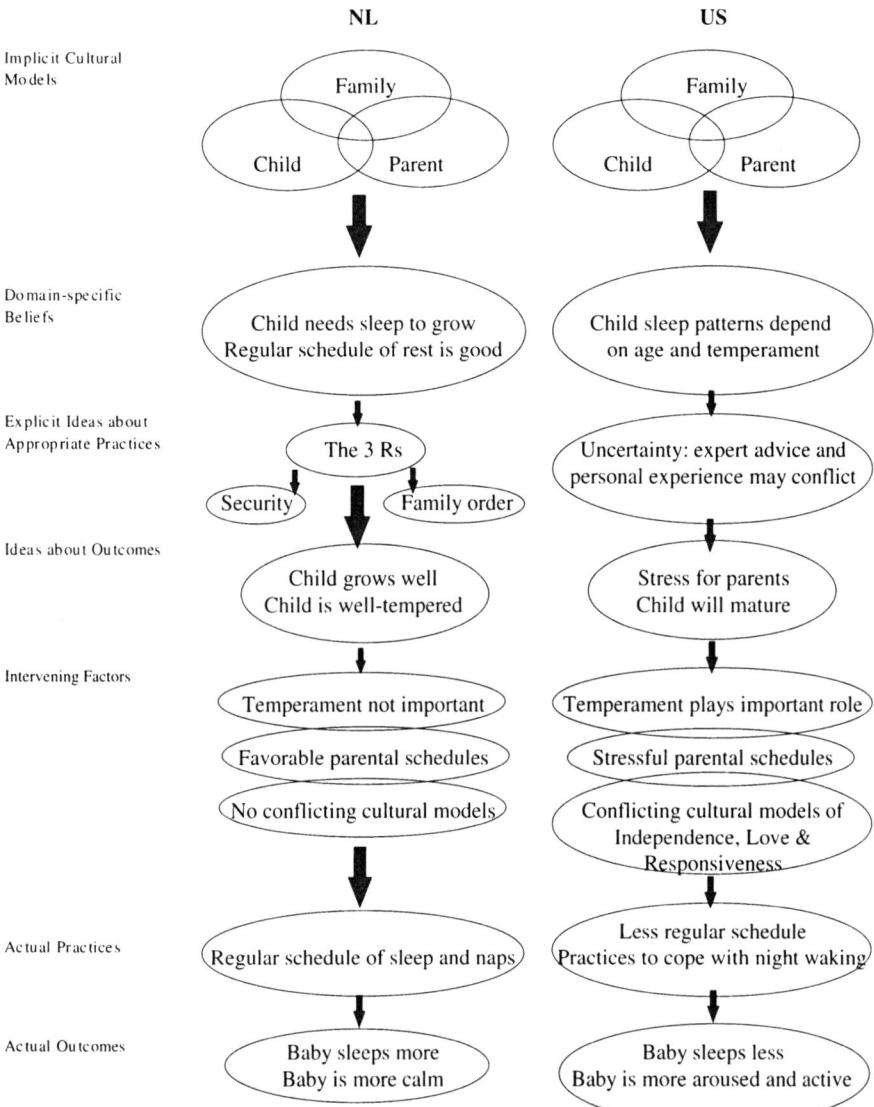

**FIGURE 3.1**   A model of parental ethnotheories, practices, and outcomes: infant sleeps.

eventually they will come to sleep through the night on their own. Parents' actual practices, and related child outcomes, are mediated differently in each cultural setting. For the Dutch parents, individual differences among children were not considered important in this regard, as all children were thought to need plenty of sleep and a regular schedule; in contrast, as we have seen, the American parents perceived themselves as captive to the child's individual behavioral style. Situational characteristics including the parents' own work schedules were more favorable for the Dutch parents, who ironically may have had less need for their children to sleep through the night.

Perhaps equally important is another intervening factor: competing cultural models and practices. For the Dutch families in our study, the "3 R's" encompassed a wide range of ideas and practices; for example, having a regular schedule was also thought to give the child a greater sense of comfort and security, as well as creating a more pleasant family environment. The "3 R's" would appear in a diagram such as this for many specific domains. For the American parents, in contrast, ethnotheories of infant sleep were connected to other broad-ranging cultural models such as the idea of independence, which could be encouraged in the child through sleeping through the night apart from the parents. This cultural model created even more of a challenge to parents whose infants presented "sleep problems" such as the one so eloquently described above, as it created a feeling of guilt about picking up a crying baby in the middle of the night. On the other hand, yet another competing American cultural model, as suggested in our discussion of "special time," was that children need responsive and attentive parenting in order to feel secure. Thus, although in principle both Dutch and American parents might be influenced by the same intervening factors, this part of the model is quite simple in the Dutch case and rather complex in the American one. Looking at the issue from this perspective may help to explain why infant sleep tends to be so much more frequent a topic of concern for the American parents we studied than it was for the Dutch parents. These differences are reflected in the last links of the model: actual practices and actual child and family outcomes.

The same analysis could be applied to the domain of parent–child relationships, including the idea of "special time." In both cases, the usefulness of the model is demonstrated through its ability to elucidate the links among parental ethnotheories, practices, and outcomes in ways that might not otherwise be evident.

## EXPLORING IMPLICIT CULTURAL MODELS OF THE CHILD

In the model presented above, implicit cultural models of the child, of parenting, and of the family are linked together and conceptualized as the source of more specific, often more conscious ideas about particular domains. These implicit models are in turn linked to themes in the larger culture, what Quinn and Holland have called "general purpose cultural models that are repeatedly incorporated into other cultural models developed for special purposes" (Quinn & Holland, 1987, p. 11). One approach that we have used to learn about these cultural models is the study of parents' free descriptions of their own children.

An early discovery in the International Study of Parents, Children and Schools was that parents in the different cultural communities tended to talk about their children's personalities and behavior in systematically different ways. For example, an American mother of a 3-year-old girl told the following story.

"I have this vivid memory when she was born of them taking her to clean her off and put the blanket around her and all that. And she was looking all around. She was looking at us. She was looking around the delivery room. She was alert from the very first second. Even when I would take her out—I took her out when she was six weeks old to a shopping mall to have her picture taken—people would stop me and say, "What an alert baby." One guy stopped me and said, "Lady, you have an intelligent baby there." And intelligent child. And it was just something about her. She was very engaging and very with the program, very observant. She's still fabulously observant."

(Harkness, Super, & Pai, 2000, p. 26).

Like many other American parents we interviewed, this mother conveyed her sense of amazement at her daughter's remarkable cognitive abilities, evident from the first moment of her life in the world. As we listened to more such stories, we came to recognize them as not only personal accounts but also cultural constructions that framed parents' experiences of their own child. In these constructions, we could see evidence for a cultural model of "the child," to which a particular child was implicitly compared. Although these cultural models are by definition as unique as the culture to which they belong, they can be indexed by patterns of descriptive words or phrases found to varying extents in parents' descriptions in various settings. The ISPCS researchers thus developed a list of common descriptors that covered virtually all the child descriptions found in parent interviews; we used this to identify descriptors produced both in response to our request to "describe your child" as well as throughout the interview. A comparison of the frequencies of these descriptors in the discourse of parents from six of the seven cultural samples shows both common themes and cultural variations. Parents from all six samples often described their children as sociable, loving, active, and strong-willed: freqencies of each of these descriptors varied from at least 5% to over 14% of all descriptors and were among the top 10 most frequently used. Beyond this common core of parental perceptions of young children, however, differences emerged in the particular kinds of qualities that parents chose to focus on, as shown in Table 3.1.

Among the American parents, the attention to cognitive abilities expressed by the mother quoted above was typical: the highest frequency American descriptors included "intelligent" and "cognitively advanced" as well as "asks questions." Along with these qualities, the American parents described their children as "independent" and even "rebellious." At the opposite extreme were the Italian parents, who rarely described their children as intelligent and never characterized them as cognitively advanced. Instead, these parents talked about their children as being easy, even-tempered, well-balanced, and "simpatico," a group of characteristics suggesting social and emotional competence further supported by the characterization "asks questions," which for these families was an aspect of being sociable and communicative. The Italian parents also described their children as "knowing what they want," a less aggressive version of strong will than the American "rebellious."

TABLE 3.1 Parents' Descriptions of Their Children in Six Cultures

| Australia | Italy | Netherland | Spain | Sweden | United States |
|---|---|---|---|---|---|
| Common Descriptors (%) | | | | | |
| Sociable 15% | Sociable 9% | Sociable 7% | Sociable 8% | Sociable 11% | Sociable 10% |
| Loving 8% | Loving 9 9% | Loving 8% | Loving 10% | Loving 6% | Loving 8% |
| Active 11% | Active 6% | Active 7% | Active 6% | Active 10% | Active 7% |
| Strong-willed 6% | Strong-willed 10% | Strong-willed 8% | Strong-willed 7% | Strong-willed 5% | Strong-willed 6% |
| Culture-Specific Patterns (%) | | | | | |
| Happy 15% | Asks questions 7% | Agreeable 5% | Easy 21% | Happy 19% | Intelligent 6% |
| Easy 6% | Easy 9% | Enjoys life 6% | Difficult 7% | Easy 10% | Cognitively advanced 5% |
| Intelligent 9% | Well-balanced 9% | Happy 8% | Socially mature 7% | Agreeable 7% | Asks questions 8% |
| Asks questions 8% | Even-tempered 9% | Long attention 8% | Good character 7% | Well-balanced 9% | Independent 5% |
| Calm 8% | Knows what he wants 6% | Asks questions 6% | Happy 10% | Even-tempered 10% | Rebellious 5% |
| Sensitive 8% | Simpatico 6% | Seeks attention 8% | Intelligent 10% | Secure 6% | Adaptable 5% |
| | | Regular 5% | Alert 9% | Persistent 5% | |

Like the Italian parents, the Dutch parents also focused more on their children's social qualities, describing them as "agreeable" and "enjoying life." The attribution of having a "long attention span" is a high-frequency descriptor only for the Dutch parents, as is being "regular," not surprisingly given these parents' concern with rest and regularity and its benefits. For the Dutch parents, the descriptor "asks questions" may be linked with "seeks attention," two aspects of dependent behavior. The profile of descriptors for these parents, then, indicates a child who is positive in mood, regular in habits, and able to entertain himself or herself for periods of time although needing attention every so often.

The Swedish parents were similar to the Dutch parents in describing their children as "persistent," a quality closely related to having a long attention span. Also like the Dutch parents, the Swedish parents described their children as agreeable; however, the Swedish profile of descriptors also includes high frequencies of "easy" and "well-balanced" and a low frequency for "attention-seeking," in contrast to the opposite trends in the Dutch sample. Most striking in the Swedish sample is the frequent use of the descriptor "happy," which is found more than twice as much as any other descriptor. Along with "secure," this profile of descriptors suggests a cultural model of the child as both pleasant and undemanding.

The highest rate of use of the "easy" descriptor occurs in the Spanish sample, where fully one-fifth of the parents used this term to describe their children. Interestingly, the Spanish sample was the only one in which the opposite characterization, "difficult," was among the top 10 most frequently used descriptors: it appears that the dimension of manageability was especially salient to these parents. The Spanish focus seems to go beyond this, however, as indicated by the high frequencies of the descriptors "socially mature" and "good character," suggesting that the cultural model of the child may center around an ideal of the good citizen and family member. This conceptual cluster of attributes is balanced by attention to the child's cognitive abilities as indexed by the descriptors "intelligent" and "alert."

The Australian parents, finally, are similar to the Swedish, Spanish, and Italian parents in describing their children as "easy," and similar to the U.S. parents in their focus on cognitive competence as indicated by the descriptors "intelligent" and "asks questions." Unlike all other samples, however, the Australian parents seemed to focus on the child's emotional state and reactivity, as suggested by the descriptors "calm" and "sensitive."

In summary, the patterns of both cross-cultural similarity and difference in parents' descriptions of their own children suggest that these descriptions are culturally constructed in the sense that there are locally shared ideas about what child qualities are most important, most worthy of note. Comparing across the six cultural samples, there is evidence of commonality in the group of descriptors that were among the most frequent in all of the samples. At the same time, the particular ways that these are combined with other, more culture-specific profiles of descriptors suggests that each community has its own unique perspective on the nature of the child.

## THEMES AND VARIATIONS

In this chapter, we have described an approach that has been developed to identify and study parental ethnotheories. This approach involves a number of different methods, including parents' diaries of their children's daily activities and routines, direct observation of children in their settings of daily life, and interviews with parents (Super & Harkness, 1999). Although the methods are diverse, they are tied together by a basic research strategy of working toward an understanding of general, abstract, or implicit ideas through specific instances. For example, parental diaries of actual days provide a level of specificity that is not available if one simply asks parents to describe "a typical day." Especially if kept over the course of several days, parental diaries provide information for both parents and researchers to reflect together on aspects of daily routines that parents might not otherwise have thought about, but that may reveal important underlying cultural beliefs. Likewise, a focus on specific customs of care as observed by researchers or described by parents provides a window into cultural beliefs about children's needs and what constitutes good parenting. Finally, parents' descriptions of their own children offer insights into implicit cultural models of "the child" in general. We have found that this strategy of seeking the general through the specific seems to work well for both parents and researchers. Parents find it easier to talk about their own child's routines and qualities than to answer questions about abstract principles—especially since because many of these may be unexamined, implicit assumptions about what is natural and right—and we as researchers are thereby blessed with an abundance of rich data that can be approached from a variety of perspectives. As has been evident throughout this chapter, capturing parents' actual discourse through transcribed tape recordings is especially important for both studying and conveying parents' culturally constructed ideas.

The concept of the developmental niche has provided a useful way to parse the culturally constructed environment of the child into empirically researchable parts, through the several lenses of physical and social settings of the child's daily life, customs, and practices of care, and parental ethnotheories. In each of these areas, we have found common themes as well as dimensions of cross-cultural variation across various Western cultural communities. Some of the common themes are undoubtedly more general than Western cultures, as they concern the universal tasks of parenting. Parents everywhere strive to bring up their children to be happy, healthy, well-functioning, and successful members of their own cultures. Parents in different cultures and circumstances, however, may ask themselves different questions related to this universal goal—How can I ensure that my child survives the first 2 years of life? How can I make sure that my child will stay connected to the family? How can I teach my child to be a responsible member of the community? How can I help maximize my child's potential for great personal achievement, and how can I give my child the strength to deal with frustration and failure in that enterprise?

In this chapter, we have seen hints of both shared themes and cross-cultural variation, first through comparative studies of U.S. and Dutch families, and then through the examination of parents' descriptions of their own children in six Western cultures. Common themes in parental ethnotheories probably also are based in part on the universal characteristics of children, in contrast to adults, such as the parents themselves. Our examination of the most frequent descriptors of children across six cultural samples suggests that parents—at least in Western cultures—often perceive children as sociable, loving, active, and strong-willed. To anyone who has spent a day with a young child, these qualities probably ring true. By contrast with adults, children are very interested in spending their time in the company of others and they are more open in their demonstrations of affection. They run around a great deal more than adults do, and they are also generally more willing to put up a fuss in order to get what they want.

Thus, the themes in parental ethnotheories probably have a range from the universal to the specific, from those that are shared by parents in all cultures, to those that are more particular to culture areas such as the Western world (or groupings therein such as northern Europe or the United States and other British-heritage cultures), and those that are specific to a particular culture. Although we have identified the level of comparison at national entities, it would of course be possible to take the same approach to studying cultural variability within countries as it relates, for example, to regional or socioeconomic differences. In fact, a great deal of research on these differences has already been carried out, but it is generally not undertaken within a cultural framework.

But what of the themes and variations *within* a single cultural community? A central premise of the development niche construct is that the child's environment is not a random collection of settings, customs, and parental beliefs, but rather that it is organized in a nonarbitrary manner as part of a cultural system, including contingencies and variable flexibility, thematic repetitions, and systems of meaning that cut across domains both within and beyond the niche (Super & Harkness, 1997, p. 26). In this chapter, we have seen evidence for thematic repetition across the three subsystems of the development niches of American and Dutch children: for example, the theme of "special time" as an American custom of care resonates with the diary-based account of an American child's actual day, which featured two special outings. This theme is also expressed through the American emphasis on cognitive precocity as evidenced by the American profile of child descriptors with its focus on intelligence and individual achievement.

Likewise, the Dutch child's well-organized, family-based day is clearly consistent with the Dutch "3 R's" system of beliefs about the importance of rest and regularity; and these qualities also emerge in the Dutch descriptions of their children as positive and sociable children who can sustain their attention for long periods of time, but who also need to be with their parents. The thematic connections among different aspects of the niche—as well as within each of its subsystems—are not always so evident, however, and this observation can lead to further discoveries about parental ethnotheories. For example, how does the Dutch emphasis on sociability and an even temper relate to the cultural emphasis on being strong-willed? Questions such as these can most successfully be addressed through collaborative research partnerships that provide perspectives from both within and outside the culture. In this case, we as American researchers learned from our Dutch colleagues that being strong-willed is considered an essential quality in order for children to be self-determined even while living in a densely populated social environment, rather than letting others make decisions for them.

Culture-specific themes also organize individual diversity within particular communities. In describing their children, for example, American parents do not produce identical lists; but they also generally do not produce lists that replicate those of another culture. The human mind can do a better job of discriminating these differences than the computer does: after one has listened to a number of descriptions of children from different cultures, one realizes that parents' descriptions in each culture have their own particular "sound." This is because descriptions from each cultural community tend to deal with the same basic set of themes, although they may use varying language to do so. Such themes tend to be consistent not only across social boundaries within a community, but also across time. The American mother who described her baby as an "alert baby" was a participant in our 1980s research on parents in the Boston area. Twenty years later, a Connecticut mother in our current research commented on how "alert" her baby is, and recounted an almost identical story of comments from others when she took the baby out to the post office, all the while expressing surprise at the term "alert," which she considered unusual for describing an infant.

As the theoretical model presented in this chapter illustrates, parental ethno-theories form part of a system that links ideas about the child, about practices, and about outcomes with actual practices and actual outcomes. Thus, parental ethnotheories by themselves cannot predict child outcomes, but it would be difficult to understand cultural differences in development without reference to how parents in different cultures think about children. While waiting in New York's Kennedy Airport to travel to Korea, we noticed a billboard picturing three different balls for different sports in the United States, Europe, and Australia, each labeled "football." The message seemed to be that one should not confuse apparent similarities with differences in underlying meaning systems; as the billboard advised, "Never underestimate the importance of local knowledge."

## REFERENCES

Axia, G., Prior, M., & Carelli, G. (1992). Cross-cultural influences on temperament: A comparison of Italian, Italo-Australian and Anglo-Australian toddlers. *Australian Psychologist, 27*(1), 52–56.

Bornstein, M. H. (Ed.) (1991). *Cultural approaches to parenting.* Hillsdale, NJ: Erlbaum.

Campbell, D. T., & Fiske, D. W. (1959). Convergent and discriminant validation by the multitrait–multimethod matrix. *Psychological Bulletin, 56,* 81–105.

D'Andrade, R., & Strauss, C. (Eds.) (1992). *Human motives and cultural models.* Cambridge, UK: Cambridge University Press.

Eliasz, A. (1990). Broadening the concept of temperament: From disposition to hypothetical construct. *European Journal of Personality, 4,* 287–302.

Goodnow, J. J., & Collins, W. A. (1990). *Development according to parents: The nature, sources, and consequences of parents' ideas.* London: Erlbaum.

Harkness, S. (1998, November). Time for families. *Anthropology Newsletter,* November, pp. 1, 4.

Harkness, S., & Super, C. M. (1996). *Parents' cultural belief systems: Their origins, expressions, and consequences.* New York: Guilford.

Harkness, S., & Super, C. M. (1992). Parental ethnotheories in action. In I. Sigel, A. V. McGillicuddy-DeLisi, & J. Goodnow (Eds.), *Parental belief systems: The psychological consequences for children* (2nd ed.) (pp. 373–392). Hillsdale, NJ: Erlbaum.

Harkness, S., & Super, C. M. (1993). The developmental niche: Implications for children's literacy development. In L. Eldering & P. Lesemen (Eds.), *Early intervention and culture: Preparation for literacy.* (pp. 115–132). Paris: UNESCO.

Harkness, S., & Super, C. M. (1996). *Parents' cultural belief systems: Their origins, expressions, and consequences.* New York: Guilford.

Harkness, S., & Super, C. M. (2002). Culture and parenting. In M. H. Bornstein (Ed.), *Handbook of parenting* (2nd ed.). Hillsdale, NJ: Erlbaum.

Harkness, S., Super, C. M., & Pai, S. (2000). Individualism and the "Western mind" reconsidered: American and Dutch parents' ethnotheories of children and family. In S. Harkness, C. Raeff, & C. M. Super (Eds.), *The social construction of the child: Understanding variability within and across contexts.* (Vol. 87, pp. 23–39). New Directions in Child Development. San Francisco: Jossey-Bass.

Palacios, J., & Moreno, M. C. (1996). Parents' and adolescents' ideas on children: Origins and transmission of intracultural diversity. In S. Harkness & C. M. Super (Eds.), *Parents' cultural belief systems: Their origins, expressions, and consequences.* New York: Guilford Press.

Quinn, N., & Holland, D. (1987). Culture and cognition. In D. Holland & N. Quinn (Eds.), *Cultural models in language and thought* (pp. 3–42). Cambridge, UK: Cambridge University Press.

Sigel, I. E., McGillicuddy-DeLisi, A. V., & Goodnow, J. J. (Eds.) (1992). *Parental belief systems: The psychological consequences for children* (2nd ed.). Hillsdale, NJ: Erlbaum.

Super, C. M., & Harkness, S. (1997). The cultural structuring of child development. In J. W. Berry, P. Dasen, & T. S. Saraswathi (Eds.), *Handbook of cross-cultural psychology: Volume 2. Basic processes and human development* (pp. 1–39). Boston: Allyn & Bacon.

Super, C. M., & Harkness, S. (1999). The environment as culture in developmental research. In T. Wachs & S. Friedman (Eds.), *Measurement of the environment in developmental research* (pp. 279–323). Washington, D.C.: American Psychological Association.

Super, C. M., Harkness, S., van Tijen, N., van der Vlugt, E., Dykstra, J., & Fintelman, M. (1996). The three R's of Dutch child rearing and the socialization of infant arousal. In S. Harkness & C. M. Super (Eds.), *Parents' cultural belief systems: Their origins, expressions, and consequences.* (pp. 447–466). New York: Guilford Press.

Welles-Nyström, B. (1996). Scenes from a marriage: Equality ideology in Swedish family policy, maternal ethnotheories, and practice. In S. Harkness & C. M. Super (Eds.), *Parents' cultural belief systems: Their origins, expressions, and consequences* (pp. 192–214). New York: Guilford.

# 4

# Parenting Beliefs and Behaviors: Initial Findings From the International Consortium for the Study of Social and Emotional Development (ICSSED)

KENNETH H. RUBIN, SHERYL A. HEMPHILL, XINYIN CHEN, PAUL HASTINGS, ANN SANSON, ALIDA LOCOCO, OCK BOON CHUNG, SUNG-YUN PARK, CARLA ZAPPULLA, SUMAN VERMA, CHONG-HEE YOON, AND HYUN SIM DOH

## INTRODUCTION

Why is it that researchers should be interested in parenting beliefs? What do we gain from asking parents about how or why they think about children and child-rearing? Wouldn't it simply be a much better idea to go straight to the point and *observe* parents as they interact with and relate to their children? Some time ago, Rubin and Mills (1992) wrote that the study of parental beliefs, ideas, or cognitions may represent little more than researchers' attempts to join a revivalist movement. After all, half a century ago, it was common practice to visit parents at their homes and proceed to interview them or provide them with questionnaires. In these ways, researchers were able to discover how parents thought that children should be socialized. We also learned why parents thought that parent–child relationships were important (e.g., Dameron, 1955; Miller & Swanson, 1958; Sears, Maccoby, & Levin, 1957).

The advantages of these procedures were obvious. Parents know their children very well. Parents also think about and interact with their children more than anyone else does, at least until late childhood and early adolescence. As a result, parents' knowledge of their children, of their child-rearing goals, preferences, and disillusionments, and of the quality of their relationships cut both across time and social contexts. Obviously then, parents can provide us with many insights about children, child-rearing, and about what they believe their role is in "creating" a well-socialized, well-adjusted child.

But there are also obvious disadvantages to studying beliefs and cognitions. Parent self-reports may be distorted by, as Messick pointed out, "the intrusion of nonfocal personal characteristics via mechanisms of self-deception, self-defense, and impression management" (Messick, 1983, p. 487). Furthermore, if the writings of social information processing theorists are to be believed, then it is probably the case that most parenting behaviors are, to a great extent, "automatic" or very much devoid of concentrated thought. As Maccoby once argued, parents may not even be aware of much of their behavior, unless it concerns highly salient events or interactions (Maccoby & Martin, 1983).

Another difficulty in the collection and understanding of parenting beliefs data concerns the issue of *memory*. If we ask parents to remember how they dealt with this situation or that, if we ask parents to think about how they reacted when their children behaved in this way or that, if we ask parents to recollect what they were thinking or feeling or what their goals were when they were trying to get their children to do this or that, if we ask parents to remember what their relationships with their children were like "some time ago," we plunge ourselves deeply into a methodological quandary. Memories are imperfect; they are often biased in both positive and negative ways dependent upon the situations, issues, and phenomena that we ask parents to recall. Retrospection is less than ideal unless one is very much aware that what one is examining *is* actually retrospection.

And finally, perhaps the worst of all possible flaws in the study of parenting beliefs, especially about child-rearing, is that whatever parents tell us they do with their children is remarkably uncorrelated with what we observe when we watch parents interacting with their children. Much of the available literature leads one to believe that there is a reasonable disconnect between thought and action, between attitude and behavior, or even between competence and performance. Parents can think one thing (and tell us, for example, that this is how they would interact with their child) and do another.

Despite these pitfalls, the truth is, of course, that asking parents about childhood in general; their children in particular; their parenting goals; their thoughts and feelings about this, that, or the other developmental phenomenon; and their thoughts and feelings about their relationships and interactions with their children provides psychologists with a wealth of precious information. For example, there is emerging evidence that parents' ideas, beliefs, and perceptions concerning child development, in general, and their ideas, beliefs, and perceptions concerning the origins of children's acceptable and unacceptable behavioral and emotional styles, in particular, contribute to, predict, and partially explain the development of adaptive and maladaptive behaviors in childhood. The basic idea is that what we *observe*, in our labs, on the playground, or in the home, insofar as parenting behaviors or the quality of the parent–child relationship is concerned, merely represents a behavioral expression or reflection of:

a.  How parents think about developmental pathways to social and emotional competence,
b.  How family contexts should be structured to shape children's behaviors, and
c.  How and when children should be taught to initiate and maintain relationships with others (Sigel & Kim, 1996).

Put another way, it is important that we know what parents think and believe, because those thoughts serve as parent-cognition "megabytes" that are eventually, in some way, retrieved and either acted upon or inhibited.

This chapter is centered on parents' expressed or reported preferences for child-rearing strategies. For the most part, we were interested in factors that may predict parents' beliefs about child-rearing. For example, we describe below a series of studies in which we examined the ways in which parents described their children's basic temperamental characteristics; we also examined whether their reported beliefs about child-rearing were associated in meaningful ways with the ways in which they viewed their children's dispositional characteristics. In keeping with previously noted views about the significance of culture (see, for example, the previous chapters by Bornstein and Cheah and Goodnow), we examined the relations between parents' beliefs about optimal child-rearing strategies and their notions about their own children's temperamental characteristics from a cross-cultural perspective.

In our research program described below, we attempt to demonstrate that depending on the culture within which parents live, they interpret or think about particular child characteristics in positive, negative, or neutral ways. We also attempt to demonstrate that parents in different cultures have very different ideas about how to go about best raising their children . . . and that these "best ways" are associated, in predictable ways, with how they view that which is normal or abnormal child behavior within their culture. Put another way, we attempt to demonstrate that if within a culture, a given behavioral characteristic is viewed as noxious or unacceptable, and if a child is viewed by parents as "having" this behavioral characteristic, then the expressed parenting preferences associated with this behavior will be of a within-culture negative variety. On the other hand, if the same characteristic is viewed as acceptable in a given culture, and if a child is viewed by parents as "having" this behavioral characteristic, then the expressed parenting preferences associated with this behavior will be of a within-culture positive variety.

To summarize, research concerned with parents' ideas about children's socio-emotional characteristics and about the ways that they should go about raising their children represents an excellent way to study culturally driven "inner working models" of that which is acceptable and that which is unacceptable. This notion fits nicely within Belsky's (1984) model of the determinants of parenting. That is, culture is one determinant of parenting. But so too are other factors. We examine some of these "other" factors below.

## Child Factors That May Influence Parenting Beliefs and Cognitions

It has been argued that parental beliefs are key determinants of parenting behaviors (e.g., Dix & Grusec, 1985; Goodnow & Collins, 1990). That is, some suggest that we behave as we do with our children because somehow, somewhere, we have retrieved in "quick-time," well-rehearsed strategies that will help us meet our parenting goals. But from where do these cognitions come?

It is theoretically and empirically unsatisfying to suggest that parental beliefs appear *de novo*. Parents' socialization beliefs must necessarily develop from a variety of preexisting factors. For example, transactional models of development have suggested that child characteristics shape the beliefs that parents develop about child-rearing and about that which is acceptable or unacceptable, normal or abnormal child behavior (Bell & Chapman, 1986). In this view, it is suggested that the best explanation for given child and parent behaviors derives from a transactional process of give-and-take between child and parent. In the following section, we describe a number of studies in which the first author and his colleagues examined child factors that predict parenting beliefs about child-rearing.

**Child Characteristics and Parenting Beliefs.**  In North America, parents appear to be very much consumed with the idea that children must be socially assertive, socially skilled, and accepted by their social community of peers, teachers, coaches, neighbors, and so on. They must be consumed with this idea, because there are countless, highly successful books written for parents on exactly this topic. Clearly then, parents want their children to grow up happy, successful, and well-adjusted. And parents can tell you what they mean by happy, successful, and well-adjusted. In North America and Western Europe, they can also tell you what less than happy, less than successful, and less than well-adjusted looks like.

For example, parents of preschoolers believe that something is amiss when their children behave consistently in socially reticent, inhibited, and withdrawn manners. North American and Western European mothers and fathers express concern when they see their children behaving consistently in a socially inhibited or reticent manner (Hastings & Rubin, 1999; Mills & Rubin, 1990; Schneider, Attili, Vermigili, & Younger, 1997). When parents feel embarrassed by, or disappointed in, or angry with their children's social reticence, they are likely to suggest that they would react to these behaviors in coercive or authoritarian ways. All of which is to suggest that if parents believe that a particular behavior as less than acceptable, and if they feel negatively about the behavior, they are more inclined to respond in a negative fashion.

As one may surmise from the preceding paragraph, the particular dispositional child characteristic that we have examined in our research program is *behavioral inhibition*. We have attempted to demonstrate that this putatively biologically based characteristic influences how parents think and feel about particular child-rearing strategies and how parenting behavior, in turn, influences the developmental course of inhibition. But what is behavioral inhibition and why have researchers been drawn to its study?

**Behavioral Inhibition.**  Behavioral inhibition (BI) may be defined as (a) a pattern of responding or behaving, (b) possibly biologically determined, such that (c) when unfamiliar and/or challenging situations are encountered, (d) the child shows signs of reactive anxiety, distress, or disorganization, and (e) the child has difficultly calming down on his or her own or being soothed by others. (Kagan, Reznick, & Snidman, 1987). Put another way, the behaviorally inhibited child shows clear signs of *emotion dysregulation*.

It has been argued that BI is a developmental precursor of social reticence, withdrawal, and anxiety proneness in childhood and adolescence (Rubin, Burgess, & Coplan, 2002). This being the case, there may be good reason to be concerned with this dispositional characteristic. Behaviorally inhibited toddlers refrain from interacting with unfamiliar adults; socially withdrawn children are those who when observed among familiar peers, such as their classmates, refrain from initiating and engaging in social interactions with them. Like behaviorally inhibited toddlers, socially withdrawn children appear socially wary and anxious and appear to be motivated to avoid social interaction. This link between behavioral inhibition and social withdrawal is rather significant because like behavioral inhibition, social withdrawal is rather stable (Rubin, 1993). Extremely withdrawn seven-year-olds are likely to maintain their status into late childhood and early adolescence. And perhaps more important, social withdrawal in midchildhood is predictive of negative self-regard, loneliness, peer rejection, and depression in early adolescence (see Rubin, Burgess, & Coplan, 2002 for a recent review).

## Behavioral Inhibition and Its Biological
## Concomitants.  Kagan and colleagues (e.g., Kagan, Reznick, & Snidman, 1987, 1988) have argued that some infants are genetically hardwired with a physiology that biases them to be cautious, timid, and wary in unfamiliar social and nonsocial situations. These "inhibited" children differ from their uninhibited counterparts in ways that imply variability in the threshold of excitability of the amygdala and its projections to the cortex, hypothalamus, sympathetic nervous system, corpus striatum, and central gray (Kagan, Snidman, & Arcus, 1993).

Consistent with Kagan's argument that there is a physiological basis to social wariness and inhibition is the research of Fox and colleagues (e.g., Fox & Calkins, 1993). These researchers began by noting that adults exhibiting relatively greater EEG activity in the right frontal lobe are more likely to express negative affect and rate emotional stimuli as negative (Jones & Fox, 1992). Moreover, adults diagnosed with unipolar depression, even in remission, are more likely to display right frontal EEG asymmetry compared with controls (Henriques & Davidson, 1990, 1991). Drawing from the adult literature on the psychophysiological underpinnings of emotion dysregulation, Fox and his collaborators have demonstrated that stable patterns of infant brain electrical activity predict temperamental fearfulness and behavioral inhibition in young children. For example, Calkins, Fox, and Marshall (1996) recorded brain electrical activity of children at 9, 14, and 24 months and found that infants who displayed a pattern of stable right frontal EEG asymmetry across this 15-month period were more fearful, anxious, compliant, and behaviorally inhibited as toddlers than other infants.

These physiological data provide evidence that unique patterns of brain electrical activity may reflect increasing arousal of particular brain centers involved in the expression of fear and anxiety (LeDoux, 1989), and appear to reflect a particular underlying temperamental type. The functional role of hemispheric asymmetries in the regulation of emotion may be understood in terms of an underlying motivational structure to emotional behavior, specifically the approach–withdrawal continuum. Infants exhibiting greater relative right frontal asymmetry are more likely to withdraw from mild stress. Infants exhibiting the opposite pattern of activation are more likely to approach. It is argued that these patterns of frontal activation represent a dispositional characteristic underlying behavioral temperamental responses to the environment.

Another physiological entity that distinguishes wary from nonwary infants/toddlers is *vagal tone*, an index of respiratory sinus arrhythmia (RSA) that assesses the functional status or efficiency of the nervous system (Porges & Byrne, 1992), and which marks both general reactivity and the ability to regulate one's level of arousal. RSA comprises the high-frequency oscillations in heart period that are associated with the breathing cycle (Porges, 1995). Higher brain centers associated with emotions and cognitions can influence brain stem cardiorespiratory control centers and thus affect RSA, with a reduction in these measures under conditions of stress or effort (Berntson, Cacioppo, & Quigley, 1993). In the context of a neurobiological model of behavioral inhibition, high inhibition might be associated with low vagal tone and low heart period variability. Indeed, Kagan and colleagues found concurrent associations between low heart period (high heart rate) and increased behavioral inhibition as assessed in infancy and childhood (Kagan, Reznick, Clarke, Snidman, & Garcia-Coll, 1984; Kagan, Reznick, & Snidman, 1988; Reznick et al., 1986). Anderson, Bohlin, and Hagekull (1999) reported similar relations between vagal tone and inhibition in a sample of Swedish toddlers.

Lastly, the hypothalamic-pituitary-adrenocortical (HPA) axis is affected largely by stressful or aversive situations that involve novelty, uncertainty, and/or negative emotions (Levine, 1983). Behaviorally inhibited infants evidence significant increases in cortisol as a function of exposure to stressful social situations (Spangler & Schieche, 1998). And, a positive relation exists between cortisol production in saliva and the demonstration of extremely inhibited behavior not only in the toddler period (Kagan, Reznick, & Snidman, 1987; Nachmias, Gunnar, Mangelsdorf, Parritz, & Buss, 1996), but also during early and middle childhood (Schmidt et al., 1997). The high cortisol levels of inhibited children may increase corticotrophin-releasing hormones in the central nucleus of the amygdala, thereby exacerbating the social fearfulness response. Furthermore, high cortisol levels may predispose inhibited children to develop a cognitive working model to expect fear and anxiety when facing novelty. It is relevant to note that exaggerated autonomic responses to novelty are associated with internalizing problems such as anxiety. Longitudinal data also suggest a link between BI in infancy and early childhood and phobic and anxiety disorders in midchildhood (Hirshfeld et al., 1992).

**Summary.**  It seems rather clear that behavioral inhibition is a phenomenon with some degree of biological underpinning. This being the case, in our research program we have asked whether there is variability in the ways in which parents respond to toddlers who have an inhibited temperament. We have argued that behavioral inhibition in infancy and toddlerhood, and its physiological markers, may be altered or strengthened through environmental means. For instance, we have suggested that a temperamentally inhibited infant or toddler may prove a challenge or stressor to his or her parents. Thus, for parents who view the inhibited child as particularly vulnerable, specific parenting cognitions and behaviors may follow. Alternatively, for parents who adopt the view that an inhibited temperament is changeable, a different constellation of parenting cognitions and behaviors may follow. And for parents who believe that behavioral inhibition is a reflection of a positive state or trait, yet another set of parenting thoughts, feelings, and behaviors may result.

## Behavioral Inhibition and Parenting

We turn now to the question, "How do North American parents think about behavioral inhibition?" We can make a guess of what the answer would be by examining the relations between observed and reported parenting practices associated with inhibited behavior.

### Study 1 (Rubin, Hastings, Stewart, Henderson, & Chen, 1997).  The children and parents who participated in the study lived in a moderately sized city, 100 kilometers from Toronto, Canada. One hundred and eight families participated in this study of 2-year-olds, their mothers, and fathers. Data collection included observations of behavioral inhibition and maternal behavior, and parental ratings of child temperament (Rubin et al., 1997). In this chapter, we focus primarily on parents' ratings of shyness and parents' reports of their preferred parenting styles.

At age 2, we observed the children in two situations: in an adaptation of Kagan's "Inhibition" paradigm (e.g., Kagan, Reznick, & Snidman, 1987, 1988), and in a play session with another 2-year-old and mother. We defined "inhibition" by referring to the toddlers' remaining in close proximity to the mother and exhibiting a lengthy latency to approach adult strangers as they entered a playroom and requested that the toddlers approach them in the Kagan paradigm; we also defined "inhibition" by referring to the toddlers' remaining in close proximity to the mother and exhibiting a lengthy latency to approach the unfamiliar toddler in the toddler–peer play paradigm.

Among the first set of findings was that maternal and paternal ratings of toddler shyness were strongly correlated with the child's display of inhibited behavior in each of the two contexts. This is actually something worth keeping in mind. The finding can be taken to mean that what researchers refer to as shy, inhibited behavior *as assessed and observed in the lab*, corresponds with parents' own judgments and beliefs about their children's dispositional temperamental characteristics.

A second finding was that inhibited behavior was associated, at two years, with the maternal display of what we referred to as "oversolicitousness." That is, the mothers of these extremely inhibited children were observed to be highly controlling, intrusive, and yet at the same time, suffocatingly warm. They were observed to remain very close to their children and often precluded their children's exploration of the playroom by their effusive kissing and hugging of them. In a way, they amply demonstrated that too much of any good thing can be quite bad.

A third finding pertained to vagal tone. In earlier work, researchers had reported that children with lower vagal tone (consistently high heart rate due to less parasympathetic influence) were more behaviorally inhibited and less able to self-regulate their emotions. We replicated this finding.

To summarize, in our first study, we found that consistently—across time and across situations—inhibited toddlers were viewed by both their mothers and fathers as shy and socially fearful; they had lower vagal tone; and their mothers were observed to be more oversolicitous than those of "average" and uninhibited toddlers.

### Study 2 (Rubin, Nelson, Hastings, & Asendorpf, 1999).

In Study 2, we followed up these same children at age 4. We asked two questions: (1) Does inhibition at age 2 predict socially reticent behavior with peers at age 4? (2) What is the role of parenting in the prediction of social reticence at four years? We know, from Study 1, that parental perceptions and beliefs about their children's shy temperament are significantly associated with their children's behavior in the laboratory at age 2. We learned, in this second study, that children who frequently exhibited socially reticent behavior among preschool-age peers during free play at age 4 were also perceived by their mothers and fathers as being shy and socially fearful. This finding was replicated in a collaborative, multiple cohort, longitudinal study with Nathan Fox at the University of Maryland. (e.g., Fox, Henderson, Rubin, Calkins, & Schmidt, 2001; Henderson, Marshall, Fox, & Rubin, 2004) In summary, from this initial body of work we discovered that in both Canada and the United States, toddlers and preschoolers who are observed to behave in socially fearful and reticent manners are viewed by their parents as socially fearful and reticent.

We then examined the longitudinal relations between shy inhibited behavior and parents' expressed socialization preferences. In this latter case, we sought to assess parents' beliefs about how best to socialize, or raise, their children. We found that: (a) observed inhibition/socially reticent behavior was stable between ages 2 and 4 years; (b) mothers' and fathers' ratings of their children's shy, socially wary behavior were stable between ages 2 and 4 years; (c) mothers' and fathers' expressed child-rearing preferences were stable between ages 2 and 4. We were particularly interested in the extent to which these North American parents indicated that they encouraged independent behavior in their children (the opposite of overly protective parenting behavior). This particular parenting belief was found to be stable between child ages 2 and 4 (e.g., the correlation for mothers' beliefs in encouraging independence between child age 2 and 4 was .64, $p < .001$). (d) Perhaps of greatest interest was our finding that parents who believed their 2-year-old toddlers were shy and socially fearful indicated that they would *not* encourage independence for these children at age 4. On the other hand, parents who believed their 2-year-old toddlers were not shy indicated that they would encourage their children at age 4 to be independent. Put another way, from age 2 to 4, the child led the "dance": parents' notions about the child's characteristics appeared to influence their beliefs about how to best raise their children. These findings suggest that perhaps, in North America, parents believe their shy toddlers to be particularly vulnerable and thus in need of protection.

**Study 3 (Kennedy, Rubin, Hastings, & Maisel, 2004).** In Study 3, we ran the same analyses as in Study 2. However, instead of using the parents' perceptions of their child's temperament, we examined the longitudinal relations between physiologically assessed vagal tone and parents' beliefs in appropriate child-rearing strategies. It has repeatedly been reported, in North America, that socially inhibited toddlers and preschoolers are emotionally dysregulated. Oftentimes, dysregulation has been assessed physiologically, and oftentimes, the preferred index of emotion dysregulation has been a baseline index of vagal tone (e.g., Burgess, Marshall, Rubin, & Fox, 2003).

The findings were an almost exact replication of the second study. (a) Physiologically assessed emotion dysregulation (vagal tone) was stable between ages two and four years ($r = .47^{\circ\circ\circ}$); (b) mothers' expressed child-rearing preferences were stable between 2 and 4 years. This time, we were particularly interested in the extent to which North American mothers indicated that they believed in discouraging their child's independent behavior (e.g., low ratings on "I encourage my child to be curious, to explore, and to question things") and in being overly protective ("I do not go out if my child must stay with a stranger"). This particular parenting belief "aggregate" was found to be stable between 2 and 4 years ($r = .47$, $p < .001$). (c) We found that vagal tone at 2 years predicted mothers' beliefs about the importance of overcontrolling/overprotective parenting at age four years; however, parenting beliefs did not predict physiological assessments of emotion dysregulation at age 4. Once again, the data suggest that in very early childhood, the child leads the dance; in this case, the child's physiological characteristics appeared to influence parents' beliefs about how to best raise their children. And once again, perhaps North American parents of toddlers who are physiologically dysregulated perceive their children to be particularly vulnerable and thus in need of protection.

**Study 4 (Hastings & Rubin, 1999).** Finally, just to strengthen this notion that one determinant of parenting beliefs is the child's temperament, we asked parents directly about what they think about socially anxious and shy behavior. Our goal was to examine if we could predict parents' beliefs about how they would react to seeing their preschool-age child behaving in a socially inhibited fashion, consistently, in the company of peers. It is important to note that the parents we interviewed were those of 4-year-olds for whom longitudinal data were available at age 2 years.

Our "predictors" of four-year maternal beliefs included the sex of the child, mothers' perceptions of their toddler's social fearfulness/shyness two years earlier, and mothers' expressed preferences for protective parenting behavior at child age 2 years. All relevant interactions were added to the regression equation as well. We found that the extent to which mothers viewed their toddlers as socially fearful and the extent to which mothers expressed a preference for protective parenting at child age two years were highly predictive of maternal beliefs about how they would respond to their preschooler's social withdrawal two years later. That is, social wariness at age 2 predicted parents' beliefs that the way to "deal with" or react to their preschoolers' social reticence was to be power-assertive (i.e., to punish, threaten, command, or disapprove of the behavior). But this connection between toddler inhibition and maternal power assertion was true *only* for mothers who, when their children were 2 years old, also exhibited overprotective parenting. For mothers who were less than protective at child age 2, the relation between toddler inhibition and maternal power assertion was nonsignificant.

To recap, inhibited social behavior is a moderately stable trait. But some researchers suggest that protective socialization patterns may contribute to that stability. Maternal interventions that involve "taking over" or directing a child who is having difficulty with social interactions, rather than encouraging the child to master the situation himself or herself, are likely to exacerbate shyness because the child is denied opportunities to practice self-regulation. A mother may not consciously want her child to be shy. And a mother may not want to expose her shy child to situations that are too arousing for him or her. In these cases, the parent may believe that by acting protectively, the child can be buffered from situations that arouse the child's distress. As a consequence, highly protective mothers of more wary toddlers may eventually come to use high-power techniques because they wish to alleviate both their children's anxiety and their own empathic anxiety. And also, by using commands in response to their preschooler's social withdrawal, mothers may be attempting to assure themselves that their child's social withdrawal is not ignored. Mothers may believe that by taking control in situations in which they believe their child to feel discomfort, they may also reduce their children's immediate anxieties. But it may also be that they are inadvertently promoting the long-term stability of their child's social wariness.

In summary, many theories of socialization are centered on the argument that there are multiple determinants of parenting cognitions and behavior (e.g., Belsky, 1984). In the studies described thus far, we have attempted to demonstrate that child characteristics and, perhaps most important, parents' beliefs about their children's temperaments are highly predictive of parents' beliefs about how to best raise their children. But there are certainly reasons other than child temperament that can account for why parents believe that they should socialize their children in the ways they do. Given the focus of this book, it is clear that one potential "cause" of parenting beliefs and behavior is that of culture.

## Culture and Parenting Beliefs

In this section, we borrow heavily from the writings of Harkness and Super (2002) about the meanings of culture and the effects that culture can have on parenting ideas and behaviors. To begin with, what is "culture"? Drawing from Bates and Plog (1991, p. 7), culture may be defined as

> a system of shared beliefs, values, customs, behaviors, and artifacts that the members of society use to cope with their world and with one another, and that are transmitted from generation to generation through learning.

Note well that this definition makes it clear that culture involves three key components: what people think, what they do, and the material products they produce (Bodley, 1994). Among these beliefs and behaviors are those that have much to do with the socialization of the society's next generation, that is, *parenting* beliefs and behaviors. Thus, it is argued that the values, beliefs, and attitudes that help define a particular culture also serve to shape and influence values and beliefs about that which is normal or abnormal, acceptable or unacceptable, and typical or atypical.

One pertinent example of the role of culture derives from the research of Xinyin Chen and colleagues (e.g., Chen, Hastings, Rubin, Chen, Cen, & Stewart, 1998; Chen, Liu, Rubin, Cen, & Li, 2002; Chen, Rubin, & Li, 1995). Chen and colleagues have argued that some forms of behavior that are viewed as unacceptable and atypical in some cultures are viewed as acceptable and typical in others. For example, as noted above, shy, socially wary, and reserved behaviors are viewed by North American parents as less than desirable.

Not only is shy, withdrawn behavior unappreciated by North American parents, but we have also demonstrated that shy, withdrawn elementary- and middle-schoolers in North America and Western Europe are rejected and victimized by their peers. Many of these shy/anxious/socially withdrawn children grow up thinking poorly of themselves, feeling lonely and depressed. They have trouble making and keeping friends. In keeping with this perspective, Harkness and colleagues have reported that Italian parents regard shyness as putting the child at a disadvantage in the social world. And Casiglia, LoCoco, & Zappulla (1998) have reported that shy, withdrawn Italian children are rejected by peers.

In Mainland China, on the other hand, Chen and colleagues argue that shy children are viewed by parents as reverential, conforming, reserved, and compliant. These characteristics are considered typical and desirous. Given the significance attached to achieving and maintaining social order and interpersonal harmony within traditional Chinese culture, it makes sense that individuals are encouraged to restrain their personal desires and to behave in a sensitive, cautious, and inhibited fashion. Indeed, children who exhibit such tendencies are described as *Guai Hai Zi* in Mandarin, which may be loosely translated as meaning "good" or "well-behaved."

According to Chen and colleagues, peers don't reject shy, reserved Chinese children and these children do not grow up to think poorly of themselves or to feel lonely. Put another way, shy, reserved Chinese children are quite capable of self-regulation. They willingly comply with the directives of adults (Chen, Liu, Rubin, Hen, Wang, & Li, 2003); they are quiet; and most important, they become good students (Chen, Rubin, & Li, 1997). Chen's research is a paradigm-case example of culturally defined normalcy and abnormalcy. And if Chen and colleagues are correct, then one can begin to see the policy implications of cultural definitions of normal and abnormal behaviors and thoughts. If a society is to be respectful of its immigrant population, it must assuredly respect these cultural definitions of normal and abnormal, acceptable and unacceptable, typical and atypical.

It was the research that Chen and colleagues were doing on the correlates of shyness in elementary- and middle-school Chinese children that led us to the next obvious questions. (a) Are there differences in the prevalence of shy, socially wary behavior among Eastern and Western children? (b) If so, how early can these differences in prevalence be detected? (c) And, are there cultural differences in parents' ideas about and reactions to their children's shy behavior? From this initial set of questions came the *International Consortium for the Study of Social and Emotional Development (ICSSED)*.

### The Cultural Prevalence of Shy Inhibited Behavior.

We begin first with the issue of *prevalence*. If a behavior is to be viewed as "normative," it should probably also be frequently produced in the population at large. If a given behavior is viewed as culturally aberrant, one might expect that it would be responded to in ways that would decrease, or certainly not increase its production. With this in mind, we considered whether behavioral inhibition or shyness carries with it psychological "meanings" that vary across cultures and how it is that culture may be involved in the development of behavioral inhibition.

In a study co-authored by Chen et al. (1998), it was discovered that Chinese 24-month-olds differed from Canadian 24-month-olds on every index of behavioral inhibition (see Table 4.1). As one can see, in Table 4.1, Chinese toddlers were significantly more behaviorally inhibited than their Canadian counterparts. But does this mean that inhibition carries with it a different meaning in the minds of Chinese and Canadian parents? Does the higher frequency of inhibited behavior suggest that Chinese parents are encouraging of it and that Canadian parents are discouraging of it? Our data could not answer the latter question directly. We could, however, address whether parents' beliefs in how to best socialize their children were associated in meaningful ways with the demonstration of behavioral inhibition in the two samples.

We found that the frequent display of inhibition in the Chinese sample was associated significantly with parents' reports that it is best to be accepting and

TABLE 4.1   Percentage of Children Who Contacted Mother or Did Not Approach Stranger

| Variables | China | Canada | $\chi^2$ |
|---|---|---|---|
| Contact with mother in free play | 41.06 | 21.91 | 10.56[a] |
| Contact with mother in truck/robot | 60.96 | 37.26 | 13.63[a] |
| Did not approach stranger | 21.09 | 5.90 | 12.21[a] |
| Did not touch robot | 43.24 | 11.77 | 30.76[a] |

[a] $= p < .001$

encouraging of achievement and independence, and not to be rejecting. The frequent display of inhibition in the Canadian sample was associated significantly with parents' reports that it is best to be punitive, highly protective, and not to be accepting or to encourage achievement.

It is important to note that each of the correlations differed significantly between the cultures. Thus, if we can believe that parents' ideas about parenting do get instantiated in their behaviors, we might argue that Chinese parents whose toddlers demonstrate shy, wary, cautious behavior socialize their children by being accepting and encouraging of achievement and independence. North American parents whose toddlers demonstrate shy, wary, cautious behavior socialize their children by being punitive, overly protective, and unaccepting.

One rather important question to ask is whether Chinese parents actually believe that their observationally inhibited toddlers are shy and wary. As noted above, our team of researchers had already discovered that North American parents of inhibited toddlers observed in the lab rated them as shy and socially fearful. But do Chinese parents rate toddlers observed to be behaviorally inhibited as shy and socially cautious and fearful? A recent analysis of our data indicates that there is a zero-order correlation between observed behavioral inhibition and parents' ratings of shy, wary behavior. This finding raises an enormous number of questions, not the least of which is whether Kagan's behavioral inhibition paradigm tells us anything about shyness, fearfulness, and wariness in cultures beyond those found in North America and Western Europe! For example, perhaps the behaviors displayed by Chinese toddlers in such situations are viewed as being primary indicators of cautiousness and reservedness. These behaviors may be viewed, by Chinese parents, as entirely appropriate in situations that bring with them the introduction of unfamiliar adults and toys.

With these findings in mind, we turn now to a new, multicountry longitudinal study being conducted in Australia, Brazil, Canada, China, India, Italy, and Korea by members of the *ICSSED*. In this project, we are comparing similarities and differences within Asian countries and within several countries representative of "Western" culture. In our first data set, we examined the prevalence of behavioral inhibition across cultures and the extent to which parents in different cultures perceived their toddlers to be shy and wary.

**The Prevalence of Observed Behavioral Inhibition.** At present, we have gathered observed behavioral inhibition data on toddlers in five countries: Australia, Canada, China, Italy (Sicily), and Korea. Two of these countries, Canada and Australia, share a relative historical "newness." Their non-Aboriginal populations left their countries of origin and struggled with rugged untamed terrains to build new nations. Ongoing immigration has continued to contribute to their ever-evolving cultural identities, both positively and with some tensions. These are very pluralistic nations. Over time, both Australia and Canada have become thoroughly industrialized and like the United States, their peoples tend to emphasize independent, achievement-oriented mores. Thus, in mainstream "Euro-"Australia and Canada, there have been parental emphases on training for independence, individualism, social assertiveness, competence, and risk-taking (e.g., Marjoribanks, 1994). Indeed, it has been demonstrated that foreigners perceive Australians as "friendly" and outgoing (McGregor, 1966); and Australian parents typically encourage their children to be friendly (Conway, 1971). Canadian parents also believe that sociability and social skills are high socialization priorities (Rubin, Mills, & Rose-Krasnor, 1989).

Like North Americans, Italians value sociability, independence, and assertiveness (Casiglia, LoCoco, & Zappulla, 1998). Perhaps one of the most important influences on Sicilian norms, attitudes, and lifestyles derives from Arab culture. In this regard, historians have written about the influence of Arabian culture vis-à-vis the importance of negotiating and bargaining, not only for "things" but also in the establishment and maintenance of relationships. Assertiveness, negotiation skills, and being able to establish social interactions and to easily approach others are viewed as desirable characteristics. Children are socialized to learn how to enter peer groups, to manage relationships with peers, to negotiate, and to be assertive (Edwards, Gandini & Giovannini, 1996).

Also, Italian culture encourages emotional expressiveness during interpersonal interaction. Thus, from the earliest years of childhood, Italians engage their young children in lively debates, or *discussione*, thereby promoting social assertiveness (Corsaro & Maynard, 1996; New & Richman, 1996). Italian mothers also promote independence and social competence during the early years of childhood (Edwards, Gandini, & Giovannini, 1996). The Italian sample in the *ICSSED* was drawn from Sicily where a primary parenting goal is to socialize assertiveness and leadership (Casiglia et al., 1998). Thus, it is conceivable that Italian toddlers may learn their lessons well and demonstrate less inhibited behavior than both Australian and Canadian children.

As noted above, in Eastern cultures such as those found in China and Korea, the emphasis shifts from the promotion of independence, sociability, and assertiveness to obedience, compliance, and a collectivistic spirit (Harkness & Super, 2002). Self-restraint, cautiousness, and cooperation are highly valued. Achieving and maintaining social order and interpersonal harmony are primary concerns. Individuals are encouraged to restrain personal desires for the benefits and interests of the collective. Furthermore, one learns to control or suppress emotions, particularly negative ones, so as to avoid social rejection and disapproval.

In both Confucian and Taoist philosophies, self-restraint is considered an index of social maturity, accomplishment, and mastery (King & Bond, 1985). The expression of individuals' needs or striving for autonomous behaviors is considered selfish and socially unacceptable (Ho, 1986). Relatedly, parents in Eastern cultures view children as extensions of themselves and thus encourage parent–child proximity and physical contact during the early childhood years (Ho, 1986).

Our sample comprised approximately 100 toddlers and their parents in each of the five countries. For the most part, the parents were from similar educational backgrounds, although the Chinese parents were more poorly educated than all others. Our observational measure of behavioral inhibition was identical in all cultures. We found the following: (a) The Chinese toddlers were observed to be more behaviorally inhibited than the Australian, Italian, and Canadian toddlers; and (b) the Korean toddlers were observed to be more behaviorally inhibited than the Australian and Italian toddlers. Thus, our observational data suggest meaningful cultural differences between the Asian and Western cultures in the expression of inhibited behavior.

## Cross-Cultural Differences in Parent Ratings of Child Shyness/Social Fearfulness.

Given that this book is, in large part, centered on parenting *beliefs*, we would argue that is important to ascertain whether parental ideas about how socially fearful and shy their children are mirror the data we obtain from our observational protocols. That is, are behaviorally inhibited toddlers viewed as shy by their parents? This is an essential question to address for several reasons. Insofar as determinants of parenting are concerned, it may be far more important to know whether parents think their children are shy or wary than to know how the children actually behave. Parents' beliefs about how to "parent" their children may have more to do with how they "see" their children than with how we, as unbiased observers, see them. With this in mind, we examined whether we obtained the same results for observed prevalence when we asked parents to rate their toddlers on an index of "social fearfulness/shyness."

Once again, the data were derived from Canadian, Chinese, Korean, and Italian mothers and their toddlers. To these samples, we added maternal ratings of shyness from India. The inclusion of Indian data allows yet another comparison of Asian cultures. Like China and Korea, Indian culture is thought to be more collectivistic and less concerned with individual pursuits. For example, in the Hindu religion, the *Ramayana* encourages *Dharma* or the understanding of the environment surrounding the individual. It also encourages the individual to see herself or himself as a part of a greater whole that includes not only the family, but the community as well (Kakar, 1978). From what we knew about Indian culture, we anticipated that the data from India would not be significantly different from those obtained in China and Korea.

It is important to note that for this particular set of data analyses, we had to exclude the Australian sample. Our Australian colleagues insisted on being "independent" and thus chose to use different measures of temperament and parenting than did the remaining researchers! From this we can conclude that our

Australian colleagues behaved very much like the Australian toddlers—extremely independent!

Our results revealed that: (a) Italian mothers viewed their toddlers as less inhibited than mothers from all other cultures; (b) Canadian and Indian mothers viewed their toddlers as less inhibited than mothers from China and Korea; (c) there were no differences in the shyness ratings of mothers from Korea and China. Perhaps the biggest surprise was that there were differences between the shyness ratings of mothers from China, Korea, and India.

These latter, within-Asia differences allowed us to ask the next obvious question: are the correlations between parent perceptions of child shyness and parental beliefs about preferred child-rearing practices more similar in China and Korea than in Canada, Italy, Australia, and India? That is, in cultures where behavioral inhibition is perceived to be relatively infrequent, or in cultures where the behavior is not well-established as "normative," is it associated with negative forms of parental behavior? For example, given prevailing parental beliefs about sociability and social wariness, one might expect that Italian parents of inhibited toddlers would be less than tolerant of their children's proclivities and demonstrate more punitive behavior than parents of less inhibited or uninhibited toddlers, as has been observed in Canada and the United States (Chen et al., 1998; LaFreniere & Dumas, 1992). And in cultures where behavioral inhibition is relatively frequent, is it associated with positive forms of parental behavior? Remember, this is what we found in the Canada versus China study described earlier. For example, given these cultural beliefs and practices, perhaps one might expect that the parents of a highly cautious, wary toddler in South Korea would respond to their child in a manner supportive of the characteristic behavior, much like what we found in China.

### Cross-Cultural Differences in the Associations Between Parent Ratings of Child Shyness/Social Fearfulness and Parenting Beliefs.

The child-rearing strategies that we obtained from the Child-Rearing Practices Report Q-Sort (CRPR, Block, 1981) included the following constructs: Acceptance, Encouragement of Achievement, Encouragement of Independence, Protectiveness, Punishment Orientation, and Rejection. We began with a simple question: do the correlations between parenting beliefs and parents' perceptions of shyness/social fearfulness differ from culture to culture? The results were rather clear in this regard: (a) Parent ratings of toddler shyness were negatively and significantly associated with parents' expressed "acceptance" (see below for examples) in Canada, India, and Italy. (b) Parent ratings of toddler shyness were positively and significantly associated with parents' expressed "rejection" (see below for examples) in India, and with parents' expressed "punitiveness" in Canada and India. Indeed, if one aggregates the constructs of rejection and punitiveness to form an "authoritarian" parenting factor, one finds a positive association with toddler shyness in Canada, India, and Italy. (c) Parent ratings of toddler shyness were negatively and significantly associated with parents' expressed "encouragement of independence" in Italy and Korea. (d) Finally, parent ratings of toddler shyness were positively and significantly associated with parents' expressed "protectiveness" in Korea.

In summary, in those cultures wherein toddler shyness was reported to be less frequent, associations were found with parental rejection, punitiveness, lack of acceptance, and discouragement of independence. Strikingly, few significant correlations were found between parents' perceptions of shyness and their reported behaviors in both China and Korea, the two countries with the highest amounts of parent-reported shyness. However, it must be noted that in Korea, the correlations obtained were very much like what one would expect in the West: parent ratings of shyness were associated positively with protectiveness and negatively with encouraging independence.

## SUMMARY

Why might cross-cultural differences in behavioral inhibition or temperamental shyness exist so early in the child's development? Perhaps the findings presented herein are in keeping with a "goodness-of-fit" model. For example, it has been suggested that Asian parents reinforce, or respond in positive fashions, to expressions of cautious reserved behavior whereas "Western" parents respond with overprotectiveness or harshness to what they view as undesirable socially wary behavior (Chen et al., 1998). The data presented in this chapter are partially in keeping with such a perspective.

## CONCLUSIONS

Cultures impart meanings to behavior, determine how individuals, including parents and peers, perceive, evaluate, and react to behavior, and eventually regulate and direct the developmental processes of behavior. In this chapter, the behavior in question was behavioral inhibition, a phenomenon that has been observed in different countries, such as Canada, China, England, Germany, Sweden, and the United States. (e.g., Asendorpf, 1994; Broberg, Lamb, & Hwang, 1990; Chen et al., 1998; Engfer, 1993; Fox, Henderson, Rubin, Calkins, & Schmidt, 2001; Stevenson-Hinde, 1989). We sought to explore the possibility of differences, not only in the prevalence of behavioral inhibition among toddlers residing in Eastern and Western cultures, but especially in how parents think about and respond to their children's behavioral inhibition.

This chapter began with some questioning statements about the study of parenting beliefs. It ends with some rather positive ones. From the data we have collected in Australia, Brazil, Canada, China, India, Italy, and Korea, we have learned that parents' views about the prevalence of a given "type" of temperament almost mirror those we would expect from Eastern and Western cultures. Strikingly, it is also the case that in the more Western cultures, the extent to which toddlers are rated as socially fearful and shy is associated with more authoritarian parenting styles. Given that these data were drawn solely from toddlers and their parents, and given the Canadian data that demonstrate the significance of toddler characteristics in predicting parental thoughts about parenting, it may be that the cultural "message" of the *ICSSED* data will prove stronger when we have our four-year data in hand. As of this writing, such data are gradually becoming available in Australia, Canada, China, India, and Korea.

As much as we view our data as "rich" and informative, they are rather incomplete in several ways. For one, we do not have father data in every country. We expect that the relations between fathers' beliefs about parenting and their sons' versus their daughters' social fearfulness and shyness would be highly informative. For another, expressed parenting practices were assessed by a measure that was developed in the United States. Might there be dimensions of parenting that are unique to given cultures? For yet another, we only reported data for two- and sometimes four-year-olds. Might the relations between parenting beliefs and child behavior vary from one age group to another? For example, Xinyin Chen has recently discovered that among Chinese adolescents, shyness is not associated with peer acceptance and other positive markers of adjustment. And finally, for another, in the cross-cultural work that we describe herein, we did not ask parents directly about how they think and feel about social fearfulness and shyness; instead, we drew inferences about their thoughts and feelings by examining the correlations between parent-rated temperament and expressed parenting practices. Through open-ended question-and-answer methodologies, we may eventually discover parenting styles that exist in some but not other cultures. And the methodology may well provide us with a "true" reactive belief response to such behaviors as shyness and aggression.

This possibility is noted because Cheah and Rubin (2004) recently reported that when Chinese parents were asked directly how they would respond if they actually viewed their children behave consistently in a withdrawn fashion, they reported that Mainland Chinese mothers regarded such behavior in a very negative fashion. In recent years, Chen and colleagues have reported that shy/wary children are accepted by their peers, viewed as leaders in school, think well of themselves, and show virtually no signs of problematic outcome (Chen, 2000). This being the case, why would the Chinese mothers studied in the Cheah and Rubin study present a negative evaluative picture of social wariness and withdrawal?

Cheah and Rubin (2004) suggested that the answer may lie in behaviors described in their vignettes in contrast to the behaviors that fall into the peer-nominated "shyness" construct that Chen and colleagues study. The "shyness/wariness" factor studied by Chen and colleagues includes items such as "shy" and "feelings get hurt easily." Perhaps such items conjure up an image of a socially sensitive child, and not one who is neither willing nor able to interact with others. Perhaps too, such items reflect being "slow to warm up" or social cautiousness. Cheah and Rubin argue that whereas shy, socially reserved, sensitive behavior may eventually be conducive to harmonious group interactions, socially withdrawn behavior that removes the child from familiar others could undermine such goals. In this regard, socially withdrawn behavior could be perceived by Chinese mothers as "nonsocial" behavior that undermines the predominant collectivistic teachings of preschool caregivers, as well as the societal goals of group harmony and close interaction (Stimpfl, Zheng, & Meredith, 1997).

Thus, as many others have noted beforehand, language and nomenclature are important in cross-cultural research. If one interviews or provides parents and children with questionnaires, a central rule of thumb must be that the construct one is interested in exists, has a label attached to it, and can be distinguished from related but different constructs. Social withdrawal, social isolation, and shyness are related phenomena, and yet not considered the same constructs in the Western literature published in the English language (Rubin, Burgess, & Coplan 2002); in cross-cultural research, one must surely ascertain whether given constructs go by the same or different names, or whether they, in fact, exist in various cultures.

Open-ended interviews and questionnaires aside, it seems clear that the time is ripe for going beyond the study of parenting beliefs and actually observing how parents respond when their children behave in this way or that. Bornstein's work with parents and infants is an excellent example of what should and could be done (see Chapter 1). However, at the present time, extant observational research paradigms and protocols appear to be more appropriate and relevant within those cultures within which they were developed. The debate about the meaningfulness of the attachment-based "Strange Situation" is a case in point (see Chapter 5 by Van IJzendoorn, Bakermans-Kranenburg, & Sagi-Schwartz). Reliable observational data will certainly help us understand similarities and differences in the ways parents respond to their children's emotions and characteristic social behaviors. The bottom line is that there is a great amount of work to do, and that is very good news to those of us interested in studying culture.

# ACKNOWLEDGMENTS

The research described herein was supported by grants, to authors Rubin and Chen, from the Social Sciences and Humanities Research Council of Canada, to Ann Sanson from Australian Research Council, to Alida LoCoco from the Italian National Science Foundation, and to Ock-Boon Chung from the Korea Research Foundation. Author Rubin was also supported by an Ontario Mental Health Foundation Senior Research Fellowship while at the University of Waterloo. We are grateful to the children and mothers for their participation and to the following individuals who aided in the collection and coding of data: AUSTRALIA–Jordana Bayer, Lisa Warren, Heather Siddons, Tammie Noy, Lisa Meehan, and Adina Kotler at the University of Melbourne; CANADA–Loretta Lapa, Kelly Lemon, Jo-Anne McKinnon, Amy Rubin, Alice Rushing and Cherami Wischman at the University of Waterloo; CHINA–Lan-zhi Liang, Yue-bo Zhang and Li Wang at Beijing Normal University; Bo-shu Li, Dan Li, Zhen-yun Li and Mowei Liu at Shanghai Teachers' University; ITALY–Rossella Bonomo, Rosanna Di Maggio, Francesca Liga, Manuela Scrima, Monica Spallino, Alice Sprini at the Università di Palermo; and KOREA–Su-Min Ha of Dongduk Women's University, Jung-Ha Lim, Hyun-Joo Hwang, Se-Jin Eom, Youn-Jung Park of Korea University.

## REFERENCES

Anderson, K., Bohlin, G., & Hagekull, B. (1999). Early temperament and stranger wariness as predictors of social inhibition in 2 year olds. *British Journal of Developmental Psychology, 17*, 421–434.

Asendorpf, J. (1994). The malleability of behavior inhibition: A study of individual developmental functions. *Developmental Psychology, 30*, 912–919.

Bates, D. G., & Plog, F. (1991). *Human Adaptive Strategies*, New York: McGraw Hill.

Bell, R. Q., & Chapman, M. (1986). Child effects in studies using experimental or brief longitudinal approaches to socialization. *Developmental Psychology, 22*, 595–603.

Belsky, J. (1984). The determinants of parenting: A process model. *Child Development, 55*, 83–96.

Berntson, G. G., Cacioppo, J. T., & Quigley, K. S. (1993). Respiratory sinus arrhythmia: Autonomic origins, physiological mechanisms, and psychophysiological implications. *Psychophysiology, 30*, 183–196.

Block, J. H. (1981). *The Child-Rearing Practices Report (CRPR): A set of Q items for the description of parental socialization attitudes and values.* Berkeley: University of California, Institute of Human Development.

Bodley, J. H. (1994). *Cultural Anthropology: Tribes, States, and the Global System.* Mountain View, CA; Mayfield Publishing.

Broberg, A., Lamb, M. E., & Hwang, P. (1990). Inhibition: Its stability and correlates in 16- to 40-month old children. *Child Development, 61*, 1153–1163.

Burgess, K. B., Marshall, P., Rubin, K. H., & Fox, N. A. (2003). Infant attachment and temperament as predictors of subsequent behavior problems and psychophysiological functioning. *Journal of Child Psychology and Psychiatry and Allied Disciplines, 44*, 113.

Calkins, S. D., Fox, N. A., & Marshall, T. R. (1996). Behavioral and physiological antecedents of inhibition in infancy. *Child Development, 67*, 523–540.

Casiglia A. C., LoCoco A., & Zappulla C. (1998). Aspects of social reputation and peer relationships in Italian children: A cross-cultural perspective. *Developmental Psychology, 34, 4*, 723–730.

Cheah, C. S. L., & Rubin, K. H. (2004). A cross-cultural examination of maternal beliefs regarding maladaptive behaviors in preschoolers. *International Journal of Behavioral Development, 28*, 83–94.

Chen, X. (2000). Social and emotional development in Chinese children and adolescents: A contextual cross-cultural perspective. In F. Columbus (Ed.), *Advances in psychology research: Vol. I* (pp. 229–251). Commack, NY: Nova Science.

Chen, X., Hastings, P. D., Rubin, K. H., Chen, H., Cen, G., & Stewart, S. L. (1998). Child-rearing practices and behavioral inhibition in Chinese and Canadian toddlers: A cross-cultural study. *Developmental Psychology, 34*, 677–686.

Chen, X., Liu, M., Rubin, K. H., & Cen, G., & Li, D. (2002). Sociability and prosocial orientation as predictors of youth adjustment: A seven-year longitudinal study in a Chinese sample. *International Journal of Behavioral Development.*

Chen, X., Liu, M., Rubin, K. H., Hen, H., Wang, L., & Li, D. (2003). Compliance in Chinese and Canadian toddlers: A cross-cultural study. *International Journal of Behavioral Development, 27*, 428–436.

Chen, X., Rubin, K. H., & Li, B. (1997). Maternal acceptance and social and school adjustment in Chinese children: A four-year longitudinal study. *Merrill-Palmer Quarterly, 43*, 663–681.

Chen, X., Rubin, K. H., & Li, Z. (1995). Social functioning and adjustment in Chinese children: A longitudinal study. *Developmental Psychology, 31*, 531–539.

Conway, R. (1971). *The great Australian stupor: An interpretation of the Australian way of life.* Melbourne, Australia: Sun Books.

Corsaro, W., & Maynard, D. W. (1996). Format tying in discussion and argumentation among Italian and American children. In D. Slobin & J. Gerhardt (Eds.), Social interaction, social context, and language. *Essays in honor of Susan Ervin-Tripp* (pp. 157–184). Hillsdale, NJ: Erlbaum.

Dameron, L. E. (1955). Mother–child interaction in the development of self-restraint. *Journal of Genetic Psychology, 86*, 289–308.

Dix, T. H., and Grusec, J. E. (1985). Parent attribution processes in the socialization of children. In I. E. Sigel (Ed.), *Parental belief systems: The psychological consequences for children.* (pp. 201–233). Hillsdale, NJ: Erlbaum.

Edwards C. P., Gandini L., & Giovannini D. (1996). The contrasting developmental timetables of parents and preschool teachers in two cultural communities. In S. Harkness & C. M. Super (Eds.), *Parents' Cultural Belief Systems.* New York: Guilford.

Engfer, A. (1993). Antecedents and consequences of shyness in boys and girls: A six-year longitudinal study. In K. H. Rubin & J. B. Asendorpf (Eds.), *Social withdrawal, inhibition, and shyness in childhood* (pp. 49–79). Hillsdale, NJ: Erlbaum.

Fox, N. A., & Calkins, S. D. (1993). Pathways to aggression and social withdrawal: Interactions among temperament, attachment, and regulation. In K. Rubin & J. Asendorpf (Eds.), *Social withdrawal, inhibition, and shyness in childhood.* Hillsdale, NJ: Erlbaum.

Fox, N. A., Henderson, H. A., Rubin, K. H., Calkins, S. D., & Schmidt, L. A. (2001). Stability and instability of behavioral inhibition and exuberance: Psychophysiological and behavioral factors influencing change and continuity across the first four years of life. *Child Development, 72*, 1–21.

Goodnow, J. J., & Collins, W. A. (1990). *Development according to parents: The nature, sources, and consequences of parents' ideas.* London: Erlbaum.

Harkness, S., & Super, C. M. (2002). Culture and parenting. In M. H. Bornstein (Ed.), *Handbook of parenting* (2d ed.). Hillsdale, NJ: Erlbaum.

Hastings, P. D. and Rubin, K. H. (1999). Predicting mothers' beliefs about preschool-aged children's social behavior: Evidence for maternal attitudes moderating child effects. *Child Development, 70*, 722–741.

Henderson, H., Marshall, P., Fox, N. A., & Rubin, K. H. (2004). Psychophysiological and behavioral evidence for varying forms of nonsocial behavior in preschoolers. *Child Development, 75*, 251–263.

Henriques, J., & Davidson, R. (1990). Regional brain electrical asymmetries discriminate between previously depressed and healthy control subjects. *Journal of Abnormal Psychology, 99*, 22–31.

Henriques, J., & Davidson, R. (1991). Left frontal hypoactivation in depression. *Journal of Abnormal Psychology, 100*, 535–545.

Hirshfeld, D. R., Rosenbaum, J. F., Biederman, J., Bolduc, E. A., Faraone, S. V., Snidman, N., Reznick, J. S., & Kagan, J. (1992). Stable behavioral inhibition and its association with anxiety disorder. *Journal of the American Academy of Child and Adolescent Psychiatry, 31*, 103–111.

Ho, D. Y. F. (1986). Chinese patterns of socialization: A critical review. In M. H. Bond (Ed.), *The psychology of Chinese people.* New York: Oxford University Press.

Jones, N., & Fox, N. (1992). Electroencephalogram asymmetry during emotionally evocative films and its relation to positive and negative affectivity. *Brain and Cognition, 20*, 280–299.

Kagan, J., Reznick, J. S., Clarke, C., Snidman, N., & Garcia-Coll, C. (1984). Behavioral inhibition to the unfamiliar. *Child Development, 55,* 2212–2225.

Kagan, J., Reznick, J. S., and Snidman, N. (1987). The physiology and psychology of behavioral inhibition in children. *Child Development, 58,* 1459–1473.

Kagan J., Reznick, J. S., & Snidman, N. (1988). Biological basis of childhood shyness. *Science, 240,* 167–171.

Kagan, J., Snidman, N., & Arcus, D. (1998). Childhood derivatives of high and low reactivity in infancy. *Child Development, 69,* 1483–1493.

Kakar, S. (1978). *The inner world: A psychoanalytical study of childhood and society in India.* Delhi: Oxford University Press.

Kennedy, A. E., Rubin, K. H., Hastings, P., & Maisel, B. (2004). The longitudinal relations between child vagal tone and parenting behavior: 2 to 4 years. *Developmental Psychobiology, 45,* 10–21.

King, A. Y. C., & Bond, M. H. (1985). The Confucian paradigm of man: A sociological view. In W. S. Teng & D. Y. H. Wu (Eds.), *Chinese culture and mental health.* New York: Academic.

LaFreniere, P., & Dumas, J. E. (1992). A transactional analysis of early childhood anxiety and social withdrawal. *Development and Psychopathology, 4,* 385–402.

LeDoux, J. (1989). Cognitive-emotional interactions in the brain. *Cognition and Emotion, 4,* 267–274.

Levine, S. (1983). A psychobiological approach to the ontogeny of coping. In N. Garmezy & M. Rutter (Eds.), *Stress, coping, and development in children* (pp. 107–131). Baltimore, MD: Johns Hopkins University Press.

Maccoby, E. E., & Martin, J. A. (1983). Socialization in the context of the family: Parent–child interaction. In E. M. Hetherington (Ed.), *Handbook of child psychology: Vol. 4. Socialization, personality, and social development* (pp. 1–102). New York: John Wiley.

McGregor, C. (1966). *Profile of Australia.* London: Hodder & Stoughton.

Marjoribanks, K. (1994). Cross-cultural comparisons of family environments of Anglo-, Greek- and Italian-Australians. *Psychological Reports, 74,* 49–50.

Messick, S. (1983). Assessment of children. In W. Kessen (Ed.), *Handbook of child psychology: Vol.1. History, theory, and methods.* New York: Wiley.

Miller, D. R., & Swanson, G. E. (1958). *The changing American parent.* New York: Holt.

Mills, R. S. L., and Rubin, K. H. (1990). Parental beliefs about problematic social behaviors in early childhood. *Child Development, 61,* 138–151.

Nachmias, M., Gunnar, M., Mangelsdorf, S., Parritz, R. H., & Buss, K. (1996). Behavioral inhibition and stress reactivity: The moderating role of attachment security. *Child Development, 67,* 508–522.

New, R. S., & Richman, A. L. (1996). Maternal Beliefs and Infant Care Practices in Italy and the United States. In S. Harkness & C. M. Super (Eds.), *Parents' Cultural Belief Systems.* The Guilford Press, New York, London.

Porges, S. W. (1995). Cardiac vagal tone: A physiological index of stress. *Neuroscience and Biobehavioral Reviews, 19,* 225–233.

Porges, S. W., & Byrne, E. A. (1992). Research methods for measurement of heart rate and respiration. *Biological Psychology, 34,* 93–130.

Reznick, J. S., Kagan, J., Snidman, N., Gersten, M., Baak, K., & Rosenberg, A. (1986). Inhibited and uninhibited behavior: A follow-up study. *Child Development, 57,* 660–680.

Rubin, K. H. (1993). The Waterloo Longitudinal Project: Continuities of social withdrawal from early childhood to early adolescence. In K. H. Rubin & J. Asendorpf (Eds.), *Social withdrawal, inhibition, and shyness in childhood.* Hillsdale, NJ: Erlbaum.

Rubin, K. H., Burgess, K., & Coplan, R. (2002). Social inhibition and withdrawal in childhood. In P. K. Smith & C. Hart (Eds.), *Handbook of Childhood Social Development.* London: Blackwell.

Rubin, K. H., Hastings, P. D., Stewart, S. L., Henderson, H. A., & Chen, X. (1997). The consistency and concomitants of inhibition: Some of the children, all of the time. *Child Development, 68,* 467–483.

Rubin, K. H., & Mills, R. S. L. (1992). Parents' ideas about the development of aggression and withdrawal. In I. Sigel, J. Goodnow, & A. McGillicuddy-deLisi (Eds.), *Parental Belief Systems* (pp. 41–68). Hillsdale, NJ: Erlbaum.

Rubin, K. H., Mills, R. S. L., & Rose-Krasnor, L. (1989). Maternal beliefs and children's social competence. In B. Schneider, C. Attili, J. Nadel-Brulfert, & R. Weissberg (Eds.), *Social competence in developmental perspective* (pp. 313–331). Holland: Kluwer.

Rubin, K. H., Nelson, L. J., Hastings, P., & Asendorpf, J. (1999). Transaction between parents' perceptions of their children's shyness and their parenting style. *International Journal of Behavioral Development, 23,* 937–957.

Schneider, B. H., Attili, G., Vermigili, P., & Younger, A. (1997). A comparison of middle class English-Canadian and Italian mothers' beliefs about children's peer-directed aggression and social withdrawal. *International Journal of Behavioral Development, 21,* 133–154.

Sears, R. R., Maccoby, E., & Levin, H. (1957). *Patterns of child-rearing.* Evanston, IL: Row, Peterson.

Sigel, I. E. and Kim, M. I. (1996). The answer depends on the question: A conceptual and methodological analysis of a parent belief-behavior interview regarding children's learning. In S. Harkness and C. M. Super (Eds.), *Parents' cultural belief systems: Their origins, expressions, and consequences* (pp. 83–120). New York: Guilford.

Spangler, G., & Schieche, M. (1998). Emotional and adrenocortical responses of infants to the Strange Situation: The differential function of emotional expression. *International Journal of Behavioral Development, 22,* 681–706.

Stevenson-Hinde, J. (1989). Behavioral inhibition: Issues of context. In J. S. Reznick (Ed.), *Perspectives on behavioral inhibition* (pp. 125–138). Chicago: University of Chicago Press.

Stimpfl, J., Zheng, F., & Meredith, W. (1997). A garden in the motherland: A study of a preschool in China. *Early Child Development and Care, 129,* 11–26.

# III

## Cultural Perspectives on Parent–Child and Family Relationships

# 5

# Attachment Across Diverse Sociocultural Contexts: The Limits of Universality

MARINUS H. VAN IJZENDOORN, MARIAN J.
BAKERMANS-KRANENBURG, AND
ABRAHAM SAGI-SCHWARTZ

## INTRODUCTION

In this chapter we address the issue of the universality and sociocultural specificity of individual differences in attachment behavior, and we try to examine whether any sociocultural limits to the emergence of organized patterns of attachment can be found. In light of the more than 1200 different cultures (past and present), and at least 186 different cultural areas, any claim to cross-cultural validity of a theory can only be considered a bold but tentative hypothesis. Nevertheless, there is some evidence for the idea that intracultural differences in the development of attachment may be larger than the cross-cultural differences (Van IJzendoorn & Sagi, 1999). The implication of this finding is that we should investigate attachment in diverging sociocultural contexts, in order to maximize the probability of a refutation of the cross-cultural hypothesis, and to test attachment theory to its limits. Here, we broaden our scope and discuss in more detail recent attachment research in Africa, the United States, Israel, and Japan in search of the sociocultural limits of attachment theory.

We begin with a description of attachment networks by taking an evolutionary and sociocultural perspective, followed by a behavior genetics analysis of father–mother–infant attachment security, showing the role of nurture versus that of nature. A number of specific cultures and contexts are then examined: the African case with infant–mother attachment in a network of caregivers; ethnicity versus socioeconomic status in explaining differences in attachment security between African-American and White children; the maladaptive sociocultural context of infants sleeping away from parents at night in Israeli kibbutzim; and, lastly, the notion of attachment and *amae* in Japan. Analyses and integration of these diverse sociocultural contexts lead us to conclude that attachment is universal and at the same time context-dependent.

## Attachment Networks in Evolutionary and Sociocultural Perspective

**What Is Attachment?.** Children are attached if they have a tendency to seek proximity to and contact with a specific caregiver in times of distress, illness, and tiredness (Bowlby, 1984). Attachment is a major developmental milestone in the child's life, and it will remain an important issue throughout the lifespan. In adulthood, attachment representations shape the way adults feel about the strains and stresses of intimate relationships, including parent–child relationships, and the way in which the self is perceived. Attachment theory is a special branch of Darwinian evolution theory, and the need to become attached to a protective conspecific is considered to be one of the primary needs in the human species. The theory is built upon the assumption that children come to this world with an inborn inclination to show attachment behavior—an inclination that would have had survival value, or better: would increase "inclusive fitness"—in an environment in which human evolution originally took place.

**Sociocultural Context of Attachment.** The evolutionary background of attachment has sometimes wrongly been interpreted as indicating strong univer-sality of patterns of attachment behavior, and as implying the indifference of attachment theory to the diverse sociocultural contexts in which attachment takes shape. It has been argued, for example, that attachment researchers have been blinded to alternative conceptions of relatedness (Rothbaum, Weisz, Pott, Miyake, & Morelli, 2000). Rothbaum and others argue that it is much too early in this game (learning about human variation in attachment behavior) to assume we know what is universal. Rothbaum suggests that attachment theory suffers from a West-ern bias, and is not open to the influences of non-Western cultures.

Ironically, empirical research using the concept of individual differences in attachment started in Uganda half a century ago (Ainsworth, 1967), and attachment researchers have ever since been studying the universality and cross-cultural validity of attachment theory. Of course, the innate bias to become attached leads to attachment behavior in almost every exemplar of the species, but in an earlier review on cross-cultural attachment research we emphasized that "from this universality thesis, it does not follow, however, that the development of attachment is insensitive to culture-specific influences . . . the evolutionary perspective leaves room for globally adaptive behavioral propensities that become realized in a specific way dependent on the cultural niche in which the child has to survive . . . " (Van IJzendoorn & Sagi, 1999, p. 714).

**Patterns of Attachment.** Attachment to a protective caregiver helps the infant to regulate his or her negative emotions in times of stress and distress, and enables the infant to explore the environment even if this environment contains somewhat frightening stimuli. The idea that children seek a balance between the need for proximity and the need to explore the environment is fundamental to the various attachment measures, such as the *Strange Situation* procedure (Ainsworth, Blehar, Waters, & Wall (1978) and the *Attachment Q-Set* (Vaughn & Waters, 1990). Ainsworth and her colleagues observed one-year-old infants with their mothers in a standardized stressful separation procedure, and used the reactions of the infants to their reunion with the caregiver after a brief separation to assess the amount of trust the children had in the accessibility of their attachment figure. The procedure consists of eight episodes of which the last seven ideally take three minutes. Each episode can, however, be curtailed on request of the caregiver, and the experimenter may also shorten an episode, for instance when the infant is crying.

In the *Strange Situation* procedure, infants between 12 and 24 months of age are confronted with three stressful components: an unfamiliar environment, interaction with a stranger, and two short separations from the caregiver. This mildly stressful situation elicits attachment behavior; three patterns of attachment can be distinguished on the basis of infants' reactions to the reunion with the parent or other caregiver. Infants who actively seek proximity to their caregivers upon reunion communicate their feelings of stress and distress openly, and then readily return to exploration are classified as *secure* (B) in their attachment to that caregiver. Infants who do not seem to be distressed, and ignore or avoid the caregiver following reunion (although physiological research shows that their arousal during separation is similar to other infants; see Spangler and Grossmann , 1993), are classified as *insecure-avoidant* (A). Infants who combine strong proximity seeking and contact maintaining with contact resistance, or remain inconsolable, without being able to return to play and explore the environment, are classified *insecure-ambivalent* (C). In Figure 5.1 the distribution of attachment classifications across some cultures is presented. In this chapter we focus on attachment studies conducted in Africa, the United States, Israel, and Japan.

In addition to the classic tripartite ABC classifications Main and Solomon (1990) proposed a fourth classification, namely, *disorganized* attachment (D). Main and Solomon (1990) used the term disorganized/disoriented attachment (D) to describe patterns of infant behavior during the *Strange Situation*, which seemed odd and lacked an organized strategy with respect to the attachment figure. *Disorganized* attachment has been associated with the infant's experience of prolonged or repeated separation from the caregiver. Approximately 80 percent of maltreated infants show this type of attachment. *Disorganized* attachment is also found with high frequency in infants whose mothers are alcoholics or depressed, and in families with high marital conflict (for a meta-analytic review, see Van IJzendoorn, Schuengel, & Bakermans-Kranenburg, 1999). Main and Hesse (1990) have suggested that infants develop disorganized attachment when they experience the parent as frightening or frightened, and that the essence of disorganized attachment is fright without solution. When the only possible base from which to explore the world

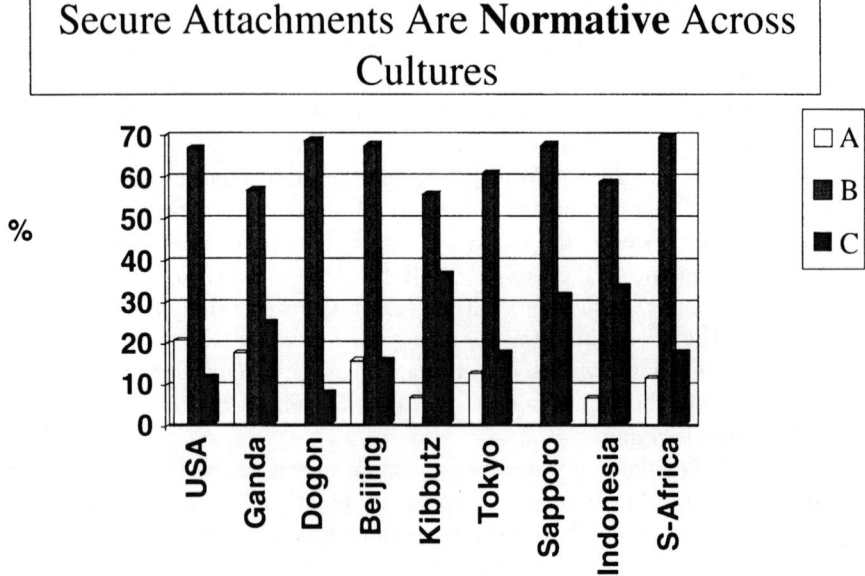

**FIGURE 5.1** Updated from Handbook of Attachment, 1999, p. 729.

(the parent) is at the same time the source of fear, the child is placed in an irresolvable paradoxical situation, with disorganized attachment as a result. Although some cross-cultural attachment studies include the disorganized attachment category, it is not central to the discussion of cross-cultural issues in attachment theory in the current chapter (see Van IJzendoorn, Schuengel, & Bakermans-Kranenburg , 1999, for a meta-analytic review of disorganized attachment).

**Attachment Networks.** One of the differences between Western and non-Western families seems to be the number of parental and nonparental caregivers available for the infants. In Western families the mother–infant bond seems to be unique and rather exclusive whereas in non-Western cultures nonmaternal care-givers seem to be important attachment figures. Attachment theory, however, is not biased toward one of these arrangements. Attachment involves part of a person's social network, namely, the affective relationships someone might have with one or more significant others who are considered stronger or wiser and may serve as sources of protection from danger and a safe haven for exploration of the environment. The attachment relationship emerges from myriad social interactions during the first few years of life, usually with the biological mother or with alternative caregivers who are genetically related to the child and interact with him or her on a regular basis. As the evolutionary perspective of attachment theory would predict, fathers, older siblings, or grandparents fulfill important roles as attachment figures in a variety of cultures and in various nonhuman primates (Lamb, 1997; Van IJzendoorn & Sagi, 1999; Hrdy, 1999).

As Bowlby argued in the second edition of the first volume of *Attachment and Loss*, "the survival of the genes an individual is carrying must always be the ultimate criterion when biological adaptedness is being evaluated" (1969, p. 56). Attachment should be evaluated from the perspective of reproduction of the genes in future generations; it was evident to Bowlby that not only the tie to the biological mother but also emotional bonds with biologically related protective others could serve this function. "Inclusive fitness" (Trivers, 1974) means that reproduction of one's genes may be promoted through promoting the survival of one's own offspring, but also by promoting the reproduction and survival of any other kin who is likely to be carrying the same genes (Belsky, 1999).

Attachment theory is quite clear-cut about the role of the biological mother, and one of the most important experiments in the history of attachment theory—Harlow's rhesus monkey experiments with wire-mesh and furry-clothed artificial mother figures—showed how the biological functions of child-bearing and feeding are separate from that of protection (Harlow, 1958). For Bowlby, the biological mother is not necessarily the most important attachment figure; early in his work on attachment he remarked that whenever he used the term "mother," "[I]t is to be understood that in every case reference is to the person who mothers the child and to whom he becomes attached" (p. 29). From his trilogy it was also clear that more than one person may play the role of attachment figure. Therefore, it is somewhat disappointing that attachment theory is still misinterpreted as exclusively dyadic, monotropic, and mother-fixated (Tavecchio & Van IJzendoorn, 1987; Van IJzendoorn & Sagi, 1999).

**Alloparenting.** What factors promote the involvement of attachment figures other than the biological mother in nonhuman primates? In her book on "Mother Nature," Hrdy (1999) coined the term *alloparenting* to indicate the care provided to the infant by biologically related nonmaternal caregivers. Hrdy demonstrated that our species may well have evolved to become dependent on maternal as well as alloparental care for its infants. Mothering should be supported by nonmaternal care in order to share the heavy burden of raising human infants. As Hrdy argued, at least three factors are important in enhancing the role of older siblings, grandparents, or fathers as attachment figures.

The *ecological* factor concerns the necessity for mothers to be near the infant in order to provide for hunger and thirst in environments that have only scarce resources. If the infant does not run the acute risk of starvation or dehydration there is room for other caregivers to set the mother free from infant caretaking and promote her freedom to forage. The *offspring* factor concerns the burden the offspring poses on the mother; in some species almost all births are twin births that occur in rapid pace, and only the support of the father can guarantee the survival of this heavy burden (as in the cooperatively breeding tamarins). The *genetic* factor concerns the certainty about one's biological relatedness to the infant. In a species in which the fathers are more certain about their paternity because "marital relationships" are monogamous (e.g., in the titi monkeys, Hrdy, 1999, p. 213) the contribution of the fathers to the survival of their offspring is larger, and their roles as attachment figures are more important. Human infants are evolutionarily built to become part of a network of attachment relationships from which they derive protection and security. Human mothers may be evolutionarily selected to share the burdens of raising their children with biologically related alternative caregivers such as the father, older siblings, or grandparents.

When evolutionary forces have shaped attachment relationships in nonhuman primates and in humans alike, one may wonder whether any room is left for influences from the sociocultural context in which infants grow up. Nature may have become predominant in shaping such an essential characteristic as attachment. Nevertheless, the selection of a fixed "traitlike" tendency to become attached in a similar way across all individuals would have made the human species rather vulnerable to drastic changes in the environment, for example, in the natural resources available. Hinde (1982; Hinde & Stevenson-Hinde, 1990) was one of the first scholars to argue that even the propensity to become insecurely attached might have evolutionary advantages in adapting to certain niches and living conditions (see also Main, 1990; Belsky, 1999). The crucial question, therefore, is whether nurture plays a role in shaping individual differences in *patterns* of attachment behavior (attachment *security*). Behavior genetics may test the validity of this (nurture) assumption in the debate about the cross-cultural validity of attachment theory.

## *Behavioral Genetics of Father–Infant and Mother–Infant Attachment Security: Nurture Instead of Nature*

Some proponents of the behavioral genetic approach have declared most findings on child development seriously flawed, because they are based on traditional research designs focusing on between-family comparisons that confound genetic similarities between parents and children with supposedly shared environmental influences (Rowe, Vazsony, & Flannery, 1994). It has been argued that there is an urgent need to rethink the role of parents in child development (Harris, 1998; but see Collins, Maccoby, Steinberg, Hetherington, & Bornstein, 2000).

Considering the amount of evidence in favor of a major role for genetics in the development of behaviors, personality traits, and attitudes, one is certainly inclined to emphasize the influences of genetics and unique environmental pressures more heavily than in the past. In a succinct summary of the advances of behavior genetic research, McGuffin, Riley, and Plomin (2001) stated that behavior genetic findings consistently converge on the conclusion that "genetic variation makes a substantial contribution to phenotypic variation for all behavioral domains" (p. 1232). More specifically, they argued that most behaviors that have been studied show moderate to high heritability, and if environment plays a role, its contribution often would be nonshared or unique because it makes people different from their relatives, rather than similar to them. Parental behavior that stimulates similar developmental patterns across siblings (shared environment) seems to be elusive, and important behaviors or characteristics without a substantial genetic component seem to be rare.

Against this strong and predominant current, attachment theory emphasizes environmental causes of individual differences in attachment security and stresses the important role of parental sensitivity. Indeed, contemporary work on attachment makes the even more specific claim that the primary causes of individual differences in attachment security are of the shared environmental kind (O'Connor et al., 2000). In particular, the model of intergenerational transmission of parental attachment representations to infant patterns of attachment behavior implies a rather strong environmental effect (Hesse, 1999; Van IJzendoorn, 1995), although this model does not preclude a genetic mechanism of transmission (Main, 1999).

From an evolutionary viewpoint, it seems to make sense that infants do not inherit a fixed attachment behavior pattern but are endowed with flexible ways to adapt to changing circumstances and especially to changing or conditional parenting strategies (Belsky, 1999; Main, 1999). Secure, resistant, and avoidant attachment behavior patterns (Ainsworth et al., 1978) are thought to result from the infants' experiences with consistently sensitive or consistently insensitive parents. These types of sensitivity would, in turn, be determined by parents' diverging (secure, avoidant, or resistant) childhood attachment experiences and more crucially their subsequent mental representations of attachment (Main, Kaplan, & Cassidy, 1985; Van IJzendoorn, 1995a). This would seem to imply a rather large role for the shared environment, not only for attachment security but also for the organized nonsecure attachment patterns, that is, resistant and avoidant attachment.

The transmission of attachment from parents to their infants may nevertheless be mediated, in part, by a genetic pathway (Main, 1999). Although several studies provide support for the basic model of causal relations among parental attachment representations, parental sensitivity, and infant attachment strategy (Main et al., 1985), a large and quantifiable "transmission gap" of about 75 percent of the intergenerational transmission still remains to be closed. If parents' attachment representations are found to be strongly associated with infant attachment strategies (Hesse, 1999; Main, 1999), even when parental attachment representations are assessed before the birth of the infant (Fonagy, Steele, & Steele, 1991), and at the same time equally strong associations between parenting behavior and infant attachment cannot be found (DeWolff & Van IJzendoorn, 1997), the gap between parent and infant attachment should be closed in other ways. Of course, genetics seems a plausible candidate for closing the transmission gap because parents and infants share 50 percent of their genes, and intergenerational transmission of attachment may (partly) be based on transmission of genes from one generation to the next.

In a recent study, Van IJzendoorn et al. (2000) reported some evidence for the idea that mothers stimulate similar attachment relationships with siblings. Attachment theory would suggest that brothers and sisters growing up in the same family are likely to relate in similar ways to their parents, at least when parental attachment representations and interactive styles remain stable across time. Attachment security was assessed for each sibling using the *Strange Situation* procedure between 12 to 14 months after birth. Sibling relationships were found to be significantly concordant when classified as secure/nonsecure. Maternal insensitivity to both siblings (shared environment) was associated with concordance of sibling insecurity, which may be consistent with a substantial role for the shared environment, that is, for similarity in parenting style to both siblings. Siblings of the same gender were more likely to form concordant relationships with their mother than those of opposite gender. In the design of this study, the role of (shared and nonshared) environment was still confounded with the role of genetics because contrast groups with varying degrees of genetic relatedness were lacking. It was impossible, therefore, to address the question of heritability of attachment with a behavior genetic approach.

Studies with kibbutz children are shedding further light on the issue with biologically unrelated infants who were raised for a large part of the day by professional caregivers (*metaplot*). In a study of family-based kibbutzim Sagi, Van IJzendoorn, Aviezer, Donnell, Koren-Karie, Joels, and Harel (1995) found concordant infant attachments to the same *metapelet* (singular for caregiver) in 17 (68 percent) of the 25 pairs. These same pairs plus another 2 pairs of infants were also observed with the second *metapelet*, with similar results: 19 pairs (70 percent) were found to have the same secure or insecure attachment to the other *metapelet*. The family-based kibbutz setting (see below) allows for the *metaplot* to be engaged with the same unrelated infants during 50 or more hours per week in a familylike context (Aviezer, van IJzendoorn, Sagi, & Schuengel, 1994). Infants in the kibbutz are not genetically related to each other nor to the *metapelet*; thus, any observed concordance is attributable to common experiential rather than genetic factors. Although this study allowed a heritability–environment confound-free test, its limitation is that the attachment figure is a professional caregiver rather than a parent; a limitation that can be overcome by adoption studies of attachment in biologically unrelated siblings in the same child-rearing environment, which are unfortunately still lacking.

Twin studies provide another unique opportunity to test the similarity of siblings' attachment relationships under conditions of similar age and child-rearing contexts, using established behavior-genetic methods. In a sample of 157 mono- and dizygotic twins, we investigated genetic and environmental influences on infant attachment and temperament. Only unique environmental or error components could explain the variance in disorganized versus organized attachment as assessed in the Ainsworth *Strange Situation* procedure. For secure versus nonsecure attachment, 52 percent of the variance in attachment security was explained by shared environment, and 48 percent of the variance was explained by unique environmental factors and measurement error. The role of genetic factors in attachment disorganization and attachment security was negligible. Genetic factors explained 77 percent of the variance in temperamental reactivity, and unique environmental factors and measurement error 23 percent. Differences in temperamental reactivity were not associated with attachment concordance.

In a first behavioral genetic study of infant–father attachment, we also estimated genetic and environmental influences on attachment as assessed with the *Attachment Q-Sort* (consisting of 90 specific behavioral descriptions of children in the natural home-setting; Vaughn & Waters, 1990; Waters, 1995). The AQS not only allows for the measurement of attachment security but also for various other constructs because only a subset of the behavioral descriptions are meant to index security. Waters and Deane (1985) included a contrasting construct, dependency, in order to test the relation between attachment security and what Ainsworth originally considered to be temperamental dependency (Ainsworth, 1969). Mothers of mono- and dizygotic twins ($N = 56$ pairs) sorted the *AQS* focusing on the infant's behaviors in the presence of the father. Genetic modeling showed that attachment was largely explained by shared environmental (59 percent) and unique environmental (41 percent) factors. For dependency, a construct that was meant to be a personality dimension indicating the children's stronger or weaker orientation to the parent in any situation, genetic factors explained 66 percent of the variance, and unique environmental factors including measurement error explained 34 percent. Attachment to father appears to be, to a significant degree, a function of the environment that twins share. In contrast, the personality trait of dependency showed a large genetic influence that marks the discriminant validity of the attachment concept.

Infant attachment behavior and dependency seem to be different in their constellations of genetic shared environmental and unique environmental factors. The model with only the shared and unique environmental factors fit the data best in both infant–mother and infant–father attachment. Genes and unique environment explained temperamental reactivity and dependency. The large role of shared environmental factors in attachment is one of the most intriguing findings of attachment twin studies. Shared environment makes siblings within the same family similar to each other and different from siblings in other families. Unique environmental factors make siblings within the same family different from each other.

Thus, we found considerable evidence to support the decisive role of environmental factors in the development of (non)secure attachment, with concordances for identical and fraternal twins that leave some room for shared and unique environmental influences. Behavior genetic modeling indicates that the heritability of attachment disorganization and security is negligible. The unique environment seems responsible for disorganization of attachment, and the shared environment counts for more than half of the variance in secure attachment. This not only represents confirmation of one of the basic assumptions of attachment theory, but also seems to fit well with research that has documented a robust association between parental representations of attachment and infant attachment security (of around $r^2 = .25$; see Van IJzendoorn, 1995b).

In an age when shared environmental theories of development have been rejected by some behavior-geneticists, the finding of a substantial shared environment influence is noteworthy. For example, in their authoritative textbook on behavioral genetics, Plomin and his colleagues (Plomin et al., 2001) clearly stated that for most domains of psychology, environment is important and explains about half of the variance in traits, attitudes, and behavior patterns, but it "is generally not shared family environment that causes family members to resemble each other" (p. 298). Bouchard and Loehlin (2001) described moderate shared environment effects in altruism, sociability, and autonomy in adolescence, and in attitudes toward love or love styles in adulthood. With regard to the latter, the authors noted that the combination of small heritability and modest shared environment of love styles belongs to "a very rare class of phenotype, one with little or no genetic variance" (p. 263). It appears that attachment security also belongs to this class of phenotype.

In sum, behavior genetics showed that differences in attachment relationships are mainly caused by nurture instead of nature. Although the bias to become attached is inborn, the way in which this inborn tendency takes shape in the first few years of life is determined by the specific sociocultural context. In fact, attachment behavior patterns appear to be rather context-dependent and to express flexible adaptations to specific niches in which the child is born and has to survive. It is therefore intriguing to study attachment patterns in non-Western societies and investigate this flexible adaptation process. The question is whether attachment is sufficiently flexible to adapt to more extreme types of living conditions, or whether there are limits to this adaptability. We start with an update of African attachment studies (see Van IJzendoorn and Sagi, 1999, for an overview of the first African studies).

## Infant–Mother Attachment in a Network of Caregivers: The African Case

As we noted in the introduction it was in Uganda, a former British protectorate in East Africa, that Mary Ainsworth (1967) started her empirical contributions to attachment theory and began to develop the now famous tripartite classification system of avoidant (A), secure (B), and ambivalent (C) infant–mother attachment relationships. Ainsworth's (1967) pioneering Uganda study was followed by a series of attachment studies in various African countries and cultures. Attachment research in Africa is particularly important for testing the idea that a multiple caregiving environment is not incompatible with a unique attachment relationship between child and parent. Cross-cultural evidence shows that in most non-Western societies, nonparental caretaking is either the norm or a frequent form, and attachment in a network of multiple caregivers is the rule rather than the exception (Weisner & Gallimore, 1977). What are the results of five decades of African attachment research?

**Uganda.** After Bowlby's (1952 ; see also Robertson & Robertson, 1971) report on the disastrous effects of fragmented institutional care, Ainsworth's (1967, 1977) Uganda study showed for the first time that it is not the number of caretakers per se, but the continuity and quality of the mother–infant interaction that is decisive for attachment security. In her Uganda study, Ainsworth showed that even in a child-rearing environment in which mothers share their caregiving responsibilities with several other adults and older children, infants nevertheless become attached to their mother and use her as a secure base to explore the world. The presence of multiple caretakers did not interfere with the development of a secure attachment (Weisner & Gallimore, 1977). The Uganda study, however, was rather small and exploratory, and certainly not representative of the various African cultures (Jackson, 1993).

More recently Peterson and his colleagues investigated attachment in Ugandan families with HIV/AIDS infection (Peterson, Drotar, Olness, Guay, & Kiziri-Mayengo, 2001). Family life in Africa has changed drastically in recent years due to the HIV/AIDS pandemic. In particular, mothers of young children often become victims of this infection for which, in Africa, no medical treatment is yet available on a large scale; many infants are born with HIV. In Zambia it is estimated that about half a million children are orphans because of the pandemic, and this figure is expected to double in the next five years. Peterson investigated a sample of 35 HIV-positive mothers with or without AIDS, and 25 HIV-negative mothers with infants in their first year of life. The researchers used the *Attachment Q-Sort* (Vaughn & Waters, 1990) to rate the attachment security of the infants during a four-hour home-visit. The *AQS* consists of 90 specific behavioral descriptions of 12- to 48-month-old children in the natural home setting, with special emphasis on secure-base behavior (Vaughn & Waters, 1990). Waters and Deane (1985) introduced the *AQS* for assessing attachment security in infants and toddlers as an alternative to the *Strange Situation (SSP)* laboratory procedure (Ainsworth et al., 1978), and it appears to have some advantages over the latter measure (Van IJzendoorn, Vereijken, Bakermans-Kranenburg, & Riksen-Walraven, in press). For the current study, it is of relevance that *AQS* observations are conducted in the home setting, and they may therefore have higher ecological validity. The *SSP* has been criticized for its lack of ecological validity (Bronfenbrenner, 1979). Furthermore, because the application of the *AQS* does not require the stressful separations used in the *SSP*, the method can be applied in cultures and populations in which parent–infant separations may be less common. Peterson and his colleagues found a remarkable percentage of predicted variance in attachment security: 32 percent variance of *AQS* attachment security was predicted by maternal affect. The findings thus support the central attachment hypothesis that maternal sensitive warmth is associated with infant attachment security.

**The Gusii of Kenya.** Among the Gusii of Kenya, mothers share their child-rearing tasks and responsibilities with other caregivers to a larger extent than in many other non-Western cultures and, in particular, child caregivers such as older siblings take care of the infants during a large part of the day. Mothers provide most of the physical care and are responsible for the child's health, whereas the activities of child caregivers are limited to social and playful interactions (Kermoian & Leiderman, 1986). Kermoian and Leiderman (1986) included 26 families in their study, with infants between the ages of 8 and 27 months (mean age: 14.5 months). A modified *Strange Situation* procedure was implemented outside the mother's hut, with two separation/reunion episodes for each of the mother, other caregiver, and stranger. The extra separations were meant to compensate for the lack of a strange laboratory environment.

Although the Gusii infants used culture-specific attachment behaviors to express their emotions about the separation and reunion (e.g., reaching out for a handshake from the attachment figure), the patterns of attachment were comparable with Western findings. Sixteen of the infants (61 percent) were classified as securely attached to the mother at the first assessment, and fourteen infants (54 percent) were classified as securely attached to the nonmaternal caregiver (Kermoian and Leiderman, 1986; Reed & Leiderman, 1981). Infants who were securely attached to their nonmaternal caregivers had higher scores on the Bayley scales for cognitive and motor development than the insecurely attached infants. Infants who were securely attached to their mothers had a recent history of higher nutritional status than insecurely attached infants. Thus, attachment security appeared to have a different impact on the infants' development, dependent on the context in which the bond had emerged. The Gusii study also provided some evidence in favor of the sensitivity hypothesis (Kermoian and Leiderman, 1986).

**The Hausa of Nigeria.** The Hausa, who populate a large market town in Nigeria, represent another polymatric culture in which the distribution of child-care tasks is somewhat less strict than among the Gusii. An average of four caregivers shares the tasks of social, verbal, and playful interactions with the mothers. The biological mothers, however, take almost complete responsibility for physical care activities such as feeding and bathing (Marvin, VanDevender, Iwanaga, LeVine, & LeVine, 1977). The Hausa live in small, round, walled compounds with separate huts for each of the wives. In the middle is an open common cooking and working area, where open fires and freely accessible tools and other utensils constitute a continuous risk for the infants.

Marvin and his colleagues (1977) included 18 infants in their descriptive study, which focused on the occurrence of attachment and exploratory behaviors in the natural setting. When not asleep, the Hausa infants were almost always in close physical contact or in the near proximity of one or more adult caregivers. All infants displayed attachment behavior to more than one caregiver, and on the average they appeared to be attached to three or four different figures, including their father. Although they were raised in a network of attachment relationships, most Hausa infants were primarily attached to one attachment figure (not necessarily the biological mother), to whom they addressed their attachment behaviors most frequently (Marvin et al., 1977). The Hausa study shows that culture-specific attachment and exploratory behaviors appear to leave room for the universal occurrence of the safe base phenomenon.

**The Dogon of Mali.** In a cross-cultural study of 25 mothers and their one-year-old infants, True (1994), in cooperation with Pisani and Oumar (True, Pisani, & Oumar, 2001), investigated attachments among the Dogon of Mali (West Africa). With a few exceptions, the infants were living in compounds with their extended families. The fathers usually have children with several co-wives. Maternal care is supplemented with care from siblings and other family members. In particular with firstborn male infants, the primary caregiver during the day is the paternal grandmother, but the mother is available when the child is hungry, and the mother sleeps with the infant at night. Infant mortality is high during the first years of life: 25 percent of the children do not survive the first five years. This threatening ecology may be one of the reasons that the Dogon mothers breast-fed their infants on demand and very frequently, and kept them in close proximity almost all the time.

The Dogon dyads were filmed in the traditional *Strange Situation* procedure, and they were also observed during a standardized well-baby examination: the Weigh-In.

The Dogon study showed a high percentage of disorganized infants (24 percent) compared to the percentages in normal Western samples (15 percent). The percentage of secure infant–mother dyads was also high: 68 percent, whereas the avoidant classification appeared to be absent and only 8 percent insecure-resistant infant–mother dyads were found. In the Weigh-In secure infant–mother dyads were found to be less liable to violate the rules of open communication as compared to the insecure infant–mother dyads (True et al., 2001). This outcome supports the validity of the *Strange Situation* in the Dogon.

### !Kung San or Bushmen of Northwestern Botswana.

!Kung San hunters and gatherers live in small semi-nomadic groups with a fluid group structure, absence of strict social rules, and flexible subsistence strategies (Konner, 1977). The general rules of child-rearing in the !Kung are indulgence, stimulation, and nonrestriction (Konner, 1977). !Kung infants are fed whenever they cry, and whenever they reach for the breast. At night, the infants sleep in close proximity to the mother, and they also suckle whenever they want, even without the mother awakening. Infants are carried around in a sling. Two- and three-year-old children are involved in multiage peer groups, in which they spend more time than with their mother, and in which they readily establish new bonds. The !Kung study provides support for the universality as well as the sensitivity hypothesis. In this hunter and gatherer society, the bond between infant and mother fulfills a unique function of protection and stimulation, even in the context of a wider social network of caregivers. Furthermore, a basic tenet of attachment theory is confirmed, namely, that sensitive responses to the infants' signals foster independence instead of dependence later on in life.

### The Efe or Pygmies of the Ituri Forest in Northeastern Zambia.

The Efe employ a system of multiple caregivers throughout the first few years of life (Morelli & Tronick, 1991). Beginning at birth, when other adult females are also suckled by the newborn, child-rearing remains the responsibility of a larger network of adult caregivers (Tronick, Morelli, & Winn, 1987). Even the physical care is shared with other caregivers, in contrast with the Hausa and the Gusii where the mothers are mainly responsible for feeding, bathing, and other physical care activities. The number of caregivers in the first 18 weeks amounts to 14.2 on average. This extremely dense social network leads to prompt responses to any sign of infant distress.

During the second half of the first year the infants began to show preference for the care of their own mother, and they were more likely to be carried by their mothers on trips out of the camp and to protest against her leave-taking. Morelli and Tronick (1991) proposed that the one-year-olds' interference with the adults' work activities would preclude nonmaternal caregivers from taking on caregiving responsibility during work. Another intriguing reason for the emergence of a special bond between infant and mother, despite the multiple caregiver context, may be the care provided during the night. At night, only the mothers cared for their infants, and sleep was regularly interrupted by episodes of playful interaction exclusively between infant and mother (Morelli & Tronick, 1991). From the perspective of attachment theory, the night may be an especially stressful time during which the infants need a protective caregiver most (see the Israeli communal kibbutzim, below).

### Black and Colored Families in South Africa.
Minde and his colleagues (Minde, Minde, & Vogel (2002) investigated the psychosocial conditions and attachment belief systems of 51 mothers of one cultural subgroup (the Northern Sotho) in a South African township. The attachment of their toddlers, aged 18 to 30 months, was assessed using the *Attachment Q-sort* (Vaughn and Waters, 1990) during a two-hour home visit. The mothers were interviewed with the *Working Model of the Child Interview* (*WMCI*; Zeanah & Benoit, 1995). The *WMCI* is a one-hour semi-structured audiotaped interview covering 22 questions that reflect parents' perceptions and subjective experiences of their relationships with their young children. The mothers lived in a very poor township where unemployment is 60 to 70 percent and 400,000 people live within an area of just over 1.5 square miles. All mothers had been the primary caretakers of their children all through their lives.

The majority of the children (53 percent) were found to have an insecure attachment, using the criteria of Waters (1995). Attachment security was not related to maternal poverty and support from the child's father but to (1) the number of available other supports of the mother, such as extended family, church, and neighbors; (2) the reported relationship of the mother with her own parents; and (3) the degree of maternal depression as assessed with the *SCL-90-R*. The concordance between the mothers' culture-specific *WMCI* pattern and the Q-sort security of their children was strong (81 percent concordance), demonstrating the validity of the *AQS* assessment of attachment in families that had recently been immigrated to an impoverished township from rural areas.

In South Africa, Tomlinson and his colleagues studied attachment in a sample of 97 colored mother–infant dyads, and assessed them at 2, 6, and 18 months postpartum (Tomlinson, 2002). Families were living in Khayelitsha, an impoverished black settlement close to Cape Town, also with a high proportion of migrants from rural areas. The following figures might demonstrate how difficult life conditions for these families are: 74 percent regard the rural area as home; 4 percent of mothers were born in Cape Town; 58 percent of the families had no regular income; only 5 percent lived in brick houses; 49 percent of the houses were unserviced; and 51 percent of the pregnancies were unplanned. In addition to the *Strange Situation*, the *HOME* inventory and a structured play procedure were used to assess sensitive responsiveness. Preliminary results suggested that the majority of infants were securely attached to their mothers (62 percent), and that a rather large number of infants did develop a disorganized attachment (26 percent). Furthermore, there was a remarkably high incidence of post-partum depression in the mothers (35 percent at infant's age of 2 months), compared to similar samples in Western countries (with about 10 percent of post-partum depression). There was a strong association between the presence of post-partum depression and attachment insecurity and disorganization, again supporting one of the basic

hypotheses of attachment theory, namely, the relation between attachment insecurity and maternal insensitivity as a consequence of maternal depression.

In sum, attachment research in several African countries and cultures has by
and large supported some of the basic tenets of attachment theory. It is clear that
without drastic changes in research design and measures, crucial associations
between attachment security and sensitivity have been replicated, even in sociocultural contexts in which the participants were confronted with increasingly
difficult life conditions (poverty, chronic diseases). Of course, the findings of the
African studies thus far cannot be considered sufficient evidence for the cross-
cultural validity of attachment theory, but falsifying data have not been presented
either. Attachment appears to be a robust phenomenon, and attachment measures
seem to be flexible enough to cover various culturally specific behaviors that
constitute the universal patterns of attachment.

## Differences in Attachment Security between African-
## American and White Children in the United
## States: Ethnicity or Socioeconomic Status?

Already in the first few years after birth, large differences between African-
American and Euro-American children have emerged in various domains of development (Garcia Coll, 1990; McLoyd, 1990a, 1998; Spencer, 1990). Do they differ
in attachment security as well; and when such differences exist, how can they be
explained? Are differences in attachment security the result of factors that are
associated with ethnicity, or should they be ascribed to socioeconomic circumstances? Presupposing the cross-cultural validity of the attachment assessment,
differences in attachment security between African-American and White children
may result from two separate processes. First, associations between attachment
quality and assumed precursors of secure attachment may be divergent in the two
different cultural contexts. Second, a third variable, related to ethnicity and attachment, may be responsible for differences in attachment security between the two
groups.

The first explanation of differences in developmental outcomes between
African-American and White children pertains to the existence of diverging developmental processes in different cultural groups. Two competing hypotheses can
be distinguished (Rowe, Vazsony, & Flannery, 1994). The *no group difference*
hypothesis is that there are few, if any, differences among ethnic groups in most
developmental processes (where evidence for such processes can be found in the
patterns of covariation among relevant variables). According to this hypothesis,
members of a society of different ethnic origins are exposed to variables common
to all ethnic groups in that society. Culturally specific experiences do not alter the
associations among developmental variables. This hypothesis allows for main effect
differences in variables, but states that the correlations among variables do not
differ between groups.

In contrast, the *group differences* hypothesis presupposes culturally relative
models of socialization (Ogbu, 1981, 1993) and it states that correlations among

developmental variables are different between groups. According to this model, development occurs within cultural contexts that are associated with qualitatively different processes. Any observed differences in developmental processes are assumed to be adaptive responses to the demands of the cultural environment (Ogbu, 1981). Some studies on the effects of parental discipline have provided evidence for the group differences hypothesis. Authoritarian parenting (a restrictive, often physical parenting style) was found to be associated with negative socioemotional outcomes for European-American children of preschool or school age, but not for African-American children (Baumrind, 1972, 1993; Deater-Deckard, Dodge, Bates, & Pettit, 1996; Dornbusch, Ritter, Leiderman, Roberts, & Fraleigh, 1987). As we indicated in the previous section, cross-cultural studies on attachment have presented some evidence for the universality of the hypothesized association between parental sensitivity and attachment security in different African cultures (the *no group difference* hypothesis), but this association was not found in all cross-cultural attachment studies (Van IJzendoorn & Sagi, 1999).

Alternatively, correlations among the pertinent variables may differ between groups (the *group differences* hypothesis), and divergent associations between attachment and sensitivity (or other precursors) may be found for African-American and White families. For instance, Jackson (1993) considered multiple caregiving as instantiated in African-American families as distinctive and without parallel in the cross-cultural literature on attachment. Childcare for African-American children is generally conducted within a relatively large social network of friends and acquaintances of the family. There are often several adult caregivers with designated responsibility for infant care and a larger set of children and adults who also provide care, comparable to the Efe system (see previous section). In Jackson's (1991) study, the number of households providing daily care for any one child ranged from one to four; and the infants encountered, on average, 15 familiar adults on a recurring weekly basis. This seems to imply a context for the infant–mother attachment formation that is rather different from the experiences of most White American infants.

The *no group difference* explanation of different developmental outcomes assumes that the patterns of covariation among relevant variables are similar in the different ethnic or cultural groups, but that a "third variable" on which the groups differ is responsible for differences in outcome. The first candidate for such an explanatory factor distinguishing African-American and White children in the United States may be socioeconomic status. African-American children generally come from families with lower incomes and a lower educational level of the parents than White children. Thus, diverging child outcomes among families with different ethnicities may as a matter of fact be caused by differences in family income (Jencks & Philips, 1998). Family income is associated with the development of children and youth (Huston, McLoyd, & Garcia Coll, 1994), and income effects are strongest during the preschool and early school years (Duncan, Yeung, Brooks-Gunn, & Smith, 1998). This early childhood effect has been found to be particularly strong when low income is persistent.

Income may have a differential effect on distinct child outcomes. Stronger effects of adverse economic conditions have been found on children's school and cognitive achievement than on children's socioemotional development (Duncan & Brooks-Gunn, 1997; Haveman & Wolfe, 1994). Nevertheless, Linver and colleagues (Linver, Brooks-Gunn, & Kohen, 2002) demonstrated that child behavior problems were also associated with low family income. Two processes were responsible for this association. First, low income was related to child behavior problems via maternal emotional distress, which was related to observed parenting practices. This mediational model is known as the *family stress model*. The family stress model postulates that low income influences children's development (measured in terms of school achievement, school engagement, or behavior problems) because of its impact on parent mental health, which then influences parenting practices, which in turn are associated with children and youth outcomes (Conger et al., 1992a, 1992b; Elder & Caspi, 1988; McLoyd, 1989). Empirical studies have demonstrated that economic hardship diminishes parental abilities to provide warm responsive parenting (Dodge, Pettit, & Bates, 1994) and contributes to an increase in the use of harsh punishment (Dodge et al., 1994; McLoyd, Jayaratne, Ceballo, & Borquez, 1994). The second process is known as the *investment model*. It hypothesizes that income is associated with child development because it enables parents to purchase materials, experiences, and services that are beneficial to children's well-being and development (Becker & Thomas, 1986; Haveman & Wolfe, 1994).

Studies on attachment have shown a high incidence of insecurity in poor families where poverty is combined with other social risks such as social isolation, maternal depression, or inadequate caretaking (e.g., Barnard et al., 1988; Lyons-Ruth, Connell, & Grunebaum, 1990). In a meta-analysis of infant attachment, (Van IJzendoorn, Goldberg, Kroonenberg, & Frenkl, 1992) the distribution of classifications in low-SES samples was not contrasted with the distribution of middle-class samples, but in a meta-analysis of adult attachment, secure representations of attachment were underrepresented in low-SES samples (Van IJzendoorn & Bakermans-Kranenburg, 1996). Research on attachment in African-American children involved, apparently without exception, only low-income families (Sims-Stanford, 1997; Nelson, 1991), which is not surprising as African-American ethnicity and low income tend to go together.

In a recent study of attachment in African-American and white American children, and on the role of ethnicity and socioeconomic status in explaining any differences in attachment security (Bakermans-Kranenburg, Van IJzendoorn, Bokhorst, & Schuengel, in press), the database was drawn from the NICHD Study of Early Child Care (see NICHD, 1996, 1999). The NICHD study covers a large, more or less representative sample of American children ($N = 1364$) who were recruited at ten different sites in the United States. Approximately 13 percent of these children had mothers who were African-American, and approximately 83 percent had White mothers. The children were followed across the first seven years of their lives, and their development was monitored at regular intervals. The recruited families came from a wide range of socioeconomic and sociocultural backgrounds and included 24 percent ethnic-minority children, 11 percent low-education mothers (less than a high school education), and 14 percent single-parent mothers. (Note that these percentages are not mutually exclusive.) Average family income was 3.6 times the poverty threshold. Income in the African-American families was almost half of the income of the White families. Average hours of nonmaternal childcare in African-American families did not differ from hours of childcare in White families.

Attachment was assessed with the *Attachment Q-Sort* (AQS; Waters, 1995) at 24 months. We included ratings of maternal sensitivity during the first two years as well as relevant background variables. African-American children's attachment security was substantially lower than in White children, with means of .20 (*SD* = .18) for African-American children's attachment security, and .30 (*SD* = .21) for White children's attachment security. The score of .20 for the African-American children is substantially lower than the average observer AQS security score for infant–mother attachment in nonclinical samples of .32 (Van IJzendoorn et al., in p ress). In fact, it is closer to the mean score of .21 that was found for children in clinical samples (Van IJzendoorn et al., in press).

The African-American children scored less secure on the attachment items of the *AQS*. However, several not-attachment-related items also yielded statistically significantly different scores. A set of items indicating children's compliance showed consistently lower mean scores for the African-American group. African-American children appeared to be less compliant to their mothers' suggestions or requests, and were less inclined to "stop misbehavior when told no." Also, African-American children showed, on average, more active and even rough behavior in the context of play. Play materials were more roughly handled and the children became more easily angry with toys. But African-American children were also more inclined to enjoy "dancing and singing along with music," and—maybe in the absence of an abundance of toys—they tended to spend more time playing with just a few favorite toys. Moreover, the African-American children were more sociable to strangers visiting their home. They enjoyed climbing all over visitors, getting their hugs, and were, in general, more oriented toward the stranger. Lastly, African-American children were less often attached to a cuddly toy or a security blanket. Our findings converge with the high sociability of African-American children reported by Jackson (1991), who notes that in the African-American culture friendliness with unfamiliar people is usually encouraged.

In spite of diverging ethnic group characteristics in attachment, activity, and sociability, we found that the pattern of covariation between attachment security and predictor variables was similar in the African-American and White subgroups. Sensitive parenting was associated with attachment security in the total group (*r* = .27) as well as in the separate groups of African-American (*r* = .20) and White families (*r* = .23). African-American mothers showed less sensitive responsiveness in the first two years of the child's life than White mothers. In both groups, maternal sensitivity was the strongest predictor of attachment security. The regression equations (including sensitivity, maternal age, and income) of the African-American and White subgroups were cross-validated in the other group and predicted attachment security in the two subsamples in a largely similar manner, and in the total group ethnicity did not add significantly to the prediction of attachment security. Our findings provide support for the *no group difference* hypothesis: children of African-American and White families in the United States may be exposed to culturally specific experiences, but these do not alter the relation between attachment security and pertinent predictor variables.

Our findings on African-American mother–infant dyads also support one of the basic tenets of attachment theory: the association between maternal sensitivity and attachment security. In De Wolff and Van IJzendoorn's (1997) meta-analysis on the association between maternal sensitivity and infant attachment security, socioeconomic status was a significant moderator. In the 18 middle-class samples, the effect size was .27, whereas in the 8 lower-class samples this figure was .15. De Wolff and Van IJzendoorn suggested that the strains and stresses of lower-class life may overburden potentially sensitive mothers. This may be the case, but in the NICHD sample the association between sensitivity and attachment security for African-Americans was similar to that of White families. African-American mothers were less sensitive to their children's signals than White mothers; and the effect size for the difference in sensitivity was substantial, $d = 1.27$.

Why are African-American children less secure than White children? We found evidence for a mediational model. Income predicted sensitivity and attachment security, sensitivity predicted attachment security, and when sensitivity was added to the equation, the association between income and attachment dropped from $\beta = .21$ to $\beta = .10$. The distributions of income in the African-American and White families differed substantially. Higher incomes were only found in White families, and the variances in the two groups were unequal. The effect size for the difference in income amounted to $r = .65$. Thus, ethnicity was related to income, which through sensitivity affected the quality of the infant–mother attachment relationship. The negative effects of economic hardship on children's developmental outcomes are well documented (Haveman, Wolfe, & Spaulding, 1991; Huston, McLoyd, & Garcia Coll, 1994; Jencks & Phillips, 1998; Keating & Hertzman, 1999). The *family stress model*, postulating that low income influences children's development through its impact on parenting practices, which in turn are associated with children and youth outcomes (Conger et al., 1992a, 1992b) seems to describe adequately what is going on in African-American families. Income effects are strongest when low income is persistent, or when poverty is deep. These characteristics are typical of African-American families in the United States. Poverty among African-American children is marked by its persistence and geographic concentration, whereas it is primarily a transitory, geographically diffuse phenomenon among White children (McLoyd, 1990b).

In sum, the findings in African-American and White families in the United States document that attachment security is not a White, middle-class American phenomenon that discriminates against non-Western or non-White cultures and ethnicities. At the same time, however, the study demonstrates that it is important to acknowledge that the development of attachment is not immune against contextual influences. In that respect, the findings converge with results from a recent Israeli study (Aviezer, Sagi-Schwartz, & Koren-Karie, 2003) demonstrating that low-quality nonmaternal care imposes ecological constraints on infant–mother attachment formation (see below). In a similar vein, low income may force mothers to become less sensitive to their infants than their cultural or ethnic background might allow them to be in optimal circumstances. This is in line with the conclusion of Zevalink and Riksen-Walraven (2001) from their comparative study of Dutch, Surinamese-Dutch, Japanese, and Sundanese-Indonesian mother–infant dyads, that socioeconomic factors have a stronger impact on the quality of parenting than cultural factors. In Belsky's process model of child development (1984) socioeconomic influences are incorporated without the implication that child-rearing and child development are completely culture-dependent and would fail to show universal, evolutionary-based characteristics (Belsky, 1999). In research on child development, the role of culture and ethnicity should not be confused with the influences of poverty. As poverty partly is a comparative phenomenon, that is, poverty is experienced as worse to the degree that the environment is more affluent, the impact of poverty in the United States might even be larger than that of poverty in African societies with homogeneously low levels of income. But even in the African-American case, basic tenets of attachment theory have been substantiated, and the African-American sociocultural context did not appear to be a limit to the generalizability of some of the most crucial findings of attachment research in more privileged contexts.

## The Limits of Attachment Universality: The Unique but Maladaptive Sociocultural Context of Sleeping Away from Parents at Night in Israeli Kibbutzim

To test the limits of attachment theory, the unique sociocultural context of the Israeli kibbutz provides one of the most stringent cases. Kibbutz childcare can be viewed as a unique and unprecedented "social experiment in nature." From the perspective of attachment theory this experiment should have failed because it disregarded the universal attachment needs of parents and children (Aviezer, van IJzendoorn, Sagi, & Schuengel, 1994; Aviezer, Sagi, & van IJzendoorn (2002); Aviezer, Sagi-Schwartz, & Koren-Karie, 2003; Sagi & Aviezer, 2001).

The Israeli kibbutz is one of the very few utopian experiments that successfully established a radically different, collective way of living and raising children for a period of almost 100 years. It is a cooperative, democratically governed, multigenerational community with an average population of 400 to 900 people. In the past kibbutzim were fairly isolated agricultural communities in which living conditions were difficult. Nowadays, kibbutz economies are based on a diversity of industries and agricultural activities, including a growing move toward privatization, and most of them provide their members with satisfying standards of living. Finally, following a major economic crisis in the 1980s, kibbutzim have been undergoing major changes affecting all facets of kibbutz life. Kibbutzim constitute a minority of about 1.5 percent of Israel's Jewish population.

In the harsh and hostile environment faced by kibbutz people in the pioneer settlements of the emerging Israeli society, the decision to raise children collectively was viewed as a contribution to the protection and well-being of the young. Children were housed in the only brick building on kibbutz grounds and never went hungry, whereas the adults of the community lived in tents and their food was rationed. This reality in early kibbutz history reinforced the collective's goals to discourage individualism, abolish gender inequality, and bring up a new type of Jewish person who would be healthy, sturdy, and productive as well as socialized to live a communal life. The kibbutz community was regarded as a "collective parent" committed to satisfying the needs of each child without the mediation of the family. Each child was, in a sense, regarded as a "kibbutz child", and part of an informal communal socialization network (Rabin & Beit-Hallahmi, 1982; for more details see Sagi-Schwartz & Aviezer, in press).

Collective sleeping for children away from their parents constituted probably the most distinctive characteristic of early kibbutz child-rearing practices. In effect the kibbutz children's houses functioned as children's homes in almost every respect. Thus, typically children's houses consisted of bedrooms that were each shared by three or four children, a dining area, showers, and a large space for play and learning. Children had their own private corners in their bedrooms where they kept their personal items. Family time was designated for the afternoon and evening (approximately 4 to 7 PM), when both parents made an effort to be available and families spent time together in the parents' dwelling. Children returned to the children's house for their night sleep and were put to bed by their parents, but were watched over throughout the night by two watchwomen who were responsible for all kibbutz children under the age of 12. These watchwomen, many of them unfamiliar figures to the children, were assigned based on weekly shifts and they monitored the children's houses via intercom and making rounds. Sensitive responsiveness to children's needs during the night thus was nearly impossible (Aviezer, Van IJzendoorn, Sagi, & Schuengel, 1994).

Although many cultures practice multiple caregiving, as we have seen in the African cases, a worldwide sample of 183 societies showed that none of them maintained a system of having infants and young children sleep away from their parents (Barry & Paxton, 1971). In fact, from the early days of the kibbutz movement, the collective sleeping arrangement was debated and the very first four kibbutzim have always maintained home-based sleeping. Collective sleeping became normative and an officially advocated practice in kibbutzim only with later immigrants who were zealous socialists emphasizing the interests of the collective over individualistic tendencies. Doubts about children's collective sleeping had been loudly voiced during the 1950s along with a rise in familistic tendencies (Lavi, 1990), which were reinforced by the Gulf War and the growing prosperity of kibbutz economies and better housing for families (see Aviezer et al., 1994 for a review of childcare practices; Aviezer et al., 2002).

From attachment theory the hypothesis may be derived that communal sleeping increases the risk for children to become insecurely attached. This unusual child-rearing practice, in which normal children of middle-class families were raised in institutionlike conditions, offered a unique opportunity for quasi-experimental observation of the impact of unusual child-rearing conditions without confounding it with SES or clinical status. Indeed we found a significantly lower rate (48 percent) of secure attachment to mothers among infants living under such conditions, compared to 80 percent in the family-based kibbutzim (Sagi et al., 1994). The ecology of the children's house during the day, maternal separation anxiety, infants' temperament, and mother–infant play interaction were similar in both arrangements. For collectively sleeping infants the mothers were largely unavailable during the nights. A longitudinal investigation of one of our kibbutz cohorts (the "kids" are now 23 years of age) revealed enduring effects of collective sleeping (Sagi-Schwartz & Aviezer, in press). Compared with young adolescents who slept at home with their parents, those exposed to collective sleeping beyond early childhood were rated by their teachers as less emotionally mature in the school context.

Transmission of attachment has been demonstrated by showing correspondence between classifications of infants' attachment relationships and classifications of their parents' internal representations, a rate of about 75 percent in several studies of Western cultures (see Van IJzendoorn, 1995, for a review). Indeed, if the collective child-rearing ecology was problematic for infants' attachment then this should be also manifested in disrupted attachment transmission. The *Adult Attachment Interview* (*AAI*; George, Kaplan, & Main, 1985) was presented to mothers from collective kibbutzim and from kibbutzim with home sleeping (Sagi et al., 1997). We found no difference in rates of security between mothers who raised their children in communal sleeping arrangement (65 percent) and mothers whose children slept at home (72 percent). However, attachment transmission in dyads whose infants were sleeping collectively was significantly weaker than attachment transmission in dyads whose infants were sleeping at home (40 percent and 76 percent, respectively).

In a multiple-caregiver environment creating attachment networks, the question is how various attachment relationships affect the children's socioemotional and cognitive development. Is only one attachment to the primary caregiver important, or should the network as a system be taken into account? Van IJzendoorn, Sagi, and Lambermon (1992) proposed four models. The *monotropy* model implies that only one attachment figure (mostly the mother) is an important attachment figure (Bowlby, 1951). The *hierarchy* model suggests that one caregiver (again mostly the mother) is most important, but other caregivers may be considered subsidiary and serve as a secure base when the primary caregiver is absent. The *independence* model states that a child can form attachments to several caregivers that will be functional in the domains in which child and caregiver interact. Finally, the *integration* model argues that in a network of attachment relationships, secure attachments will compensate for insecure ones and the absence of any secure attachments would be most difficult (Van IJzendoorn et al., 1992).

Based on the kibbutz experience, we examined the predictive power of an extended network of attachment relationships (mother, father, and caregiver) in comparison with the family network (mother and father) and separate mother- or father–infant relationships. The extended attachment network was the best predictor of later socioemotional and cognitive functioning at age 5 years, and it was interpreted as support for the integration model. In later phases of development across middle childhood, adolescence, and adulthood the situation becomes more complex, with inconsistent predictions from early relations with individual attachment figures, from family network and extended network. For instance, infant security with the mother but also with the extended network was associated with a higher sense of attachment coherence at age 21 years (Sagi-Schwartz & Aviezer, 2003). Thus, the quality of early relationships is connected to future adaptations; yet, in an environment of multiple relationships, the combination of attachment relations to primary caregivers is important as well as the particular setting in which an attachment relation developed. This integration pattern was most pronounced in the kibbutz ecology (Van IJzendoorn et al., 1992) in which the influence of the caregiving network was ideologically based and was given a considerably large part in children's daily life compared to the regular family-based child-rearing settings using professional childcare.

Following a visit to kibbutzim in the early 1950s, Bowlby (1953) already identified the rich opportunities for research provided by kibbutz upbringing and cautioned that this child-rearing context, although clearly different from institutional care, may produce higher rates of attachment insecurity. Aviezer et al. (2002) suggest that Bowlby was, in fact, correct in predicting the deleterious effects of the kibbutz experience, and that communal sleeping was an experiment destined to fail because it deviated too much from the original environments of evolutionary adaptedness in which the universal need for attachment emerged. However, it is important to point out that collective sleeping cannot be considered to be similar to institutionalized and fragmented care leading to the maternal deprivation that was observed by Bowlby after visiting kibbutzim in the 1950s (Bowlby, 1953). All observed kibbutz children were indeed attached to their mothers. Through painstaking investigations in the kibbutz context, Bowlby's prediction has been made much more specific and grounded. Larger rates of infant insecurity were found as well as an enduring influence of sleeping away from parents at night during infancy on coping mechanisms for later adjustments, and a disrupted transmission of attachment across generations in the communal kibbutzim. No wonder that this unique experiment was not acceptable to its participants, although it took quite some time before this was realized.

## Japan, Attachment, and Amae: A Case Study in Invalid Cross-Cultural Attachment Assessment

One of the most severe critiques of current attachment theory and research was the accusation of "cultural blindness" to alternative conceptions of relatedness (Rothbaum et al., 2000). The accusation of a Western bias in attachment theory was based, in particular, on the Japanese case. In 1985, Miyaki, Takahashi, and others published their widely discussed paper on attachment in which they showed that Japanese infants are much more often ambivalently/resistantly attached to their mothers than infants in comparable Western samples. Insecure-avoidance of the mother just did not emerge in the stressful *Strange Situation* procedure that confronted the Japanese infants with the culturally unusual experience of being separated from their mother in an unfamiliar environment.

In the often heated debates of the Japanese case usually only two studies (Miyake, Chen, & Campos, 1985; Mizuta, Zahn-Waxler, Cole, & Hiruma, 1996) are used as evidence. To our knowledge, however, at least six empirical studies on attachment in Japan have been published (Durrett, Otaki, & Rich ards, 1984; Kazui, Endo, Tanaka, Sakagami, & Suganuma, 2000; Posada et al., 1995; Vereijken, 1996). What findings are overlooked and make the "cultural blindness" accusation implausible?

First, as is the case in many other cultures (Van IJzendoorn & Sagi, 1999), Japan is not one homogeneous culture, and attachment studies in different regions of Japan have yielded diverging results. For example, Durrett et al.'s (1984) Tokyo study showed an attachment distribution that is similar to the distribution found in Western-European and Northern-American samples. The small Sapporo study (Miyake et al., 1985) showed an overrepresentation of insecure-resistant infants (although the majority of the children were securely attached), and it had insufficient statistical power to falsify the sensitivity hypothesis. More important, however, is the procedure of assessing attachment quality in this study. According to the guidelines, the *Strange Situation* should only create "mild stress". Unfortunately, the *Strange Situation* separations in the Sapporo study were not curtailed when infants became distressed for more than about 20 seconds (a time limit set in most attachment research), but episodes were curtailed only after full two minutes of crying (Van IJzendoorn & Sagi, 1999). Grossmann and Grossmann (1990) remarked after reviewing many of the original Japanese videotaped *Strange Situation* procedures:

> In the 15 reviewed cases, episode 6 (when the infant is alone) was skipped twice but in the rest of the cases it was at least 55 seconds long and at most 3 minutes long even if the infant was extremely upset. Also episode 7 (when the infant is alone with the stranger) was not curtailed to less than one minute even if the infant cried from the beginning very intensely. . . . Thus adding up the crying time of episode 6 and episode 7, some infants cried as long as 4 minutes and 40 seconds in extreme despair.

With this rigid two-minute rule as the minimum length of time for the second separation, the flexibility of the *Strange Situation* to create only mild stress across cultures disappears.

The second finding that most authors favoring the "cultural blindness" idea have overlooked derives from strong Japanese support for the concept of secure attachment instead of *amae* or dependence (Vereijken, 1996). Vereijken (1996) asked eight native Japanese behavioral scientists to describe the concepts of *amae*, attachment, and dependence with the help of the 90 behavioral descriptions provided by the *Attachment Q-Sort* (Posada et al., 1995). It should be noted that the *AQS* descriptions are not theory-specific and not restricted to attachment but cover a large variety of basic behaviors typical for 1- to 4-year-old children. The experts agreed strongly about the different descriptions of the three concepts. Then Vereijken asked Japanese mothers to describe their most ideal child with the items of the *AQS*, and compared this description with the experts' definitions of *amae*, attachment, and dependence. The Japanese mothers clearly favored the secure child as close to their ideal. According to the Japanese mothers their ideal child was not similar at all to a child who would especially show behaviors indicative of *amae* or dependence. This finding constitutes an independent replication and extension of the Posada et al. (1995) investigation which found a similar appreciation of secure attachment behaviors across a large set of cultures. Lastly, the Vereijken study also showed a strong association in Japan between maternal sensitivity and infant attachment security.

A third set of findings that Rothbaum et al. (2000) and others failed to take into account in their scathing critique of attachment theory was reported by Kazui et al. (2000). Their pioneering study on the intergenerational transmission of attachment in 50 Japanese mothers and their preschool-age children is the first Japanese replication of the well-established association between mothers' attachment security and their children's security. They showed that the children of secure mothers as assessed with the *Adult Attachment Interview* (*AAI*) had the highest security scores on the *Attachment Q-Sort*, whereas the children of unresolved mothers had the lowest *AQS* scores. The children of the dismissing and preoccupied mothers scored in between. The majority of the mothers were classified as secure (66 percent). It is remarkable that the assessment of discourse coherence developed in the English language shows similar predictive validity in the Japanese language. Of course, this exciting investigation should be further replicated, but the study clearly shows that competent researchers are able to go beyond cultural as well as language boundaries in confirming basic hypotheses in attachment theory in a non-Western culture.

We must conclude that the Japanese case is not yet a falsification of the nomological network that constitutes attachment theory's claim to cross-cultural validity. The concept of secure attachment is appreciated, even in Japan, beyond related concepts such as *amae* or dependency. Most importantly, the *Strange Situation* procedure seems only cross-culturally valid if used in its original sense, namely, as a setting arousing feelings of *mild* stress. If cross-cultural attachment researchers implement the *SSP* in a culturally insensitive way by applying it rigidly adhering to the format of three-minute episodes, chances are high that the findings will be invalid, not only in the cross-cultural sense but also in a general scientific sense. Of course, the Sapporo study was one of the first to use the *SSP* outside the United States, and the pioneering Japanese researchers were only able to rely on written protocols that were implicitly addressing the issue of flexibly conducting the procedure with the goal of creating mild stress. With the wisdom of hindsight we now know that proper implementation of the *SSP* is crucial for the cross-cultural validity of its findings.

## CONCLUSION: ATTACHMENT IS UNIVERSAL AND CONTEXT-DEPENDENT

In testing the cross-cultural validity of attachment theory, three related issues are at stake (Van IJzendoorn, 1990; Main, 1990; see Figure 5.1 and Table 5.1). The first issue concerns the *normativity* of attachment across cultures. We now have evidence across a variety of cultures that secure attachments represent the majority across cultures (NORM), and that insecure attachments represent a sometimes rather large minority of the participants. Of course, this numeric normativity of secure attachments does not imply that secure attachments would constitute the norm in any other sense, for example, in terms of ethical or adaptive value (see Belsky, 1999). The second issue concerns the *predictive validity* of the theory; that is, is attachment security associated with parental sensitivity (SENS) in similar ways across cultures?

TABLE 5.1. Evidence or the Cross-Cultural Validity of Attachment Theory from Africa and Japan

| Culture: Africa | Norm | Sens | Change |
|---|---|---|---|
| Uganda (Ainsworth, 1967) | + | + | +/– |
| Gusii (Kermoian & Leiderman, 1986) | + | + | + |
| Dogon (T rue, 1996) | + | + | + |
| Hausa (Marvin et al., 1977) | 0 | 0 | + |
| !Kung San (Konner, 1977) | 0 | (+) | + |
| Efe (Morelli & Tronick, 1991) | 0 | (+) | + |
| Sotho (Minde et al., 2002) | (–) | + | + |
| Khayelitsha (Tomlinson, 2002) | + | (+) | +/– |
| Culture: Japan | | | |
| Tokyo (Durrett et al., 1984) | + | +/– | – |
| Sapporo (Miyake et al., 1985) | + | – | – |
| Tokyo (Verejken, 1996) | + | + | + |
| Osaka (Kazui, 2000) | + | + | + |

Note: + = positive evidence; 0 = no evidence available; +/– = mixedpositive/negative evidence; – = negative evidence; (+) = indirect positive evidence.

We found evidence for this association in most cross-cultural studies, and certainly in each and every country in which attachment research has been conducted thus far.

Third, in most cross-cultural attachment studies researchers did not feel much need to use drastic, *culture-specific changes* in the design of the study or in the attachment and sensitivity measures (CHANGE). Of course, distinct attachment behaviors may be specific to the sociocultural context (e.g., reaching for the mother's hand instead of seeking proximity), but attachment patterns can be described in similar ways across cultures. Studies with the *Attachment Q-Sort* showed that parents and experts from diverse sociocultural contexts view attachment security similarly, and that even in Japan, attachment security rather than *amae* is preferred when parents describe their ideal-typical child (Posada et al., 1995; Vereijken, 1996).

In fact, the issue of the universality versus cultural specificity of attachment is not much different from the question of whether our language ability is universal or culturally specific. Pinker elaborated his evolutionary model of the *Language Instinct* (19 94) from the perspective of an inborn and universal language acquisition device, in the Chomskian sense. But he also incorporated environmental input, and argued for the cultural specificity of this input in the development of a specific language. Analogous to this language model, the development of attachment may also be described in terms of the interplay between evolutionarily based, inborn biases to become attached that are universal, and environmental input that stimulates the development of a specific attachment pattern or relationship (see Figure 5.2, derived from Van IJzendoorn, 2003).

The innate bias to become attached is universal. The environmental input is culturally specific, determining individual and group differences in becoming

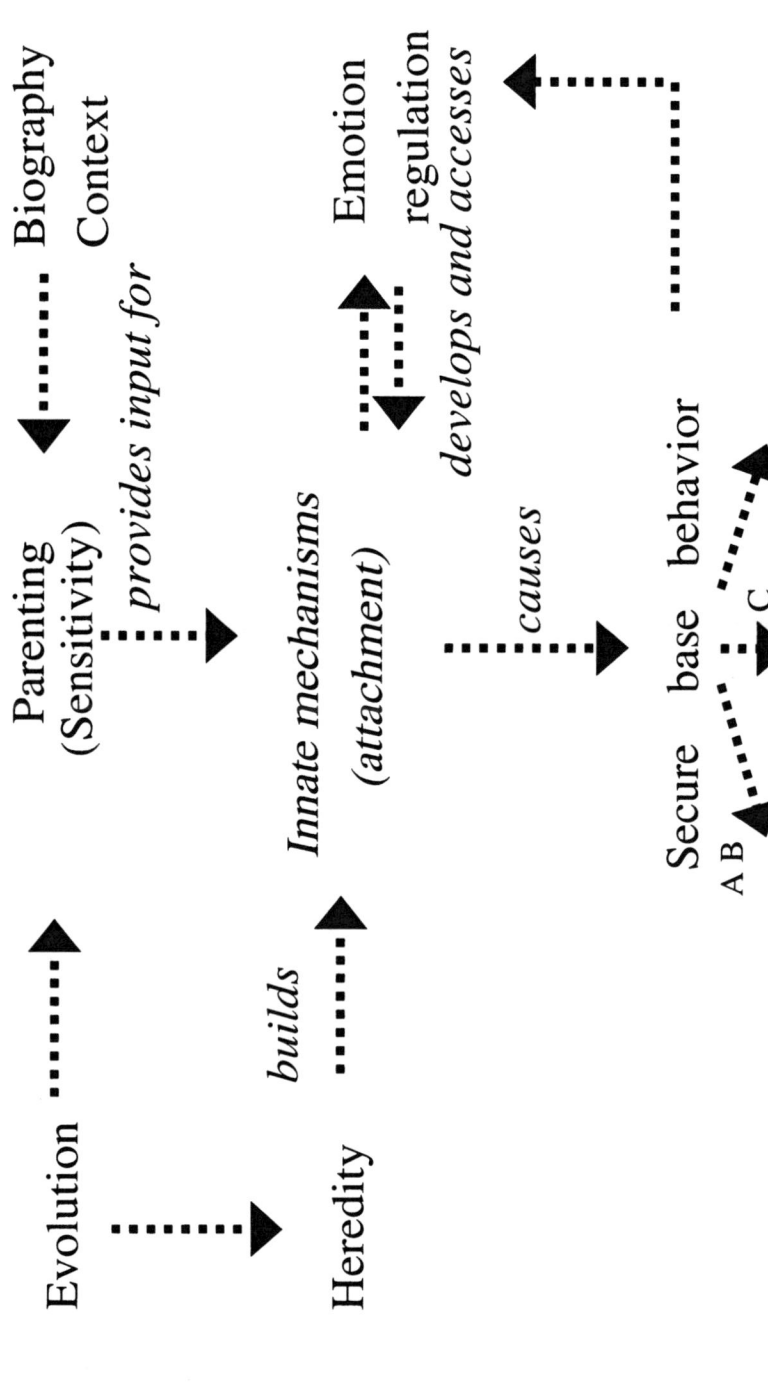

FIGURE 5.2  Evolutionary attachment model.

attached in a certain way, even to the extent that under unusual life events (e.g., poverty, low-quality early daycare, infants sleeping away from parents at night) normative transmission processes in parent–child relationships might be interrupted.

In our *Evolutionary Attachment Model*, (Van IJzendoorn, 2003) these universal and cultural-specific influences have been delineated. Variation and selection are supposed to have been the mechanisms through which the universal inclination to become attached was established. The advantage of this attachment bias may have been protection of offspring who were unable to survive on their own. Inclusive fitness would have led to a species-wide genetic bias to cling to an attachment figure. In a similar way, parents' sensitive protection of their helpless offspring would have been selected because of its advantages for inclusive fitness. But the environment is important because it provides parents with a culturally specific history of attachment experiences and with culturally based child-rearing attitudes, behaviors, and norms that influence their parenting style of responding to the child's attachment needs, preparing these children for adaptation to the specific niche in which they were born (Belsky, 1999).

The *Evolutionary Attachment Model* also emphasizes the close relation between attachment and emotion regulation (Cassidy, 1994). In fact, within the context of an attachment relationship, the infant is capable of regulating his or her overwhelming emotions of distress in times of hunger, illness, or other stresses. Only within the scaffold of an attachment relationship can the infant deal with the strains and stresses of an otherwise unpredictable environment, and develop the basic trust needed to survive the hardships of environments with scarce resources. The specific niche in which the infant happens to be born shapes parental behavior and the resulting individual differences in attachment relationships, parallel to the acquisition of a specific language on the basis of an inborn and universal language acquisition device (Van IJzendoorn, 2003).

The *Evolutionary Attachment Model* incorporates both the universal and cultural-specific dimension of attachment, and demonstrates the interplay between nature and nurture in the development of patterns of attachment behaviors. Attachment theory indeed integrates both the evolutionary perspective and the sociocultural influences on human development. Cross-cultural evidence as discussed in this chapter shows how fruitful such an integrated model has been in the past half century.

## ACKNOWLEDGMENTS

Parts of this chapter have been derived from the following papers.

Aviezer, O., Sagi, A., & Van IJzendoorn, M. H. (2002). Balancing the family and the collective in raising Kibbutz children: Why the communal sleeping experiment was predestined to fail. *Family Process, 41*, 435–455.

Bakermans-Kranenburg, M. J., Van IJzendoorn, M. H., Bokhorst, C. L., & Schuengel, C. (in press). The importance of shared environment in infant-father attachment: A behavioral genetic study of the Attachment Q-Sort. *Journal of Family Psychology*.

Bakermans-Kranenburg, M. J., Van IJzendoorn, M. H., & Kroonenberg, P. M. (in press). Differences in attachment security between African-American and White children: Ethnicity or socio-economic status? *Infant Behavior and Development, 3*.

Bokhorst, C. L., Bakermans-Kranenburg, M. J., Fearon, P., Van IJzendoorn, M. H., Fonagy, P., & Schuengel, C. (2003). The importance of shared environment in mother-infant attachment security: A behavioral genetic study. *Child Development, 74*, 1769–1782.

Van IJzendoorn, M. H., & Sagi, A. (1999). Cross-cultural patterns of attachment: Universal and contextual dimensions. In J. Cassidy & P. R. Shaver (Eds.), *Handbook of attachment: Theory, research, and clinical applications* (pp. 713–734). New York: Guilford.

Van IJzendoorn, M. H., & Sagi, A. (2001). Cultural blindness or selective inattention? *American Psychologist, 56*, 824–825.

## REFERENCES

Ainsworth, M. D. (1969). Object relations, dependency, and attachment: A theoretical review of the infant-mother relationship. *Child Development, 40*, 969–1025.

Ainsworth, M. D. S. (1967). *Infancy in Uganda. Infant care and the growth of love.* Baltimore: Johns Hopkins Press.

Ainsworth, M. D. S. (1977). Infant development and mother-infant interaction among Ganda and American families. In P. H. Leiderman, S. R. Tulkin, & A. H. Rosenfeld (Eds.), *Culture and infancy* (pp. 119-150). New York: Academic.

Ainsworth, M. D. S., Blehar, M. C., Waters, E., & Wall, S. (1978). *Patterns of attachment.* Hillsdale, NJ: Erlbaum.

Aviezer, O., Sagi, A., & Van IJzendoorn, M. H. (2002). Balancing the family and the collective in raising Kibbutz children: Why the communal sleeping experiment was predestined to fail. *Family Process, 41*, 435–455.

Aviezer, O., Sagi-Schwartz, A., & Koren-Karie, N., (2003). Ecological constraints on the formation of infant-mother attachment relations: When maternal sensitivity becomes ineffective. *Infant Behavior and Development, 26*, 285–299.

Aviezer, O., van IJzendoorn, M. H., Sagi, A., & Schuengel, C. (1994). "Children of the dream" revisited: 70 years of collective early child care in Israeli kibbutzim. *Psychological Bulletin, 116*, 99–116.

Bakermans-Kranenburg, M. J., Van IJzendoorn, M. H., & Kroonenberg, P. M. (in press). Differences in attachment security between African-American and White children: Ethnicity or socio-economic status? *Infant Behavior and Development, 3*.

Bakermans-Kranenburg, M. J., Van IJzendoorn, M. H., Bokhorst, C. L., & Schuengel, C. (in press). The importance of shared environment in infant-father attachment: A behavioral genetic study of the Attachment Q-Sort. *Journal of Family Psychology.*

Barnard, K. E., Magyary, D., Summer, G., Booth, C. L., Mitchell, S. K., & Spieker, S. (1988). Prevention of parenting alterations for women with low social support. *Psychiatry, 51*, 248–253.

Barry, H. I., & Paxton, L. M. (1971). Infancy and early childhood: Cross-cultural codes 2. *Ethnology, 10*, 466–508.

Baumrind, D. (1972). An exploratory study of socialization effects of Black children: Some Black-White comparisons. *Child Development, 43*, 261–267.

Baumrind, D. (1993). The average expectable environment is not good enough: A response to Scarr. *Child Development, 64*, 1299–1317.

Becker, G. S., & Thomes, N. (1986). Human capital and the rise and fall of families. *Journal of Labor Economics, 4*, S1–S139.

Belsky, J. (1984). The determinants of parenting: A process model. *Child Development, 55*, 83–96.

Belsky, J. (1999). Modern evolutionary theory and patterns of attachment. In J. Cassidy & P. R. Shaver (Eds.), *Handbook of attachment: Theory, research, and clinical applications* (pp. 141–161). New York: Guilford.

Bokhorst, C. L., Bakermans-Kranenburg, M. J., Fearon, P., Van IJzendoorn, M. H., Fonagy, P., & Schuengel, C. (2003). The importance of shared environment in mother-infant attachment security: A behavioral genetic study. *Child Development, 74*, 1769–1782.

Bouchard Jr., T.J. & Loehlin, J. C. (2001) Genes, evolution, and personality. *Behavioral Genetics, 31*, 243–273.

Bowlby, J. (1951). *Maternal care and mental health*. Geneva: WHO.

Bowlby, J. (1952). *Maternal Care and Mental Health: A Report Prepared on Behalf of the World Health Organization as a Contribution to the United Nations Programme for the Welfare of Homeless Children* (2nd ed.). Geneva: World Health Organization.

Bowlby, J. (1953). *Child care and the Growth of Maternal Love*, Penguin Books, London.

Bowlby, J. (1969). *Attachment and loss: Vol. I. Attachment*. London: Hogarth.

Bowlby, J. (1969/1989). *Attachment*. London: Penguin.

Bowlby, J. (1989). *Attachment and loss. Attachment* (Vol. 1, 2d ed.). London: Penguin.

Bronfenbrenner, U. (1979). *The ecology of human development*. Cambridge, MA: Harvard University Press.

Cassidy, J. (1994). Emotion regulation: Influences of attachment relationships. *Monographs of the Society for Research in Child Development, 59*, 2–3, 228–249.

Collins, W., Maccoby, E. E., Steinberg, L., Hetherington, E., & Bornstein, M. H. (2000). Contemporary research on parenting: The case for nature and nurture. *American Psychologist, 55*(2), 218–232.

Conger, R. D., Conger, K. J., Elder, G. H., Lorenz, F. O., Simons, R. L., & Whitbeck, L B. (1992a). A family process model of economic hardship and adjustment of early adolescent boys. *Child Development, 63*, 526–541.

Conger, R. D., Conger, K. J., Elder, G. H., Lorenz, F. O., Simons, R. L., & Whitbeck, L. B. (1992b). Family economic stress and adjustment of early adolescent girls. *Developmental Psychology, 29*, 206–219.

De Wolff, M. S., & van IJzendoorn, M. H. (1997). Sensitivity and attachment: A meta-analysis on parental antecedents of infant attachment. *Child Development, 68*, 571–591.

Deater-Deckard, K., Dodge, K. A., Bates, J. E., & Pettit, G. S. (1996). Physical discipline among African-American and European American mothers: Links to children's externalizing behaviours. *Developmental Psychology, 32*, 1065–1072.

Dodge, K. H., Pettit, G. S., & Bates, J. E. (1994). Socialization mediators of the relation between socioeconomic status and child conduct problems. *Child Development, 65*, 649–665.

Dornbusch, S. M., Ritter, P. L., Leiderman, P. H., Roberts, D. F., & Fraleigh, M. J. (1987). The relation of parenting style to adolescence performance. *Child Development, 58*, 1244–1257.

Duncan, G. J., & Brooks-Gunn, J. (Eds.). (1997). *Consequences of growing up poor*. New York: Russell Sage Foundation.

Durrett, M. E., Otaki, M., & Richards, P. (1984). Attachment and the mother's perception of support from the father. *International Journal of Behavioral Development, 7*, 167–176.

Elder, G. H., & Caspi, A. (1988). Economic stress in lives: Developmental perspectives. *Journal of Social Issues, 44*, 25–45.

Fonagy, P., Steele, H., & Steele, M. (1991). Maternal representations of attachment during pregnancy predict the organization of infant-mother attachment at one year of age. *Child Development, 62,* 891–905.

Garcia Coll, C. T. (1990) Developmental outcome of minority infants: A process-oriented look into our beginnings. *Child Development, 61,* 270–289.

George, C., Kaplan, N., & Main, M. (1985). *The Adult Attachment Interview.* Unpublished manuscript, University of California at Berkeley.

Grossmann, K. & Grossmann, K. E. (1990). In the *Annual Report Occasional Papers No 2, July 1990,* of the Research and Clinical Center for Child Development, Faculty of Education, Hokkaido University, Sapporo, Japan, pp. 6–17.

Harlow, H. (1958). The nature of love. *American Psychologist 13,* 673–685. Haveman, R., & Wolfe, B. (1994). *Succeeding generations: On the effects of investments in children.* New York: Russell Sage Foundation.

Haveman, R., Wolfe, B., & Spaulding, J. (1991). Child events and circumstances influencing high school completion. *Demography, 28,* 133–158.

Hesse, E. (1999). The Adult Attachment Interview: Historical and current perspectives. In J. Cassidy & P. R. Shaver (Eds.), Handbook of attachment: Theory research, and clinical applications (pp. 395–433). New York: Guilford Press.

Hinde, R. A. (1982). Attachment: Some conceptual and biological issues. In J. Stevenson-Hinde & C. M. Parkes (Eds.), *The place of attachment in human behaviour.* New York: Basic.

Hinde, R. A., & Stevenson-Hinde, J. (1990). Attachment: Biological, cultural and individual desiderata. *Human Development, 33,* 62–72.

Hrdy, S. B. (1999). *Mother nature. A history of mothers, infants, and natural selection.* New York: Pantheon.

Huston, A. C., McLoyd, V. C., & Garcia Coll, C. T. (Eds.). (1994). Children and poverty. Special Issue. *Child Development, 65* (2).

Jackson, J. F. (1991). Multiple caregiving among African-Americans and infant attachments: Issues and an exploratory study. *ERIC Document Reproduction Service No. PS 019488.*

Jackson, J. F. (1993). Multiple caregiving among African-Americans and infant attachment: The need for an emic approach. *Human Development, 36,* 87–102.

Jencks, C., & Philips, M. (Eds.). (1998). *The Black-White test score gap.* Washington, DC: Brookings Institution Press.

Kazui, M., Endo, T., Tanaka, A., Sakagami, H., & Suganuma, M. (2000). Intergenerational transmission of attachment Japanese mother-child dyads. *Japanese Journal of Educational Psychology, 48,* 323–332.

Keating, D., & Hertzman, C. (Eds.). (1999). *Developmental health and the wealth of nations: Social, biological, and educational dynamics.* New York: Guilford.

Kermoian, R., & Leiderman, P. H. (1986). Infant attachment to mother and child caretaker in an East African community. Special Issue: Cross-cultural human development. *International Journal of Behavioral Development, 9,* 455–469.

Konner, M. (1977). Infancy among the Kalahari desert San. In P. H. Leiderman, S. R. Tulkin, & A. H. Rosenfeld, (Eds.), *Culture and infancy* (pp. 287–328). New York: Academic.

Lamb, M. E. (1997). Fathers and child development: an introductory overview and guide. In M. E. Lamb (Ed.), *The role of the father in child development* (3d ed., pp. 1–15). New York: Wiley.

Linver, M. R., Brooks-Gunn, J., & Kohen, D. E. (2002). Family processes as pathways from income to young children's development. *Developmental Psychology, 38,* 719–734.

Lyons-Ruth, K., Connell, D. B., & Grunebaum, H. U. (1990). Infants at social risk: Maternal depression and family support services as mediators of infant development and security of attachment. *Child Development, 61*, 85–98.

Main, M. (1990). Cross-cultural studies of attachment organization: Recent studies, changing methodologies, and the concept of conditional strategies. *Human Development, 33*, 48–61.

Main, M. (1999). Epilogue: Attachment Theory: Eighteen points with suggestions for future studies. In J. Cassidy & P. R. Shaver (Eds.), Handbook of attachment Theory, research, and clinical applications (pp. 845–887). New York: Guilford Press.

Main, M., & Solomon, J. (1990). Procedures for identifying infants as disorganized/disoriented during the Ainsworth Strange Situation. In M. T. Greenberg, D. Cicchetti, & E. M. Cummings (Eds.), *Attachment in the preschool years: Theory, research, and intervention. The John D. and Catherine T. MacArthur Foundation series on mental health and development* (pp. 121–160). Chicago: University of Chicago Press.

Main, M., & Hesse, E. (1990) Parents' unresolved traumatic experiences are related to infant disorganized attachment: Is frightening parental behavior the linking mechanism? In M. T. Greenberg, D. Cicchetti, & E. M. Cummings (Eds.), *Attachment in the preschool years* (pp. 161–182). Chicago: University of Chicago Press.

Main, M., Kaplan, N., & Cassidy, J. (1985). Security in infancy, childhood, and adulthood: A move to the level of representation. *Monographs of the Society for Research in Child Development, 50*, 66–104.

Marvin, R. S., VanDevender, T. L., Iwanaga, M. I., LeVine, S., & LeVine, R. A. (1977). Infant-caregiver attachment among the Hausa of Nigeria. In H. McGurk (Ed.), *Ecological factors in human development* (pp. 247–259). Amsterdam: North Holland.

McGuffin, P., Riley, B., & Plomin, R. (2001). Toward behavioral genomics. *Science* 291: 1232–124.

McLoyd, V. C. (1989). Socialization and development in a changing economy: The effect of paternal job and income loss on children. *American Psychologist, 44*, 293–302.

McLoyd, V. C. (1990a) Minority children: Introduction to the special issue. *Child Development, 61*, 263–266.

McLoyd, V. C. (1990b). The impact of economic hardship on black families and children: Psychological distress, parenting, and socioemotional development. *Child Development, 61*, 311–346.

McLoyd, V. C., Jayaratne, T. E., Ceballo, R., & Borquez, J. (1994). Unemployment and work interruption among African-American single mothers: Effects on parenting and adolescent socioemotional functioning. *Child Development, 65*, 562–589.

Minde, M. D., Minde, R., & Vogel, W. (July, 2002). *Attachment patterns of mothers and toddlers in a South African Township*. Paper presented at the World Association for Infant Mental Health's Eighth World Congress, Amsterdam, The Netherlands, July 17–20, 2002.

Miyake, K., Chen, S. J., & Campos, J. J. (1985). Infant temperament, mother's mode of interaction, and attachment in Japan: An interim report. *Monographs of the Society for Research in Child Development, 50*, 276–297.

Mizuta, I., Zahn-Waxler, C., Cole, P. M., & Hiruma, N. (1996). A cross-cultural study of preschoolers' attachment security and sensitivity in Japanese and U.S. dyads. *International Journal of Behavioral Development, 19*, 141–159.

Morelli, G. A., & Tronick, E. Z. (1991). Efé multiple caretaking and attachment. In J. L. Gewirtz & W. M. Kurtines (Eds.), *Intersections with attachment* (pp. 41–52). Hillsdale, NJ: Erlbaum.

Nelson, J. Q. (1991). Case studies of black adolescent mother-infant attachment in the culture of poverty. *Dissertation Abstracts International, 51*, 4619.

NICHD Early Child Care Research Network (1996). Characteristics of infant child care: Factors contributing to positive caregiving. *Early Childhood Research Quarterly, 11*, 269–306.

NICHD Early Child Care Research Network (1999). NICHD Study of Early Child Care. Phase I Instrument Document. (CD-ROM, NICHD; see also http://public.rti.org/secc).

Ogbu, J. U. (1981). Origin of human competence: A cultural-ecological perspective. *Child Development, 52*, 413–429.

Ogbu, J. U. (1993). Differences in cultural frame of reference. *International Journal of Behavioral Development, 16*, 483–506.

Peterson, N. J., Drotar, D., Olness, K., Guay, L., & Kiziri-Mayengo, R. (2001). The relationship of maternal and child HIV infection to security of attachment among Ugandan infants. *Child Psychiatry and Human Development, 32*, 3–17.

Pinker, S. (1994). *The language instinct: How the mind creates language.* New York: William Morrow.

Plomin, R., DeFries, J. C., McClearn, G. E. & Rutter, M. (2001). *Behavioral Genetics.* New York: Freeman.

Posada, G., Gao, Y., Wu, F., Posada, R., Tascon, M., Schöelmerich, A., et al. (1995). The secure base phenomenon across cultures: Children's behavior, mothers' preferences, and experts' concepts. In E. Waters, B. E. Vaughn, G. Posada, & K. Kondo-Ikemura (Eds.), Constructs, cultures and caregiving: New growing points in attachment theory and research. *Monographs of the Society for Research in Child Development, 60*, 27–48.

Rabin, A. I., & Beit-Hallahmi, B. (1982). *Twenty years later.* New York: Springer.

Reed, G., & Leiderman, P. H. (1981). Age-related changes in attachment behavior in polymatrically reared infants: The Kenyan Gusii. In T. M. Field, A. M. Sostek, P. Vietze, & P. H. Leiderman (Eds.), *Culture and early interactions* (pp. 215–236). Hillsdale, NJ: Erlbaum.

Robertson, J., & Robertson, J. (1971). Young children in brief separation: A fresh look. *Psychoanalytic Study of the Child, 26*, 264–315.

Rothbaum, F., Weisz, J., Pott, M., Miyake, K., & Morelli, G. (2000). Attachment and culture. Security in the United States and Japan. *American Psychologist, 55*, 1093–1104.

Rowe, D. C., Vazsony, A. T., & Flannery, D. J. (1994). No more than skin deep: Ethnic and racial similarity in developmental process. *Psychological Review, 101*, 396–413.

Sagi, A., & Aviezer, O. (2001). The rise and fall of children's communal sleeping in Israeli kibbutzim: An experiment in nature and implications for parenting. *An Invited Target Essay for ISSBD Newsletter, 1*, serial no. 38, 4–6.

Sagi, A., Lamb, M. E., Lewkowicz, K. S., Shoham, R., Dvir, R., & Estes, D. (1985). Security of infant-mother, -father, and -metapelet attachments among kibbutz-reared Israeli children. *Monographs of the Society for Research in Child Development, 50* (1–2), 257–275.

Sagi, A., van IJzendoorn, M. H., Aviezer, O., & Donnell, F. (1994). Sleeping out of home in a kibbutz communal arrangement: It makes a difference for infant-mother attachment. *Child Development, 65*, 992–1004.

Sagi, A., Van IJzendoorn, M. H., Aviezer, O., Donnell, F., Koren-Karie, N., Joels, T., & Harel, Y. (1995). Attachments in a multiple-caregiver and multiple-infant environment: The case of the Israeli kibbutzim. In E. Waters, B. E. Vaughn, G. Posada, & K. Kondo-Ikemura (Eds.), Caregiving, cultural, and cognitive perspectives on secure-base behavior and working models: New growing points of attachment theory and research (pp. 71–91). Special issue in the *Monographs of the Society for Research on Child Development, 60,* (Serial #244 No. 2–3).

Sagi, A., van IJzendoorn, M. H., Scharf, M., Joels, T., Koren-Karie, N., Mayseless, O., & Aviezer, O. (1997). Ecological constraints for intergenerational transmission of attachment. *International Journal of Behavioral Development, 20,* 287–299.

Sagi-Schwartz, A., & Aviezer, O. (in pr ess). Longitudinal correlates of attachment to multiple caregivers and of communal sleeping for kibbutz children. In K. K. Grossmann, K. Grossmann, & E. Waters (Eds.), *The power and dynamics of longitudinal attachment research.* New York: Guilford.

Sagi-Schwartz, A., & Aviezer, O. (July, 2003). Longitudinal correlates of attachment to multiple caregivers and with communal sleeping. *Invited lecture at the conference on attachment from infancy and childhood to adulthood (ATICA),* Regensburg University, Regensburg, Germany.

Sims-Stanford, B. E. (1997). Patterns of attachment and caregiving among low-income African-American families. *Dissertation Abstracts International, 57,* 7760.

Spangler, G., & Grossmann, K. E. (1993). Biobehavioral organization in securely and insecurely attached infants. *Child Development, 64,* 1439–1450.

Spencer, M. B. (1990). Development of minority children: An introduction. *Child Development, 61,* 267–269.

Takahashi, K. (1990). Are the key assumptions of the "Strange Situation" procedure universal? A view from Japanese research. *Human Development, 33,* 23–30.

Tavecchio, L. W. C., & Van IJzendoorn, M. H. (1987). *Attachment in social networks: Contributions to the Bowlby-Ainsworth attachment theory.* Amsterdam: North-Holland.

Thompson, R. A. (1993). Socioemotional development: Enduring issues and new challenges. Special Issue: Setting a path for the coming decade: Some goals and challenges. *Developmental Review, 13,* 372–402.

Tomlinson, M. (July 2002). *Challenges in assessing attachment and associated factors in a South African peri-urban settlement.* Paper presented at the World Association for Infant Mental Health's Eighth World Congress in Amsterdam.

Trivers, R. L. (1974). Parent-offspring conflict. *American Zoologist, 14,* 249–264.

Tronick, E. Z., Morelli, G. A., & Winn, S. (1987). Multiple caretaking of Efe (Pygmy) infants. *American Anthropologist, 89,* 96–106.

True, M. M. (1994). *Mother-infant attachment and communication among the Dogon of Mali.* Unpublished dissertation, University of California at Berkeley.

True, M. M., Pisani, L., & Oumar, F. (2001). Infant-mother attachment among the Dogon of Mali. *Child Development, 72,* 1451–1466.

Van IJzendoorn, M. H. (1990). Developments in cross-cultural research on attachment: Some methodological notes. *Human Development, 33,* 3–9.

Van IJzendoorn, M. H. (1995). Adult attachment representations, parental responsiveness, and infant attachment: A meta-analysis on the predictive validity of the Adult Attachment Interview. *Psychological Bulletin, 117,* 387–403.

Van IJzendoorn, M. H. Schuengel, C., & Bakermans-Kranenburg, M. J. (1999). Disorganized attachment in early childhood: Meta-analysis of precursors, concomitants, and sequelae. *Development and Psychopathology, 11,* 225–249.

Van IJzendoorn, M. H (2003). *Cross-cultural aspects of attachment in infants and young children: Universal and culture-specific component.* Invited keynote presented at the ISSBD Asian Regional Workshop, Seoul, South Korea, June 6–10, 2003.

Van IJzendoorn, M. H., & Bakermans-Kranenburg, M. J. (1996). Attachment representations in mothers, fathers, adolescents, and clinical groups: A meta-analytic search for normative data. *Journal of Consulting and Clinical Psychology, 64,* 8–21.

Van IJzendoorn, M. H., Goldberg, S., Kroonenberg, P. M., & Frenkl, O. J. (1992). The relative effects of maternal and child problems on the quality of attachment: A meta-analysis of attachment in clinical samples. *Child Development, 63,* 840–858.

Van IJzendoorn, M. H., & Kroonenberg, P. M. (1988). Cross-cultural patterns of attachment: A meta-analysis of the strange situation. *Child Development, 59,* 147–156.

Van IJzendoorn, M. H., & Sagi, A. (1999). Cross-cultural patterns of attachment: Universal and contextual dimensions. In J. Cassidy & P. R. Shaver (Eds.), *Handbook of Attachment: Theory, research, and clinical applications* (pp. 713–734). New York: Guilford.

Van IJzendoorn, M. H., Moran, G., Belsky, J., Pederson, D., Bakermans-Kranenburg, M. J., & Kneppers, K. (2000). The similarity of siblings' attachments to their mother. *Child Development, 71.* 1084–1096.

Van IJzendoorn, M. H., & Sagi, A. (2001). Cultural blindness or selective inattention? *American Psychologist, 56,* 824–825.

Van IJzendoorn, M. H., Sagi, A., & Lambermon, M. W. E. (1992). The multiple caretaker paradox: Data from Holland and Israel. In R. C. Pianta (Ed.), *Beyond the parent: The role of other adults in children's lives.* New Directions for Child Development, 57, 5–24. San Francisco: Jossey-Bass.

Van IJzendoorn, M. H., Vereijken, C. M. J. L., Bakermans-Kranenburg, M. J., & Riksen-Walraven, J. M. (in prep.) *Assessing Attachment Security with the Attachment Q-Sort: Meta-Analytic Evidence for the Validity of the Observer AQS.* Manuscript submitted for publication.

Vaughn, B. E., & Waters, E. (1990). Attachment behavior at home and in the laboratory: Q-sort observations and Strange Situation classifications of one-year-olds. *Child Development, 61,* 1965–1973.

Vereijken, C. M. J. L. (1996). *The mother-infant relationship in Japan: Attachment, dependency and amae.* Unpublished doctoral dissertation, Catholic University of Nijmegen, The Netherlands.

Waters, E. (1995). The attachment Q-set. In E. Waters, B. E. Vaughn, G. Posada, & K. Kondo-Ikemura (Eds.), Constructs, cultures and caregiving: New growing points in attachment theory and research. *Monographs of the Society for Research in Child Development, 60,* 234–246.

Waters, E., & Deane, K. (1985). Defining and assessing individual differences in attachment relationships: Q-methodology and the organization of behavior in infancy and early childhood. In I. Bretherton & E. Waters (Eds.), Growing points of attachment theory and research. *Monographs of the Society for Research in Child Development, 50,* 41–65.

Weisner, T. S., & Gallimore, R. (1977). My brother's keeper: Child and sibling caretaking. *Current Anthropology, 18,* 169–190.

Zeanah, C.H., & Benoit, D. (1995). Clinical applications of a parent perception interview in infant mental health. *Child and Adolescent Psychiatric Clinics of North America, 4,* 539–554.

Zevalkink, J., & Riksen-Walraven, J. M. (2001). Parenting in Indonesia: Inter- and intrac-ultural differences in mothers' interactions with their young children. *International Journal of Behavioral Development, 25,* 167–175.

Zevalkink, J., Riksen-Walraven, J. M., & Van Lieshout, C. F. M. (1999). Attachment in the Indonesian caregiving context. *Social Development, 8,* 21–40.

# 6

# Parent–Child Relations Over the Lifespan: A Cross-Cultural Perspective

## GISELA TROMMSDORFF

## INTRODUCTION

In previous research on parent–child relationships the focus has been on childhood and adolescence, and the question of how parents and their adult offspring relate to each other over the lifespan and in changing environments and different cultural contexts has received far less attention. Lifespan and culture-informed studies on parent–child relationships over the lifespan are rare. This is surprising because it has become a widely shared goal in developmental psychology to take a lifespan perspective and to take contextual factors into account. The importance of a lifespan and contextual perspective on parent–child relationships is obvious in light of the ongoing dramatic sociodemographic changes and related economic, social, and political problems. Increased longevity all over the world affects the prolonged time span that parents and their adult children share.

Therefore, the present chapter explores parent–child relationships over the lifespan and from a culture-informed perspective. The way parents and their children relate to each other in the context of social change and of culture is seen here as an important aspect of individual development. The present chapter first discusses parent–child relationships beyond childhood and adolescence on the basis of selected studies in the Western world. Second, social changes and different cultural contexts are taken into account. Third, a culture-informed theoretical framework for parent–child relationships is suggested in order to specify different developmental pathways for the development and function of parent–child relationships over the lifespan. Finally, selected results from an ongoing cross-cultural study on "The Value of Children and Intergenerational Relations" are discussed, followed by suggestions for further research.

## Changes in Family Systems and in Developmental Contexts

Parent–child relationships are biologically based, they are influenced by developmental and contextual conditions, and they affect individual development beyond childhood and adolescence. Due to increased average life expectancy in industrialized countries, adults can expect to share on the average almost five decades with at least one surviving parent while becoming a parent oneself. However, it is unclear whether sharing an increasing length of overlapping lifetime also includes increasing interactions between parents and their adult children, and what the quality and function of the parent–child relationships beyond childhood and adolescence is like.

In some countries old aged people outnumber the younger generation; in other countries it is the other way round. Given the decreasing fertility and the uneven relation between the old aged and the younger generation, the question arises whether this implies an increasing burden of the younger generation to support the older generation, an obligation that may induce intergenerational conflict. Although fertility is declining in highly industrialized countries, it remains high in the very poor regions of the world. These changes are presumably related to changes in social institutions, including the family, and the role of the parent–child relationship.

# DEVELOPMENTAL STUDIES ON PARENT–CHILD RELATIONSHIPS OVER THE LIFE COURSE: WESTERN APPROACHES

## Theoretical Approaches to Relationships

Parent–child relationships differ from other relationships. They are not the same as intergenerational relations, which are usually studied from a sociological perspective on the aggregate level of cohorts ("generations"; cf. Mannheim, 1952 [1928]). Also, parent–child relationships are not the same as intimate personal relationships but they can be viewed as a special case of close relationships (Trommsdorff, 1991). Therefore, social psychological theories on interpersonal relations (for an overview see Duck, 1997) are relevant for our topic.

*Exchange* theories were dominant for decades, focusing on the role of cognition and assuming rationality in intimate social interactions (e.g., Kelley & Thibaut, 1978). Here, the function of emotions and the role of prosocial behavior and altruism were neglected. *Interdependence* theory (Rusbult & Arriaga, 1997) suggests an integrated novel approach in order to overcome these deficits. Here, "relationship-specific motives" such as trust and commitment are seen as affecting prosocial tendencies and the persistence of the relationship. The "*investment model*" of close relationships assumes that commitment and satisfaction of the partners predict the degree of investment in the relationship. Commitment describes the person's intention to continue in a relationship and it predicts the focus on maximizing *dyadic* outcomes (as compared to maximizing self-benefits). Even in the case of dissatisfaction, the expectancy of equitable outcomes is not seen as a necessary precondition to continue mainly nonvoluntary kin relationships.

From the point of view of developmental psychology, personal relationships are of interest with respect to their implications for individual development (the unit of analysis usually being the individual). For example, the relationships of siblings and peers have been studied with regard to their impact on individual development in childhood and adolescence (e.g., social competence) (Dunn, 1999). Also, close relationships in adulthood have attracted increasing interest. Laursen and Bukowski (1997) differentiate among various types of close relationships on the basis of permanence, power, and gender. More recently, Lang and Fingerman (2004) have suggested a developmental approach to relationships. However, all these approaches have so far ignored the cultural context; furthermore, it is unclear whether they are useful in explaining parent–child relationships over the lifespan.

## Theoretical Approaches to Parent–Child Relationships

Before parent–child relationships became a topic in developmental research, most studies focused either on the behavior or on the beliefs of parents and their children. A change of this focus has been based on the observation that individual development starts in the context of parent–child interactions. Only later, parenting and parent–child interactions were seen as not only influenced by the parents' behavior and goals but also by the child's activity thus assuming bidirectionality in the interaction of parents and children (Grusec & Goodnow, 1994; Kuczynski, 2003). However, bidirectionality in interaction still cannot account for the quality of the parent–child relationship.

### From Parenting to Parent–Child Interactions and Parent–Child Relationships.

Research on parenting has long attempted to differentiate between various styles of *parental behavior* in order to account for individual differences in parenting and its effects on child development. Lewin's (1951) work on leadership styles (authoritarian, democratic, laissez-faire) has partly influenced research on "dimensions" of parenting (parental acceptance, firm control, psychological control, parental warmth and control, acceptance and rejection, warmth, demandingness, and responsiveness; e.g., Rohner, 1976; Steinberg, 1990). It was debated whether parenting should be studied by disaggregating the complex parenting dimensions (e.g., Barber, 1996), or by aggregating parenting styles into composite scores in order to assess the influence of parenting on child development. *Authoritative* (as compared to authoritarian and laissez-faire) parenting, a combination of warmth and control, was recognized as the optimal parenting style (Baumrind, 1967, 1991). Inasmuch as parental behavior could not explain the effects of parenting on child and adolescent development, studies on *parental beliefs* (Sigel, 1985) gave further insight into the complex issue of parenting.

At present, the child's active role in parenting has been recognized. The child's needs and competence are important elements in the process of successful parenting, including the way in which the child experiences the parents' behavior. Social cognitive learning theory has pointed to the active involvement of the child, including the child's perception and choice of the parents' behavior as a model for his or her own behavior, and the child's motivation to imitate this behavior (Bandura, 1986). Accordingly, children are viewed as "active producers" of their development, who are adapting to their environments (Lewis, 1997). This view of the active child has been expanded by Grusec and Goodnow's (1994) theory of socialization, which integrates social learning theory and cognitive, motivational, and affective factors to explain the child's imitation and internalization. At the same time, the activity of the parents is taken into account. The authors assume two basic prerequisites for the child's imitation and internalization: clarity in parents' communication and the child's acceptance of the parents' message.

In this line of reasoning, ecological developmental theories view parents and children as (phylogenetically advanced), self-constructing organisms in an environment that regulates (coregulates) complex developmental processes (Bradley & Corwyn, 1999; Ford & Lerner, 1992). Here, genetic and contextual influences and interactive effects are recognized.

The focus on the active participation of children in the process of parenting (Bell, 1979; Lerner & Busch-Rossnagel, 1981) has shifted the attention to further aspects of development such as parent–child interactions and relationships. Instead of assuming direct effects from parents on the development of their children, indirect effects and the mutual influences between parents and their offspring are studied (Grusec, 2002; Kuczynski, 2003). Although the focus of past research in parenting was either on the child or on the parents but rarely on both, the view on *bidirectionality* has opened the perspective for the role of parent–child interactions and moreover on their relationship in development. Studies on *interactions* make it necessary to shift the perspective to the child's activity, taking into account both parents' and their child's beliefs and behavior and the mutual effects in *interaction processes* over time (Bell, 1979; Bornstein, 1991). These interactions are the basis for shared experiences in the past and for expected outcomes in the future thus constituting core elements of personal relationships.

The study on relationships with the focus on both parent and child therefore includes the past interactions and their expected outcomes for need fulfillment. The role of parent–child relationships for development has been suggested by attachment theory (Bowlby, 1969). From an evolutionary point of view, the infant's biological needs of survival and security and the caretaker's need to ensure the offspring's survival affects the infant–caretaker's attachment relationship and individual differences in attachment. This approach predicts further individual development on the basis of early mother–child relationships (Thompson, 1999; Van IJzendoorn & Sagi, 1999). It takes into account both the behavior of parents and children as well as the subjective representation of the relationship in terms of an "internalized working model." Thus, attachment theory differs significantly from behaviorists' attempts to study parent–child relationships in terms of "objective" criteria such as frequency of interactions, time spent with each other, ecological distance from each other, and the like.

Parent–child relationships have been described as being based on stability and power (Laursen & Bukowski, 1997), as obligatory (Maccoby, 1999), and vertical in structure due to the hierarchical and authoritative interactions. However, these studies describe parent–child relationships in childhood and adolescence. A developmental model of parent–child relationships has to take into account stabilities and changes in the relationship system, its preconditions, and its functions for both the parents and the children. A simple developmental view of parent–child relationships over the lifespan assumes that the parent–child relationship is initially hierarchically structured, and organized around the satisfaction of the child's basic needs (usually in accordance with the parents' goals); during further development, the child's dependency on the parent diminishes, and more symmetric relationships based on bidirectionality arise that may change again later in development when aging parents become dependent on their children.

Parent–child relationships thus can be conceptualized as lifelong, biologically constituted personal relationships that are based on interconnected experiences in the past and the expectation of interconnected experiences in the future. They constitute the most extended relationships even if their quality may change over the life course. Like many other social relationships, parent–child relationships provide resources for individual development while they may also imply constraints for each other's need fulfillment. Also, they are only partially voluntary and start from an asymmetric distribution of resources. Depending on the personalities involved, the given developmental stage, and the context, parent–child relationships imply a wide variety of individual differences and of variations over time.

## LIFESPAN APPROACHES TO PARENT–CHILD RELATIONSHIPS

Theoretical approaches to lifespan individual development have centered on developmental tasks and normative life events (Havighurst, 1972); on life stages, transitions, and crises (Erikson, 1959); on continuity and change of biological, cognitive, emotional, motivational, and social domains of the person; and on optimization and selection in multidimensional development (Baltes & Baltes, 1990). To what extent these concepts may also be valid for a lifespan perspective on parent–child relationships after childhood and adolescence has not yet been investigated systematically. Studies of parent–child relationships usually lack a lifespan perspective. Specifically, the developmental period of adulthood has largely been ignored and the focus has been on the period of childhood and adolescence. Little is known of the development and of individual differences of parent–child relationships over the life course.

The preference for specific developmental stages is connected to certain research interests: studies of the relationships of young parents and their infants or children usually focus on the implications of parent–child relationships for the individual (child or adolescent) development (Bugental & Goodnow, 2000; Collins, Maccoby, Steinberg, Hetherington, & Bornstein, 2000; Maccoby, 2000). In contrast, studies of parent–child relationships in later adulthood are more likely to focus on family life (e.g., Rossi & Rossi, 1990), and on caregiving by adult children for their old aged parents (Cooney, 1997; Zarit & Eggebeen, 2002). Life course theories have pointed out early that parent–child relationships underline the importance of development after childhood and adolescence, emphasizing previous socialization experiences as factors influencing intergenerational (e.g., parent–child, grandparent–grandchild) relationships. Furthermore, studies on "linked lives" of family members over the life course take into account the socioeconomic and historical contexts (e.g., Elder, 1998). In the following section, a brief overview of studies from Western countries on parent–child relationships over the lifespan is given.

### Parent–Child Relationships in Childhood and Adolescence.

From a developmental psychological perspective, individual differences in parent–child relationships can be seen as a result of individual development. In a similar way, one can assume differences over the lifespan due to effects of different developmental tasks. Western studies of parent–child relationships in childhood often take the view that the child is dependent on the parents even when children are more or less actively influencing their parents' behavior. At the same time, the parents are viewed as pursuing the goal of establishing their children's independence. Thus, to begin with, the parent–child relationship is asymmetric in character inasmuch as it is based on differences in resources to cope with environmental and developmental demands. Gradually, over time, formerly asymmetric parent–child relationships are transformed (e.g., through negotiations between parents and their children in the pursuit of individual need fulfillment). In line with this Western approach, the developmental task of adolescence is to establish a unique identity distinct from parents in order to achieve autonomy. Emotional, attitudinal, conflictual, and functional independence are described as core elements for the process of separation and individuation that are regarded as the relevant conditions for achieving identity.

Recent studies argue that both autonomy and relatedness to the parents is a more appropriate description for parent–child relationships in this developmental period: by the rebalancing of individuality and connectedness individuated relationships can develop. Thus, the connection to the parents is considered relevant for the individuation process (Cooper, Grotevant, & Condon, 1983). Accordingly, adolescent individuation is seen as associated with developing parent–child relationships. In recent Western theories, the development of autonomy is seen as associated to relatedness (Rothbaum & Trommsdorff, in press). However, the focus of Western approaches on autonomy, achieved identity, and independence in adolescence often tends to disregard the reciprocal nature of the parent–child relationship. In this process, the parents themselves have to undergo certain developmental changes, for example, from their role of caretaker to the role of a facilitator of their child's development (Cooney, 1997). Thus, a lifespan approach underlines the bidirectionality in the parent–child relationship.

## Parent–Child Relationships in Adulthood and Old

**Age.** A lifespan approach assumes that parent–child relationships are part of individual development over the lifespan. The question arising from the previous discussion is whether parent–child relationships during childhood and adolescence can be characterized rather by interdependence, and whether beyond childhood and adolescence independence prevails.

Young adulthood has been described by processes of negotiation between parents and their offspring with respect to independence in their relationship. These negotiations include issues of specifying privacy and boundaries between the generations in order to reduce conflicts (Cooney, 1997). Parent–child relationships in middle adulthood are usually characterized by the adult offspring having their own children ("the sandwich generation"). Neugarten (1968) conceives of midlife development as involving an increasing responsibility of the adult role in the extended family. This developmental task changes the quality of the parent–child relationship on the basis of a third separation-individuation process with increasingly "realistic" awareness of the (independent and interdependent) self in relation to the parents. A further change of parent–child relationships over the lifespan is generated when the adult parents are growing older, retire from work, or take on the role of grandparents (by taking care, providing support and advice for the grandchildren; cf. Szinovacz, 1998). When parents grow older they may experience increasing frailty and related physical, psychological, and cognitive dependency.

These kinds of changes may turn into a stressful transition for adult children and their aging parents, inducing challenges for their relationship. The transition between midlife and old age thus can be characterized by the personal needs of the aging parents for filial care. According to Blenkner (1965) this gives rise to a new developmental task of achieving "filial maturity." Marcoen (1995) assumes that the amount and quality of filial care is based on filial love and closeness; these again are assumed to be influenced by the early childhood experience of attachment and a sense of filial obligation. Further influential factors are seen in filial autonomy, parental consideration (degree of reciprocity between the caregiver and the receiver of care), and family solidarity (collaboration among siblings and family members). Some of these concepts underlie the influential model of family solidarity proposed by Bengtson (e.g., Rossi & Rossi, 1990). The authors explain family solidarity on the basis of intergenerational family structure and associational, affectional, consensual, functional, and normative solidarity. Their model appears to downplay conflict and negotiation, and instead focuses on interdependence and similarity between parents and children in adulthood.

## Parent–Child Relationships Over the Lifespan in

**Changing Context.** Parent–child relationships develop within a wider family system, and they are affected by the wider socioeconomic and cultural context (e.g., Schaie & Willis, 1995). A contextualized view of human development thus takes into account socioeconomic, political, and historical changes and their effects on the development of individual persons and on relationships in the family (Cooney & Uhlenberg, 1992; Elder, 1998). Life course studies of intergenerational relations in changing contexts have demonstrated how parent–child relationships are affected by contextual changes (e.g., Elder, 1998). Empirical studies provide insight into risk and buffering factors for the development of family members as they interact in a context of linked lives that are affected by the wider socioeconomic and cultural context (cf. Trommsdorff, 2000, 2001a, 2002).

A contextual view on parent–child relationships over the lifespan seems especially relevant in times of ongoing dramatic socioeconomic and demographic change that is related to increasing longevity (and a gender gap in life expectancy), decreasing fertility, increasing postponement of first childbirth, decreasing family stability, and increasing diversity of family structure (due to divorce, single-parent family, second or third marriage, or changing gender relations). Thus a central question is whether and how intergenerational relationships will be affected by such changes.

Examples of the impact of social and economic change on intergenerational relationships include changes in vertical or horizontal economic transfers and investments (Kohli, in press), changes in relationship quality (exchanges, support, emotional closeness, solidarity between the generations, patterns of intergenerational assistance, or systems of family elder care), the continuity or discontinuity of intergenerational relationships over time, similarities and differences between the generations with respect to values, and mutual perceptions between generations, intergenerational solidarity and support, including grandparents and grandchildren (e.g., Bengtson & Robertson, 1985; Cooney, 1997; King & Elder, 1997; Zarit & Eggebeen, 2002).

To summarize, a lifespan perspective on parent–child relationships in context allows for perspectives on development and change. However, any such lifespan perspective is incomplete unless the impact of context and culture is considered. Developmental research is on the way to discover the study of relationships (e.g., Lang & Fingerman, 2004). However, this research is confined mainly to Western countries. It is therefore unclear whether the results from these studies are applicable to the understanding of parent–child relationships in other parts of the world. Before a "relationship science" (Reis, 1998) can be established, further research that takes into account cultural contexts is needed. The question addressed in the present chapter, therefore, is how parent–child relationships can be characterized as part of the individual development over the life course in cultural contexts.

## PARENT–CHILD RELATIONSHIPS IN CULTURAL CONTEXT

### Culture-Informed Empirical Studies on Parent–Child Relations

Most studies of parent–child relationships are confined to the context of the Western (North American and European) world. This is surprising because early anthropological studies have demonstrated a wide variety of parenting, parents' roles, and parent–child relationships. In addition to universal goals of parenting with respect to fulfilling the basic needs of the newborn child, parental beliefs of what constitutes the characteristics of a competent child and how this can be promoted vary considerably, thus affecting the quality of the parent–child relationship.

Parent–child relationships are the biologically based universal starting point for all further development. A closer look at parent–child relationships in different parts of the world demonstrates inter- and intracultural variations. This contradicts certain axiomatic assumptions in Western research on the nature of parent–child relationships, for example, the assumption of face-to-face interactions between infants and parents, of a partner-like equality of infant and parents, of the infant–adult dyad as the main unit of social interaction, or of infant–adult interaction as a goal in itself (cf. Valsiner, 1989). During the last two decades, systematic cross-cultural and culture-psychological research on parenting and child development has provided empirical data on universalities and culture-specificities pointing to the role of cultural factors for parent–child relationships.

To give an example, mothers from different cultures do not react to the child's primary needs in the same way (Bornstein, Toda, Azuma, Tamis LeMonda, & Ogino, 1990; LeVine et al., 1994). Maternal responsivity to the child's needs can have a very different meaning in various cultures: more physical proximity by African and more verbal input (talking) by U.S. mothers (Richman, Miller, & LeVine, 1992). Infant carrying, which may also serve as an index of responsiveness, may partly depend on subsistence organization (hunting, gathering) and/or climate (Whiting & Whiting, 1975; Harkness & Super, 2002). In the case of the child's signaling stress, Japanese mothers focus the attention of their child more onto themselves whereas German mothers tend to focus their child's attention onto objects (e.g., Friedlmeier & Trommsdorff 1998; Trommsdorff & Friedlmeier, 1993; Trommsdorff & Kornadt, 2003). Also, Japanese mothers react even before the child signals distress (proactive sensitivity) whereas the German mothers only react after their child demonstrates distress (Friedlmeier & Trommsdorff, 2004; see also Hess, Kashiwagi, Azuma, Price, & Dickson, 1980, for comparisons between Japanese and North American mothers). Both interaction strategies are qualitatively different; but each strategy is successful in its respective context in that the child is calmed. The mothers' behavior differs in accord with relevant cultural values (e.g., of how to display emotions) and the respective parental goal of establishing a qualitatively positive relationship to the child.

Cross-cultural studies show that the "same" parenting may have different meanings in different cultures; and different parenting may have the same meaning in different cultures (Trommsdorff & Kornadt, 2003). For example, harsh punishment of children is seen as harmful for child development in Western cultures; however, it is positively valued in traditional Chinese families (Stevenson, Chen, & Lee, 1992; Stevenson & Zusho, 2002). The same parenting behavior and goals (e.g., psychological control) may have different functions in different cultural contexts thus underlining the cultural specificity of parent–child relations (e.g., Chao & Tseng, 2002; Miller, 2003; Rothbaum & Trommsdorff, in press). Our own studies of adolescents from different cultures have shown that Japanese as compared with German youth felt rejected by their parents when experiencing low parental control (Trommsdorff, 1985). Japanese youth experience parental control as part of a positive and warm relationship (Trommsdorff, 1995). Similar results of Koreans living in North America and Koreans in the Republic of Korea have been reported by Rohner and Pettengill (1985). Thus, conclusions about negative effects of parental control on children and adolescents cannot be generalized across cultures. In several East Asian (Japan) and Southeast Asian (Indonesian) as compared with Western (German) cultures, adolescents report more parental control and at the same time less conflict and more harmony in the parent–child relationship (Trommsdorff, 1995). Thus, bidirectionality in parent–child relationships can have different characteristics and functions in different cultures (e.g., in relation to the cultural norms for developmental tasks) (cf. Trommsdorff & Kornadt, 2003). The psychological meaning of parenting and parent–child interactions can be explained in reference to the experienced and expected parent–child relationship in the given cultural context.

A typical example is an interaction sequence between a mother and a child in the case of conflicting goals (resulting in "misconduct" of the child) in a Japanese and a German dyad. Usually this interaction sequence ends with the Japanese mother giving in whereas a conflict prevails in the German dyads (Trommsdorff & Kornadt, 2003). This different behavior occurs because of culture-specific parent–child relationships that have evolved in the course of past development, and which are based on certain culture-specific beliefs and values. In Japan, the value of interdependence and maintaining harmonious relationships prevails, whereas in Germany the value of independence dominates. On the basis of this generalized cultural value of an optimal parent–child relationship, the interaction between mother and child in the case of the child's misbehavior evolves in very different ways depending on different beliefs and attributions. The Japanese mother interprets her child's behavior as immature and as indicating an inability to follow the rules; the German mother assumes that her child is testing the power structure. The Japanese mother believes that her model of "giving in" herself makes the child aware of the necessity of (sometimes) giving up one's own goals in order to reduce conflict and maintain harmony; accordingly, her child learns to act in accordance with the culturally valued goal of fostering a harmonious relationship. In contrast, the German mother believes that the child must obey her orders and accept her authority even though (at the same time) she wants her child to become independent. Thus, the conflict in German dyads continues or even escalates.

These studies of Japanese and German mother–child interactions clarify the different *cultural meaning of parent–child relationships* in the process of social development. Japanese mother–child dyads are characterized by harmonizing conflicting needs whereas German dyads engage in escalation of conflict. In accordance with this culture-specific relationship quality, the mother's and the child's behavior significantly differ in regulating the conflict and the final interaction outcome. These typical interaction sequences affect further social and emotional development. Children learn different ways to handle conflicts in line with the prevailing cultural values, and they develop different social motivations; for example, there is less aggression in Japan than in Germany (Kornadt, Hayashi, Tachibana, Trommsdorff, & Yamauchi, 1992; Kornadt & Trommsdorff, 1990; Trommsdorff & Kornadt, 2003). The cultural differences in Japanese and German mothers' values, beliefs, intentions, and behaviors provide the basis for differences in the quality of the parent–child relationship and related further development.

Therefore, the question of what constitutes a "good" parent–child relationship is related to the question of "successful" parenting, "successful" development, and "social functioning." In order to answer these questions empirically it is necessary to study the culture-specific meaning of these concepts. The qualities and the effects of parent–child relationships must therefore be studied in the context of specific cultures, taking into account the cultural values, parental beliefs, child-rearing goals, ethnotheories, behavior, and parent–child interactions.

Studies of the parent–child relations in adolescence in different cultures also point out a large variability (e.g., Chao & Tseng, 2002; LeVine et al., 1994; Rothbaum, Pott, Azuma, Miyake, & Weisz, 2000; Trommsdorff & Kornadt 2003; Whiting & Whiting, 1975). Many culture-informed studies directly or indirectly question the assumption that striving for autonomy and independence is the most relevant task in adolescence, with autonomy indicating maturity and affecting the symmetrical quality of parent–child relations. In many non-Western cultures, maturity is achieved when the children are able and willing to fulfill their roles and responsibilities in the hierarchical structure of the family. This responsibility may consist of taking care of younger siblings and/or aging parents. Even when maturity in this sense is achieved, parent–child relationships are not characterized by autonomy of the children but instead by interdependence of both, parents and their children.

The few cross-cultural studies dealing with relations between adult children and their old parents demonstrate considerable variety (e.g., Lin et al., 2003). Some anthropological studies on the relations over three generations, including grandparents, show considerable diversity among various cultures including the gender-specific role of parent–child relations in adulthood. For example, early studies of grandparents' relationships with grandchildren by Radcliffe-Brown (1940) describe these as relaxed ("joking relationship") in contrast to the more tense relations between parents and their children. This has been attributed to the more marginal position of grandparents and children and the related special affinity of members of alternate (as opposed to adjacent) generations who may view each other as natural allies against the middle generation of powerful and privileged parents. In other societies, the grandparent generation retains authority and power over the parents also after the grandchildren are born. The relationship of grandchildren with either their maternal or their paternal grandparents differs according to the larger cultural and kinship context.

To summarize, cross-cultural studies demonstrate the heterogeneity of parent–child relationships in different age groups, revealing similarity and variability across cultures. However, systematic comparative, lifespan, cross-cultural studies have been rare. A culture-informed, lifespan approach to a parent–child relationship has to specify which factors influence the quality of the relationship and its continuities and changes. Therefore, a theoretical framework to explain the culture-specific qualities of parent–child relationships over the lifespan in different cultures is needed.

## THEORETICAL APPROACHES ON PARENT–CHILD RELATIONS OVER THE LIFESPAN IN CULTURAL CONTEXT

### Culture and Development: A General Theoretical Framework

The culture-informed study of parent–child relationships over the lifespan as suggested herein is partly indebted to ecocultural theories (e.g., Whiting & Whiting, 1975) that take into account the constraints and resources of the proximate and distal contexts and place a special focus on cultural values (Hofstede, 2001; Schwartz, 1994; Schwartz & Sagi, 2000; Triandis, 1995). Accordingly, it is assumed that individual development is embedded in interconnected levels of society, often described as the micro-, meso-, exo-, and macrosystems (Bronfenbrenner, 1979). Therefore, descriptions of the ecological and cultural context (Segall, Dasen, Berry, & Poortinga, 1999; Trommsdorff & Dasen, 2001), and the specific cultural values and related self-construals (Markus & Kitayama, 1991) are needed. The culture-informed perspective is also indebted to the theoretical approach of the developmental niche by Harkness and Super (2002) (also see Harkness & Super, Chapter 3, this volume), who assume that individual development takes place in three subsystems: the physical and social settings of the child's daily life, the culturally regulated customs of child-rearing, and the psychology of the caretakers, which are interconnected and embedded in the larger ecology.

A culture-informed theory on parent–child relationships must first of all take into account the culture-specific meanings of behavioral indicators. One example is the culture-informed modification of attachment theory by Rothbaum, Weisz, Pott, Miyake, and Morelli (2000); the authors have questioned the universality of the concepts underlying attachment theory (e.g., caretaker sensitivity). Another example is the study on culture-specificities of bidirectionality in parent–child relationships (Trommsdorff & Kornadt, 2003). The Western view is usually confined to assuming interpersonal negotiations between parents and their children on the basis of relatively independent positions. However, in many traditional and also modern (e.g., East Asian) cultures, parents' and children's roles are embedded in a hierarchical structure; the level and function of these roles prescribe certain behavior as part of interdependent relationships (Chao & Tseng, 2002; Trommsdorff & Kornadt, 2003).

### Elements of a Culture-Informed Approach to Parent–Child Relations Over the Life Course

A culture-informed theory on parent–child relationships over the lifespan investigates both (a) the factors affecting the parent–child relationship, and

(b) the functions of parent–child relationships. The first issue pertains to factors that affect the quality of the relationship in the various life stages, from childhood to old age. These factors may be life-stage-specific, such as the biological dependence of the infant on the parents, or the instrumental dependence of the aged parents on their adult children. These factors may also depend on the personalities of the interacting partners, on the situational and wider socioeconomic context, and the relevant cultural values. The second issue pertains to the effects of parent–child relationships on various outcomes. Both issues take into account universal and culture-specific factors and relationships.

What predictions can be derived for parent–child relationships on the basis of Western and of culture-informed theories? To give an example of Western theorizing, parent–child relationships are based on striving for autonomy and independence; negotiation between "independent" partners prevails and conflicts have to be dealt with. During adolescence, exchanges between adolescent children and their parents become increasingly voluntary. At the same time, peer relationships gain in importance and become the basis to renegotiate relationships with parents. Thereby, increasing independence and the need for autonomy emerge as new elements of the parent–child relationships (Laursen & Bukowski, 1997).

Rusbult and Ariaga (1997) offer a different theoretical perspective. They assume that the fulfillment of basic social needs such as trust and commitment ensures the prosocial quality and persistence of the parent–child relationship. Trust emerges as a consequence of observing the altruistic prosocial behavior of the partner and as part of the belief that the partner intends to promote one's well-being independently of the partner's self-interest. Trust reduces the perceived risk of reciprocating benevolence and departing from self-interest. According to this theory, the quality of parent–child relationships over the lifespan can increase. A precondition, however, is the child's belief (trust) in the altruistic benevolence of the parents. Whether this belief is established depends on the subjective experience of the parent–child relationship.

From the perspective of non-Western cultures, both predictions miss the essential preconditions to explain parent–child relationships over the lifespan: the fundamental belief in assurance that gives rise to a pathway of interdependent parent–child relationships over the lifespan, beyond childhood and adolescence. The explicit focus on autonomy, independence, and trust in close relationships can be seen as a bias in Western theorizing. Rothbaum, Pott et al. (2000) and Rothbaum and Trommsdorff (in press), in line with Yamagishi (Yamagishi, Cook, & Watabe, 1998), argue that trust provides the typical basis for (close) relationships in individualistic, Western cultural contexts where independence and autonomy prevail, whereas assurance provides the basis for close relationships in non-Western cultural contexts where interdependence and relatedness prevail. The question therefore arises whether the above-mentioned theoretical approaches are invalid in non-Western contexts.

### A Culture-Informed Psychological Framing of Parent–Child Relationships Over the LifeSpan

How can cultural differences be interpreted in an integrating culture-informed theoretical framework on parent–child relationships? From a culture-informed point of view, it is essential to understand whether observed behavior patterns are intended to establish and stabilize interdependent relationships based on cooperation and harmony, or whether they are intended to develop independent relationships including conflicts and negotiations of power (see also Rothbaum, Pott et al., 2000). Thus, it would appear important to examine the self-construal, intentions, goals, and related values of parents and their children. These intentions and self-construals may rather focus on independence or on interdependence (cf. Markus & Kitayama, 1991). It is assumed here that the parent–child relationships are the basis for the development of such culture-specific self-construals and values as part of the socialization process.

**Independence and Interdependence as Basic Values.** The relations between values and parent–child relationships can be seen on various levels: cultural values can influence and regulate parent–child relationships over the lifespan; parent–child relationships can influence development and changes of value orientation in the child and in the parents, and thus can affect the transmission of values to the next generation, thereby affecting the cultural value system (Trommsdorff, in press). Thus, value orientations can be seen as input and output variables but also as moderators affecting the quality of the parent–child relationship. Accordingly, values can be studied on various levels: on one level, value orientations are represented in cultural meaning systems, rituals, and artifacts; on another level, individual value orientations have an impact on belief systems, goals, intentions, and individual behavior. Such research profits when taking into account both the level of culture and the level of the individual person (Matsumoto, 1999; Triandis, 1995; Trommsdorff & Friedlmeier, in press).

Cultures and individuals differ with respect to shared values and beliefs in regard to the role of the person in the family and society. In certain cultures, the person tends to experience himself or herself as rather separate from others (independence); in other cultures the person experiences himself or herself as interconnected, especially with members of the family and the in-group (interdependence; Markus & Kitayama, 1991). In some cultures, a clear preference for independence and autonomy is highly valued, whereas in other cultures interdependence and relatedness are preferred. This distinction has proven useful for the explanation of cultural differences in the development of the self, of emotions, cognitions, interpersonal interactions, relationships (Fiske, Kitayama, Markus, & Nisbett, 1998; Greenfield, Keller, Fuligni, & Maynard, 2003; Trommsdorff & Dasen, 2001), and in family systems (Kagitcibasi, 1996). It seems fruitful to study interpersonal relations in general and parent–child relationships in particular as being influenced by these culture-specific values of independence and interdependence.

Several aspects of parent–child relationships are especially sensitive to cultural values. These include the value and the role of the family, the parents, the child, gender, and the elderly. Furthermore, these values are related to the role of the self, of interpersonal relationships in general and over the lifespan, and they include the value of parent–child relationships. Cultural values concerning the family thus influence parent–child relationships. In many traditional societies, the "family model of interdependence" is rather typical (Kagitcibasi, 1996). Here, the value of the family is strong; usually extended families prevail. A higher rate of coresidence of elderly parents with their adult children (at least one adult child) is observed in East Asia as compared with the West (Hareven, 1996). Ancestors are seen as part of present family life, and ancestor service is a duty of the family members. Parents and the elderly experience great respect; they are treated as authorities, and enjoy high status because they are believed to symbolize wisdom and authority. An example for traditional parent–child relationships according to Christianity and Judaism can be seen in the words, "Honor thy father and thy mother." Confucianism emphasizes filial piety and obedience toward the parents. In the traditional patriarchal Chinese family, children were expected to be obedient toward their parents (especially toward their father) throughout their lives. The child was traditionally regarded as the property of the parents. Accordingly, parents had the right to demand fulfillment of their wishes and to punish the child in the case of misbehavior. Although these beliefs are changing, parent–child relationships are still based on the mutual expectation of support: "Parents have the duty to rear and to educate their children; the children have the duty to support and assist their parents" (Stevenson et al., 1992, p. 25).

In many traditional but also modern East Asian societies, especially with the Confucian tradition, social status increases with increasing age. Even in Japan, the value of seniority is still predominant (The Research Committee on the Study of the Japanese National Character, 1997). The identity of the person is defined according to the person's status within the family. This can be reflected in the assignment of the name (the family name is put first; seniority and gender are specified). Cultural values also differ with respect to the role of women. In some traditional cultures, women are not considered to have full female status unless they are mothers and have given birth to a male child. Male children are often more highly valued and parents invest more in their upbringing because they take care of ancestor worship and their elderly parents (cf. Nauck & Suckow, 2003; Trommsdorff, Zheng, & Tardif, 2002). Family lineage is maintained through the son in many traditional patrilineal family systems (for traditional China see Stevenson et al., 1992).

In most industrialized modern societies, family systems vary in structure and stability. Emphasis is placed on the importance of the individual and his or her development as an independent, self-directed person. Children are valued for emotional reasons rather than for socioeconomic reasons (Trommsdorff et al., 2002). Gender differences are rather discounted, women are supposed to have a career of their own, they do not have to marry, and they can decide whether to have children, and to live alone or together with the father of their children.

Whether these changes in family systems imply changes to a "family model of independence" (Kagitcibasi, 1996), is an empirical question. Kagitcibasi (1996) suggests a third model for societies in transition from traditional to modern systems: the "family model of emotional interdependence."

The model of interdependence is characterized by extended families, high fertility, high economic value of children (especially of sons), high loyalty and family orientation, authoritarian parenting, and economic support of parents through children. This model is widely known in the traditional rural areas of the "Majority World." The model of independence, which is more typical for industrialized Western societies, is characterized by a nuclear family structure, low fertility, high status of the women, low preference for sons, high emotional value and high financial costs of children, permissive parenting, transfer of financial resources from parents to children, and low solidarity in the family. The model of emotional interdependence is characterized by changing family structure and value orientations as can be observed in societies in transition. The economic value of children and the economic dependence between parents and children decrease; instead an emotional interdependence rises, authoritarian parenting is more pronounced, and a combination of autonomy and interdependence can be found.

Thus, the cultural value of the family characterizes the quality of the parent–child relationships which can be seen as part of the cultural value of independence and interdependence. It can be assumed that values of independence allow for more flexible and unstable family and parent–child relations. In contrast, values of interdependence foster family orientations and obligations; here the individual is embedded in a tightly knit social network of duties including the mutual support between parents and children. The cultural values of independence and interdependence underlie many aspects of human development, interpersonal relations, and parent–child relations in particular.

**Developmental Paths in Close Relationships.** Starting from cultural differences in parent–child and adult mate relationships, Rothbaum, Pott et al. (2000) have suggested a culture-specific model of the development of close relationships. These authors combine their observations of cultural differences in conflicts and struggles as part of close relationships, starting with parent–child relationships. Relationships are described as being based on needs for separation or closeness, for independence or interdependence, for autonomy or relatedness. Furthermore, the authors assume that conflicting tendencies to follow self-oriented versus other-oriented goals are typical patterns of cultural differences in close relationships. Rothbaum, Pott et al. (2000) describe typical developmental paths to close relationships by focusing on the United States and Japan by describing cultural differences in the meaning and dynamics of close relationships. The authors view the biological predispositions for relatedness as "passing through cultural lenses," for example, cultural values that emphasize interdependence and accommodation or independence and individuation. These different cultural lenses affect the development of close relationships. Accordingly, they identify two prototypes: the "symbiotic harmony" that can be seen in the Japanese mother–child relationship, based on the mother's indulgence and the child's *amae* (dependence on the mother; see Azuma, 1986; Doi, 1973). In contrast, the prototype of "generative tension" is described as typical for the mother–child relationship in the United States (see the assumption in attachment theory on separation and proximity seeking). Starting from these descriptions, Rothbaum, Pott et al. (2000, pp. 1123ff) suggest the following changes in the development of parent–child relations over the lifespan:

1. Infancy: the opposing processes of separation and *reunion* versus self-other *union*.
2. Childhood: the prioritizing of personal preferences in relationships and resulting conflicts between self and partner versus adherence to obligations and to others' expectations. 3. Adolescence: *transferability* of attachment from parents to peers leading to increased distance from parents versus stability of relationships with both parents and peer. 4. Adulthood: a trust (hope and faith) in relationships which, ironically, "helps people out of committed relationships" and into new ones versus *assurance* about relationships—a role-based, socially supported sense of commitment.

Empirical evidence for the development of parent–child relationships along these two pathways demonstrates that in Japan as compared with the United States, more interdependence and less independence is established in parent–child relationships in childhood. In adolescence, stable filial piety is the basis for parent–child relations in Japan whereas conflicting relations and transfer of close relations from parents to peers is typical in the United States (cf. Rothbaum, Pott et al., 2000). Although the authors focus on parent–child relationships in childhood and adolescence, one may adapt their model of culture-specific different pathways to later life stages of parent–child relationships. In line with Greenfield et al. (2003), in a Western cultural context, parent–child relationships are based on independence where partnership, acceptance of conflicts, and negotiations of individual interests are highly valued. In contrast, in East Asian cultures, parent–child relationships are based on interdependence where children's obedience, filial piety, their compliance with the parents' wishes, and their lifelong duties and obligations in honor of the parents are highly valued. Parent–child relationships based on interdependence are characterized by harmony, cooperation, and importantly, the obligation and motivation to reciprocate.

To summarize, according to the pathway of "symbiotic harmony," parent–child relationships are characterized by maintaining interdependence; this goal is achieved by fulfilling one's duties and obligations, and meeting the other person's expectations. In contrast, parent–child relationships that are based on "generative tension" pursue the goal to establish and maintain independence and the fulfillment of individual goals. Thus, different relationship qualities are assumed to characterize parent–child relationships over the life course in different cultures.

## Culture-Specific Meaning of Relatedness and Autonomy.
A further culture-specific difference in basic values underlying parent–child relationships may be described by the concept of *assurance* versus *trust* (Yamagishi, Cook, & Watabe, 1998). In cultures based on the need for assurance, close kin networks and an incentive structure for members of the

in-group build up a sense of obligation, unconditional loyalty, and filial piety; in contrast, in security-based cultures that are characterized by changing in-groups and weak group ties, and subjective hope and faith in commitment (in the absence of assurance), the establishment of contracts or intimacy serves as the basis for relationships. These different types of relationships can be characterized by *different meaning* and *dynamics of relatedness* (Rothbaum & Trommsdorff, in press).

From this point of view, influential Western theories have to be modified. The often-used description of parent–child relationships as developing primarily around autonomy, and the assumption of autonomy as being fostered by relatedness, seem to be biased. Empirical data from anthropological and cross-cultural studies contradict the assumption of a universality of primacy of autonomy in development. Several studies on adolescence in the United States have pointed out that the combination of both autonomy and relatedness are necessary bases for the relationship between adolescents and their parents (Grotevant & Cooper, 1986; Youniss & Smollar, 1985). Along the same lines but starting from a culture-informed perspective, Kagitcibasi (1996) has criticized the assumption that the dimension of autonomy is characterized by two opposite poles, autonomy and relatedness. Adolescents may strive for autonomy without, however, giving up relatedness with their parents.

However, the culture-specific perspective on autonomy and relatedness as suggested by Rothbaum and Trommsdorff (in press) suggests a different approach. According to a description of culture-specific meanings of relatedness, one has to take into account that in cultures where independence (autonomy) and security are highly valued, relatedness can correlate positively with autonomy. However, in cultures where interdependence and assurance are highly valued, autonomy undermines relatedness (although both can occur together in specific selected situations). Thus, the assumption of a universal balance between autonomy and relatedness in different cultures has to be questioned. Instead, Rothbaum and Trommsdorff (in press) suggest a different meaning of both, relatedness and autonomy, depending on the cultural context. The authors demonstrate that in the West, relatedness and autonomy can go together: for example, individuation depends on autonomy and relatedness. In East Asia, however, relatedness and autonomy are in conflict with each other: relatedness precludes autonomy. The respective cultural and situation context give a certain meaning to autonomy and relatedness: in the case of independence, both can go together; in the case of interdependence, relatedness undermines autonomy. Accordingly, relatedness and autonomy are part of parent–child relationships only in the respective cultural context with its specific developmental pathway. Thus, a culture-informed conceptualization of parent–child relationships is suggested here that specifies whether a combination of both autonomy and relatedness or the mutual exclusion is typical for the parent–child relationship.

The meaning of relatedness depends on the culture-specific context (Rothbaum & Trommsdorff, in press). Relatedness combined with autonomy can fulfill the need for security in the Western context; however, in non-Western cultures, (e.g., in East Asia) relatedness excluding autonomy can fulfill the need for assurance.

This different view on relatedness and autonomy may be illustrated in the following way. Security needs are basic in both cultural contexts; however, in the context of independent selves it makes more sense to negotiate security in order to come to an agreement on the kind of relationship where security needs can best be fulfilled. Because relationships are not necessarily stable, commitment is an important precondition for ensuring security. Whereas in a context within which socialization to interdependent selves takes place, assurance is the best way to ascertain fulfillment of security needs. This is provided in a cohesive and tightly knit group where clear rules direct one's behavior and where emotional connections and harmonious relations provide the basis for experiencing assurance. In the first-mentioned context of independence, relationships are based on trust, and the exchange of goods and services follows the principle of reciprocity. In contrast, in the interdependent context, relationships are based on assurance; accommodation to other persons' needs, and the obligation to fulfill these needs (beyond reciprocity norms) guides one's behavior. Assurance arises from the experience of being part of the in-group of interconnected persons sharing the same beliefs. Thus, a culture-informed theory on parent–child relationships over the lifespan should take into account these different values and meanings of relationships.

To summarize, the approaches presented here differ in some ways. Kagitcibasi (1996) focuses on models of family relations in different cultures and social change, whereas Rothbaum, Pott et al. (2000) and Rothbaum and Trommsdorff (in press) analyze the characteristics of parent–child relationships in different cultures. The latter approach seems especially promising for a culture-informed approach on life-course development of parent–child relationships. The authors go beyond the established Western approach that has assumed a balance between relatedness and autonomy; instead, they demonstrate that culture specificities in parent–child relationships can be better explained on the basis of different meanings given to autonomy and relatedness depending on the cultural value of independence or interdependence.

## VALUE OF CHILDREN AND INTERGENERATIONAL RELATIONSHIPS IN DIFFERENT CULTURES

In the following section, the goals, methods, and first results from an ongoing cross-cultural, lifespan study of parent–child relationships are described.

### Goals of the Study

The present study was conceived of as a contribution to the questions of whether, why, and how parent–child relationships are part of individual development over the lifespan, and whether this is a universal or culture-specific phenomenon. The main goal of our ongoing research is to test the culture-informed model of intergenerational relationships over the lifespan (Trommsdorff, 2001a, 2003) (see Figure 6.1). Thus, the focus is on the universal and culture-specific relationships among general and specific value orientations, the quality of

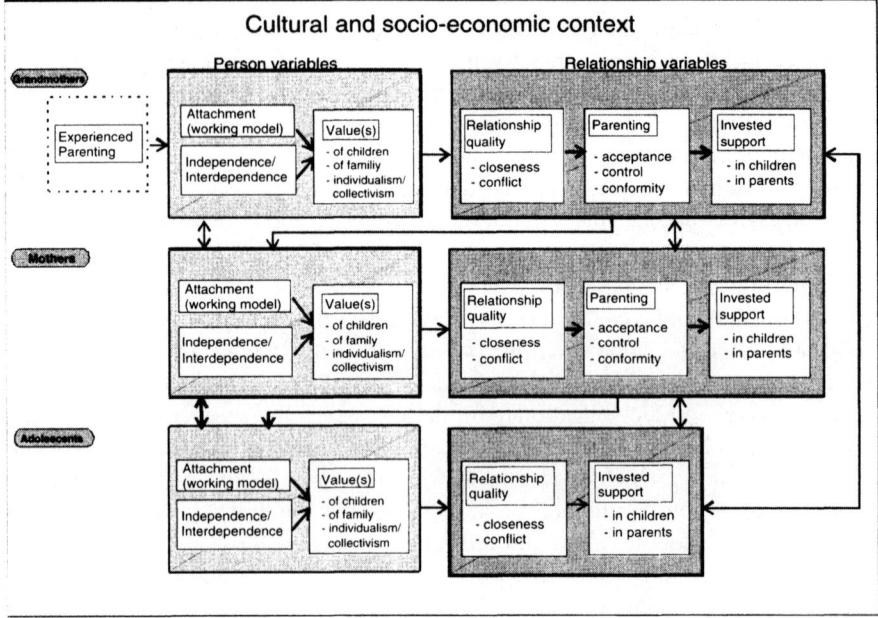

FIGURE 6.1

parent–child relationships, the intention to support one's parents and one's children, and the transmission of values to the next generation. The patterns of these relations are studied cross-culturally in order to specify the function of the cultural context (e.g., values, family systems) for parent–child relationships over the life course.

It is assumed here that the predominant sociocultural values influence the relationships between parents and their children over the lifespan and among more than one generation. These values give a culture-specific psychological meaning to the respective relationships and constitute the specific pathways in the development of parent–child relationships. The parent–child relationships are assumed to result from the past socialization experiences of parents and their children and the present value system (including general cultural values, e.g., independence or interdependence and, more specifically, the value of the child, of the parents, of family). According to the ecocultural and value-theoretical approach, it is assumed that parents transport the cultural values into the developmental niche of the child. Both parents and children are assumed to influence the parent–child relationship, and thereby affect their future development. The quality of the parent–child relationship is assumed to contribute to mutual trust or assurance, to the long-range goal of fostering the well-being of the other person, and to the experience and the effective transmission of shared values, interests, and activities (see Figure 6.1).

In order to test the culture-informed model of intergenerational relationships over the lifespan (Trommsdorff, 2001a, 2003) (see Figure 6.1), a multigeneration and a cross-cultural design is necessary (a longitudinal study would be optimal, of course). The main assumptions of this model are as follows. (A) Universalities: Parent–child relationships in different (biologically related) generations share certain similarities due to their developmental conditions and their functional properties. More specifically, the following universal relationships (independent of cultural context) are assumed: (1) Values and socialization experiences (including attachment) affect the quality of the parent–child relationship. (2) Parent–child relationships (a) function as a transmission belt between the generations (Trommsdorff, in press); and (b) influence the degree and kind of support given to the older and/or younger generations. (B) Culture Specificities: Parent–child relationships are affected by the cultural context and values; they function as a transmission belt for those values that are consistent with the cultural and the individual values. And the cultural context influences the extent and kind of support exchanged among the generations (reciprocity).

## Methods: Sample, Procedure, and Instruments

**Participating Countries.** The countries included in this study represent different economic, social, and political systems, and different aspects of individualistic and socially oriented cultural values: Republic of China, Germany (West and East), Indonesia, Israel, the Republic of Korea, and Turkey (see Table 6.1). More countries are presently being added to the study: France, India, Czechoslovakia, South Africa, and Ghana.

TABLE 6.1 Design of the VOC Main Study (Including the Three-Generation Sample)

|  | Republic of Korea | Indonesia | Republic of China | Turkey | Israel | Germany | Sum |
|---|---|---|---|---|---|---|---|
| Mothers of (2- to 3-year-old) Children | | | | | | | |
| Number | 300 | 300 | 300 | 300 | 300 (+100) | 300 | 1800 (+100) |
| Mothers of Adolescent (14- to 17-year-old) Children | | | | | | | |
| Number | 300 | 300 | 300 | 300 | 300 (+100) | 300 | 1800 (+100) |
| Adolescents | | | | | | | |
| Number | 300 | 300 | 300 | 300 | 300 (+100) | 300 | 1800 (+100) |
| Maternal Grandmothers | | | | | | | |
| Number | 300 | 300 | 300 | 300 | 300 (+100) | 300 | 1800 (+100) |
| Total Sample | | | | | | | |
| Sum | 1000 | 1000 | 1000 | 1000 | 1300 | 1000 | 6300 |

Three-generation study

*Note:* Further participating countries: Czech Republic, France, Ghana, India, Japan, South Africa.

## Design and Sample Size

The participants included approximately 300 adolescents and their biological mothers as well as approximately 100 grandmothers from these families (biological mothers of these mothers). Furthermore, a sample of 300 mothers with young children (target children not older than 5 years) was interviewed. This design allows for partial replication of the Value of Children (VOC) sample plus a study of social change and, furthermore, an extension to the study of intergenerational relations.

**Sample Description.** The samples include persons from urban and rural areas and persons from middle and low SES when possible. The adolescent participants were 14 to 17 years old (see Trommsdorff, 2001b; also see Table 6.1).

**Procedure and Instruments.** The data were collected in 2000 (pilot study) and 2002/3 (main study). Face-to-face structured interviews were carried out. Because the concepts needed to be operationalized with respect to culture-specific meanings, a pilot study was first carried out in five countries. The relevant constructs (including measures of value of children, family, socialization experience, attachment, relationship quality, and investment in old parents) were measured by instruments that were first tested with respect to reliability and validity.

To give a few examples of instruments that were tested in the pilot study and then used in the main study: the value of children was measured according to the instruments used in the original Value of Children Study (Arnold et al., 1975) by asking for advantages and disadvantages in having children (presenting a list of items that had to be evaluated on four-point scales). Value orientations were measured according to (a) the instrument of Singelis (1994), which was designed to measure the degree of independence/interdependence, and (b) collectivism/individualism was measured by the instrument of Schwartz (1994). The quality of the parent–child relationship was measured according to Furman and Buhrmester (1985, 1992). Support given to parents (in the pilot study) was measured, for example, by the answer to the question: "When your aging mother is in need: (a) would you become in debt in order to help her, or (b) would you give up your employment in order to help." Also, the participants were asked to indicate the reason for their decision in order to measure aspects of their motivation. The same set of core items was used in all three generations and also in the sample of the young mothers. Furthermore, some specific questions were added for specific samples (e.g., the adolescents' future orientation). (For more details on the main study and description of the participating countries see Trommsdorff & Nauck, 2004; for details on the instruments used see Schwarz, Chakkarath, Fecher, Mayer, & Trommsdorff, 2001).

## Selected Results

In the following section, some selected questions, analyses, and results are summarized in order to illustrate some steps for testing aspects of the culture-informed model of parent–child relationships over the lifespan. First, the role of values and of attachment for the quality of the relationship, and second, the function of parent–child relationships for (a) the transmission of values and for (b) the given support is discussed.

## (1) The Role of Values and of Attachment for Parent–Child Relationships

### Changing Value of Children: From Economic to Emotional Values.

Taking into account the massive changes in parent–child relationships occurring as a result of the ongoing socioeconomic and demographic changes, the question arises as to whether parent–child relationships are following the same developmental path in most parts of the world, or whether diverse culture-specific developmental pathways exist. In line with the above-mentioned ecocultural approach, it is assumed that the cultural context, including the economic and ecological situation, provides certain constraints and chances for the development of parent–child relationships.

For example, in subsistence societies and most traditional societies, children are responsible from an early age for contributions to the economic resources of their parents (and other family members). This obligation becomes even more pronounced in the course of development and constitutes the basis for the "economic value" of children. In contrast, in highly industrialized Western societies, adult children are not usually regarded as an economic resource for old parents, whereas the parents are held responsible for providing the resources so that their children can achieve economic independence (cf. Kagitcibasi, 1996). The socioeconomic and cultural context thus provides constraints and opportunities, including values and norms in which development and parent–child relationships take place.

Results from our pilot study have shown that the emotional value of children has increased in most countries during the period from 1970 to 2000, and at the same time the economic value of children decreased in importance (Trommsdorff et al., 2002). When comparing the two generations of mothers and grandmothers, we find that this value orientation is rather similar in industrialized countries in both generations (e.g., in Japan and Germany; Makoshi & Trommsdorff, 2002). In less industrialized countries (e.g., Turkey) economic values are still partially preferred (Nauck & Suckow, 2003). These results are in line with results from worldwide fertility surveys. Although in most countries the importance of the emotional value of children (VOC) is quite high (relative to other VOC), some intracultural differences occur (e.g., urban–rural differences and differences between the older and younger generations; cf. country reports in Trommsdorff & Nauck, 2004). For example, with respect to Old-Age-Security, VOC mothers of adolescent children reported higher values in East as compared to West Germany (Mayer & Trommsdorff, 2003, July).

The question presently being tested in the main study asks how far preferences and changes in the value of children affect the parent–child relationship over the lifespan in different cultures. Results from the German sample showed that mothers high in emotional VOC preferred independence as parental goals (Trommsdorff, Mayer, & Albert, 2004). Also, universal and culture-specific effects of the value of children on, parenting and the parent–child relations have been shown (Trommsdorff & Nauck, 2004).

## Adult Daughters' and Their Mothers' Perception of Relationship Quality: A Test of the "Intergenerational Stake Hypothesis."

The aim of this study was to analyze the quality of the relationships of adult daughters with their mothers in cultures that differ with respect to socioeconomic conditions and cultural values (Schwarz & Trommsdorff, 2004; Trommsdorff & Schwarz, 2003). We tested the general hypothesis that parents and their children systematically differ with respect to the perception of their relationship (Bengtson & Kuypers, 1971). According to the "intergenerational stake" thesis parents consistently report higher levels of closeness and harmony in the parent–child relationships as compared with their children. These differences have been explained as a result of different developmental concerns of each generation. Parents are assumed to be more interested in a stable continuation of positive relationships in the family, including continuity of values, and therefore overstate the positive aspects of their relationship with their children. In contrast, adolescent and adult children are assumed to achieve autonomy and become independent from their parents, thus feeling less commitment to the parent–child relationship and perceiving more negative aspects in their relationship to their parents. Furthermore, according to reciprocity assumptions, the parents' higher investment in the relationship should be balanced by a positive relationship quality (Giarusso, Stallings, & Bengtson, 1995). So far, the intergenerational stake hypothesis has not yet been tested in different cultures.

In our study, we assumed that the quality and the perception of parent–child relationships are influenced by culture-specific value orientations. In line with the "intergenerational stake" hypothesis, parent–child differences are expected in a context preferring independence and "generative tension" as compared with a context preferring interdependence and "symbiotic harmony." We assume that parents from cultures with high values of interdependence believe in their children's close relationship to parents; they do not worry much about possible risks and their stake in the relationship, and thus do not see a reason to overstate positive aspects of their relationship to their children.

Mothers and their adult daughters from Germany and Indonesia ($N = 400$; main study) participated in this study. German mothers reported greater intimacy and less conflict than their adult daughters, whereas the two generations within the Indonesian sample did not differ. In Indonesia an intergenerational difference occurred for emotional support: emotional support given by the mother was more frequently reported by mothers than by their adult daughters.

Intergenerational relations can be analyzed by mean differences. However, these means may be based on different patterns of relationship quality. Therefore, we carried out a cluster analysis including difference scores of the four indicators of relationship quality. The results revealed three clusters. Only one cluster (comprising 35 percent of the dyads) was consistent with the intergenerational stake hypothesis. A second cluster comprised 39 percent of the mother–daughter dyads and can be characterized as revealing the opposite pattern, in which daughters perceived the relationship more positively than the mothers. A third cluster comprised 26 percent of the dyads and was characterized by a tendency of the mothers toward less self-disclosure.

These analyses point out that the study of simple mean differences in intergenerational differences conceals complex patterns of mothers' and daughters' perspectives on the relationship. The patterns of results showed some culture-specific characteristics. We included value orientations in our further analyses in order to explain the cultural variations in intergenerational differences. As expected, Indonesian as compared with German mothers and their adult daughters favored values of interdependence and collectivism more and values of individualism less. The analyses revealed one significant effect of the mothers' value orientation: the higher the mothers' collectivism, the less likely the dyad was to belong to the cluster that was characterized by less maternal self-disclosure. Thus, the individual value orientations did not show strong correlations with the patterns of mother–daughter perspectives on the relationship.

Finally, it has to be discussed why the Intergenerational Stake Hypothesis was only confirmed in the respective cultures with respect to certain aspects: in the German sample with respect to intimacy and conflict and in Indonesian sample with respect to emotional support given by the mother. The items on intimacy in the parent–child relationship refer to the tendency of the participants to engage in self-disclosure (talk about personal experiences). Self-disclosure has often been described as more prevalent in individualistic than in collectivistic cultures. This communication style seems to be less acceptable in collectivistic cultures, in which hierarchical relationships and clear role definitions regulate interactions. Our results show that this pattern can be replicated for adult mother–child relationships in our Indonesian and German samples: less maternal self-disclosure is more typical among dyads with collectivistic mothers.

These results can be interpreted as supporting the assumption of cultural differences in parent–child relationships in adulthood. In line with the often-reported cultural value of harmony in the Javanese family, less conflict between Indonesian mothers and daughters occurred; here the dyads did not differ in their respective evaluations. Furthermore, filial piety and values of seniority foster the respect for the older generation; thus, the adult children experience relatively fewer conflicts with their parents. Our results show that Indonesian daughters report less conflict with their mothers than do German daughters. With regard to other aspects of the relationship such as the emotional support the mother has given to her daughter, the Indonesian mothers' reports turned out to be more positive than those of their daughters. This is in line with the cultural values of prosocial orientation to kin. To give support and help to the children is part of Javanese ethics (Magnis-Suseno, 1997).

When comparing samples with regard to values of interdependence and independence in such sociocultural contexts that are undergoing massive changes, one should take into account different patterns and combinations of these values in order to account for the differential function for coping with ongoing change and for the parent–child relationship. The culture-specific meaning of relatedness and autonomy in parent–child relations may undergo changes in times of transition.

### Attachment and the Relationship Between Adult Daughters (Mothers) and Their Mothers

(Grandmothers). It was assumed that socialization experiences affect parent–child relationships. Attachment (as a quasi-stable personality variable in the sense of a working model that has developed on the basis of early socialization experiences and parent–child relationship) was assumed to be related to the quality of the parent–child relationship over the lifespan. It was also assumed that any attachment style that does not coincide with the cultural norm (thus representing an individual deviation from the normal distribution) will be negatively related to parent–child relationships. Results from the pilot study showed that in the three cultures (Germany, Korea, and Japan) the ratings for the *secure* attachment were highest as compared with the other prototypes of attachment. In line with our expectations, the least preferred insecure attachment styles were significantly and negatively related with relationship quality. In the Korean and German sample, this negative relation occurred for preoccupied attachment, and in the Japanese sample it occurred for dismissive attachment. These results support the notion that early parent–child experiences underlying later attachment (working model) affect the way in which parent–child relationships develop over the lifespan.

### (2) The Role of Parent–Child Relationships in the Intergenerational Transmission

### Intergenerational Transmission of Values and

Attitudes. The transmission of values from parents to their children can be seen as a result of a positive parent–child relationship (Grusec & Goodnow, 1994). Cultural values and socioeconomic changes may affect the transmission of values between the generations, and also the parent–child relationship over the lifespan. In accordance with the model of Kagitcibasi (1996) and the model of culture-specific developmental paths (Rothbaum, Pott et al., 2000), we assume that in countries where values of interdependence are high, the transmission of value orientations from parents to their children will be stronger than in modern individualistic societies. Similarities in values of parents and their children have often been used as an indicator of successful transmission of values (for a critical discussion of the validity see Trommsdorff, in press). It was assumed that in societies undergoing a transition to modernity, the older generation prefers traditional values more than the younger generation. Here, only selective transmission of values was expected. Also, a value change may be indicated by intergenerational differences in value orientation.

In one study, we tested intergenerational differences and similarities with respect to parental goals. *Developmental timetables* (the preferred age levels for when children should show a certain behavioral competence) were used as indicators for values. Tests of value similarities between mothers and their biological mothers (grandmothers) in the German, Korean, and Indonesian samples (pilot study; Schwarz, Chakkarath, & Trommsdorff, 2002) showed differences only between the Korean and the German mothers' and grandmothers' expectations, and not for the Indonesian dyads. These results support our hypotheses that disagreements between the grandmother and mother generation are less pronounced in a traditional interdependent culture. In line with this reasoning, we also tested similarities in developmental goals among German mothers and grandmothers (main study). Again, differences between the two generations occurred in the expected direction: developmental goals of obedience were more preferred and goals of independence were less preferred by grandmothers as compared to mothers (Trommsdorff et al., 2004).

In addition to the testing of mean differences in value orientations, the comparison of value structures (e.g., by latent class analysis) can indicate whether and in which way generations differ. In a country undergoing significant socioeconomic and cultural change, the Czech Republic, we found that grandmothers belonged to a group (profile) with high values on all VOC dimensions but none of their adult daughters (mothers of adolescent children) belonged to this group; these adult daughters were represented in a group in which only the emotional value of children was high (Mayer & Trommsdorff, 2003, September). Whether these differences indicate effects of value changes or of individual development is a question that cannot be answered by these analyses.

In a further study on a German sample (main study) of mothers and their adolescent children (Albert & Trommsdorff, 2003, August) we focused on the question of whether intergenerational similarities and differences in value orientations are related to the parent–child relationships (see Figure 6.1). We tested the extent of transmission of values (general and domain-specific values such as individualism/collectivism, value of family, and interdependence), and the moderating effect of the parent–child relationship quality. As suggested in our model of intergenerational relations over the lifespan, the relationship quality between mothers and adolescents should influence the extent of transmission. According to Grusec and Goodnow (1994) the internalization of values follows two steps: the accurate perception of a value and its acceptance. Accordingly, it was assumed here that intimacy in the relationship and perceived acceptance ("admiration") enhances communication between adolescents and their mothers and thereby increases the accurate perception of maternal values and the acceptance of maternal values. In contrast, conflict between adolescents and their mothers increases the communication about values (Knafo & Schwartz, 2003) but at the same time reduces the accuracy of perception and the acceptance.

The results showed that all four value orientations of the adolescents were predicted by the value orientations of mothers. The prediction of individualism, however, was relatively weak, indicating a rather selective transmission of values. At the same time, mean values of mothers and adolescents on all scales differed;

this indicates relative as opposed to absolute transmission. Apart from that, intimacy and admiration turned out to be transmission belts for values of collectivism and the value of the family, but not for individualism and interdependence. Conflict had no moderating effect on value transmission. Furthermore, all aspects of relationship quality had direct effects on the value orientations of the adolescents. These results support the notion that relationship quality has an important impact on the development of value orientations of adolescents beyond its role as a moderator. Thus, relationship quality can be seen as an important transmission belt (Trommsdorff, in press).

### Intergenerational Transmission of Relationship Quality.

Can parent–child relationships also function as a transmission belt for the relationship quality in the nonadjacent generations? Intergenerational relations do not only consist of parent–child relations, but also of relations of nonadjacent generations such as grandparents and grandchildren. These extend the parent–child relationship over the life course to the next generation. The relationship between grandparents and grandchildren is becoming more and more important as a consequence of demographic changes; increasing life expectancy increases the probability of experiencing grandparenthood and the duration of grandparent–grandchild relations. Our aim here was to analyze in the German sample (main study) aspects of the relationship quality of grandchildren to their maternal grandmothers with respect to patterns of intergenerational relationships (Albert & Trommsdorff, 2004, July). The most important result was that the relationship quality between the mother and the grandmother (her own mother) had an important impact on the relationship quality between adolescents and their grandmothers. All aspects of relationship quality between grandchildren and grandmothers could be predicted by the relationship quality between mothers and grandmothers. This underlines that a transmission of relationship quality can occur between nonadjacent generations. Further analyses will show if these results can be replicated in other cultures, and whether universal or culture-specific patterns can be observed in the relationship among more than two generations of one family.

### Intergenerational Relationship and Support.

Further analyses dealt with the question of parent–child relationships over the lifespan in different cultures, taking into account behavioral aspects and functions of intergenerational relations. In several studies, an important role of parent–child relationships has been seen in the exchange of support between the generations (e.g., "intergenerational solidarity," Bengtson, Giarusso, Marby, & Silverstein, 2002). However, the model of intergenerational solidarity has rarely been tested cross-culturally.

### Giving Support to Parents.

In a study comparing German and Japanese adult parent–child dyads (Albert & Trommsdorff, 2003, September; Trommsdorff, 2003), we examined factors influencing intended support for old parents. The underlying theoretical question was: is the adult children's support for their aged parents based on past socialization experience or on the present emotional qualities of the relationship to the parents? The sample (pilot study) consisted of Japanese and German mothers and grandmothers.

First, cultural similarities and differences with respect to the intended support for old parents were analyzed. The results showed cultural differences in support between German and Japanese adult daughters regarding the variable "willingness to become in debt to help parents," but not in the variable "taking frail mother in one's own house and partly giving up employment." German adult daughters were more willing than their Japanese counterparts to go into debt in order to help parents. Second, we studied the relation between adult daughters' socialization experiences and their intended support for their parents. Both German and Japanese adult daughters showed more intended support for their mothers when they had experienced more sensitivity on the part of their mothers in their earlier development. Third, we studied the relation between mother–daughter relationship quality and intended support for the old mother. The results showed that the quality of the present emotional mother–daughter relationship as reported by Japanese and German adult daughters was related to their intended support for their old mothers. However, for German as compared to Japanese adult daughters, their emotional relation to their mother was significantly more related to the degree of intended support (investment by taking frail mother in one's own house and partly giving up employment). These results demonstrate the culture-specific effect of emotional relationship quality and its culture-specific function for investment in old parents. Fourth, we examined the relation between family interdependence and intended support. The analyses showed significant correlations between family interdependence and intended support for old mothers only in the German sample of adult daughters.

Fifth, in accordance with attachment theory, we assumed that secure attachment of adult daughters was related to higher support for their old parents. As a matter of fact, in the Japanese sample, secure attachment was correlated positively with intergenerational investment. This did not occur for the German sample. In order to test the hypothesis on the culture-specific effects of the relationship quality and attachment, stepwise regression analyses were carried out. Indeed, culture-specific effects of these two variables on the investment in aged mothers occurred. Japanese and German adult daughters invested in their old parents on the basis of different factors: Adult daughters' experience of their mothers' sensitivity in socialization predicted the Japanese adult daughters' intended support, and the present emotional relation between adult daughters and their mothers as well as family interdependence of the adult daughter predicted the German adult daughters' intended support of their aging mothers. For both samples, the adult daughters' experience of their mothers' sensitivity in socialization was related to support; however, for the German sample, this relation was mediated by the present emotional mother–daughter relation (see Figure 6.2).

Sixth, we examined the willingness to provide support the other way around, from aged mothers to their adult daughters. The results showed that Japanese mothers' willingness to help their adult daughters was related to their secure attachment, whereas for German mothers it was related to their emotional

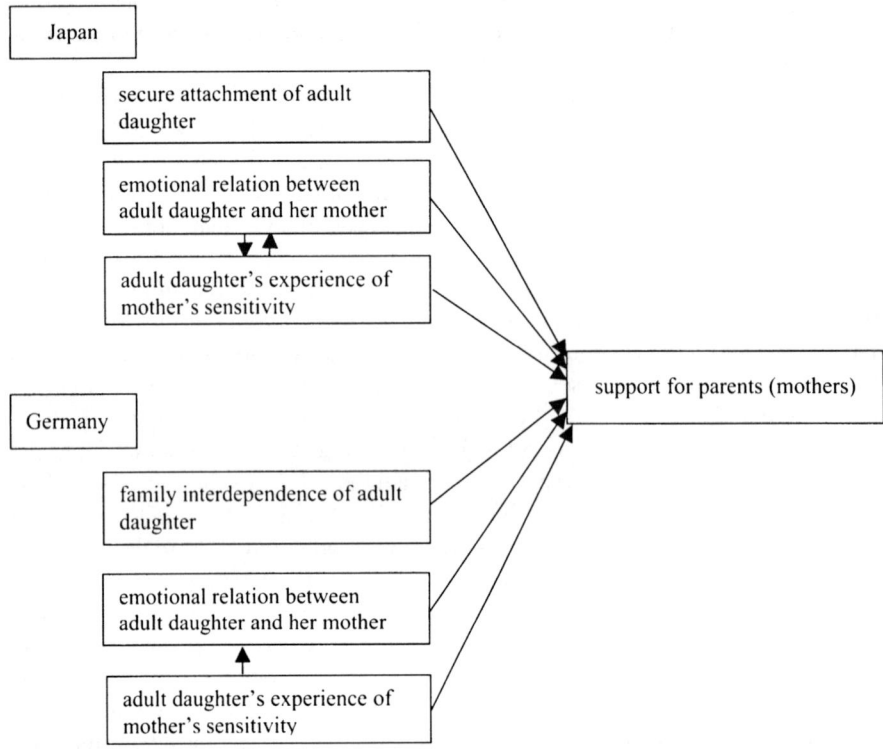

FIGURE 6.2

relationship quality with their daughters. These results underlined our assumption that there are cultural differences in the function of attachment and relationship quality for intended support.

To summarize, our results showed significant differences between adult daughters in Japan and Germany with respect to support of parents as a function of intergenerational relationships. The willingness to support the older parents was influenced by culture, socialization, attachment, aspects of the relationship quality, and family interdependence. For the Japanese adult daughters (and their mothers) secure attachment was relevant, and for the German adult daughters (and their mothers) high quality of their relationship with their own mother was most predictive of their intention to support their old parents. For German adult daughters family interdependence was also related to intended support. For German and for Japanese adult daughters, the remembered experience of their mothers' sensitivity in the past was influential for the willingness to support the old mother, but in the German sample the intention to support was mediated by the present emotional mother–daughter relation.

These results can be interpreted within the theoretical framework of Rothbaum, Pott et al. (2000) where cultural differences in parent–child relationships are described as "symbiotic harmony" as compared to "generative tension"; the results are also in line with the notion of the cultural meaning of relatedness by Rothbaum and Trommsdorff (in press). For the German dyads, a positive quality (based on emotional warmth) has to be achieved in order to give support; in an individualistic context characterized by generative tension, parent–child relationships are negotiated and vary with respect to its quality. In Japan, however, the quality of the relationship is assured, and relatedness is part of the interdependent and symbiotic harmony; therefore, the relationship quality does not significantly contribute to (and mediate) support. However, in the Japanese case, the individual attachment security of adult daughters and especially their experience of their mothers' sensitivity in the past are influential for the prediction of their support for their mothers. Although the relationship is assured, these are individual experiences that affect individual behavior. Parent–child relationships obviously entail culture-specificities that are organized around basic values of security and assurance and which affect the meaning of relatedness.

**Reciprocity in Support.**   In further analyses we studied the role of reciprocity in parent–child relationships over the life course in different cultures, assuming that reciprocity may have a different meaning in different cultures and therefore affect the exchange of support between the generations differently. A recent study on German adult daughters and their mothers shows that perceived reciprocity is associated with the intergenerational exchange of support; imbalance in support has negative effects on the quality of the adult parent–child relationship (Schwarz, Trommsdorff, Albert, & Mayer, 2004). These results are very much in line with Western theories assuming a close association between reciprocity and quality of relationship. The next question therefore is whether these results can be replicated in non-Western cultural contexts. First results from the pilot study (Schwarz, Trommsdorff, & Chakkarath, in press) showed that cultural differences occurred with respect to the effect of reciprocity (in regard to past experience of help and support by adult daughters/mothers) on the relationship quality: Indonesian adult daughters who gave more than they received from their mothers evaluated the relationship to their mother as more positive than other cultural samples. In the main study on adult daughters' and their mothers' relationships and exchange of support we further investigated the associations among reciprocity of support and the quality of the relationship comparing samples from South Korea, Republic of China, and Germany. The associations were positive in East Asian samples, however, German adult daughters evaluated their relationship with their mothers more negatively when they felt they had received less. Here, a Western conceptualization of reciprocity as a balanced exchange among independent partners seems to prevail whereas the East Asian samples rather perceive of giving support to the parents as part of a lifelong interdependency. This interpretation is supported by the result that the value of interdependence is associated with the degree of emotional and instrumental support which adult daughters give to their parents (Schwarz, Trommsdorff, Kim, & Park, 2004).

These results are in line with the traditional value of "filial piety" in East Asia and Indonesia, and the children's lifelong obligation to take care of their parents' well-being. Even though this value may be undergoing certain changes in a country like Korea, which is in a process of transition to modernity, it remains to be empirically tested whether the value of filial piety is declining (Ho, 1994), or whether it is changing its meaning in the process of other changes. A promising approach seems to specify the psychological aspects of this concept and to differentiate "reciprocal" and "authoritarian" filial piety (Yeh & Bedford, 2003).

So far, the above-mentioned results clearly demonstrate a different cultural meaning of "reciprocity" (in Germany as compared to East Asian countries) as is suggested by the model of cultural pathways (Rothbaum, Pott et al., 2000) and by Rothbaum and Trommsdorff (in press) who assume that a primacy of relatedness undermines autonomy. In the case of assurance and the primacy of relatedness, calculations of a balanced exchange of individual input and output do not meet the requirement as a valid indicator of reciprocity and the quality of the relationship. When the cultural context is characterized by interdependence and relatedness, the quality of the parent–child relationship is rather characterized by symbiotic harmony, filial obligation, and lifelong assurance. Therefore, an imbalance of parent–child relationships with respect to (given or received) support does not induce dissatisfaction and frustration. On the contrary, because parents have given so much in the past, the child can never really pay back and create a balance. Embedded in a relationship of interdependence and harmony, the child's lifelong loyalty to the parents is more than simply a duty to honor the parents' investment; this kind of parent–child relationship does not allow for compensation and balance except for adult children's investing in the next generation. Therefore, the Western concept of reciprocity in terms of a balanced exchange does not necessarily hold for non-Western countries. This underlines the necessity of culture-informed theorizing on parent–child relationships.

## SUMMARY AND CONCLUSIONS

The empirical results presented here are based on our first analysis of the data from the cross-national study on "Value of Children and Intergenerational Relationships" (VOC), which focuses on parent–child relationships over three generations. Further analyses are needed to better understand cultural differences as well as similarities in intergenerational relationships. In order to explain parent–child relationship quality over the life course, contextual and person variables will be taken into account; on this basis, the question is dealt with in how far individual value orientations and the quality of the parent–child relationship will be transmitted to the next generation.

Major socioeconomic environmental and demographic changes have recently pointed to the need to better understand the quality and function of intergenerational relationships. Parents and their children share about five decades as adults; they are mutually connected by a relationship that may impose constraints and resources and may change according to the respective developmental tasks, and personal and contextual factors. Furthermore, the study of parent–child relationships over the lifespan is important for its contribution to improved theorizing on relationships and development in cultural context.

The present study on "Value of Children and Intergenerational Relationships" attempts to analyze the effects of cultural context and individual values on parent–child relationships and their function for the transmission of values. First data analyses underline the role of value orientations and the socialization experiences for parent–child relations in different generations and cultural contexts. Also, the role of parent–child relationships for the transmission of values and for support given to parents differs according to the cultural context. These studies may be seen as a first approach to the empirical testing of the theoretical notion of culture-specific developmental paths for parent–child relationships over the lifespan, contrasting symbiotic harmony and generative tension (Rothbaum, Pott et al., 2000) and taking into account the culture-specific value of relatedness (Rothbaum & Trommsdorff, in press) for parent–child relationships. This may allow a better understanding of the development of parent–child relationships over the lifespan in the different cultural contexts and in processes of sociocultural change. According to Rothbaum and Trommsdorff (in press), for non-Western countries, values of assurance affect interpersonal relationships including the meaning of relatedness and reciprocity. Thus, reciprocity as a characteristic of a relationship is not necessarily a universal value based on rules of a balanced exchange of resources among independent persons. This perspective is valid in cultures based on security and where a positive association between autonomy and relatedness prevails. However, reciprocity may have a different meaning in cultures based on assurance and where a negative association between relatedness and autonomy prevails. In these cultures, the meaning of reciprocity can be associated with the unquestioned obligation (or even subjective need) to invest in the other person's (parents or children) well-being for the sake of maintaining the interdependent bonds of the in-group or the bonds of the parent–child relationship.

Whether the relations among parents and children from different generations will follow a different developmental path in the course of sociocultural change in different cultures needs to be investigated in future research. It is assumed that environmental changes will influence intergenerational relations while at the same time intergenerational relations will affect the cultural context and social change on the basis of transmission processes. Although the related demographic changes presumably constitute the most urgent global environmental problems, developmental psychology has to face the task of engaging in testing theories that may contribute to both a "science of culture and parenting" (Bornstein, 2001) and a "science of development and relationships in culture."

## NOTES

The study on "Value of Children and Intergenerational Relations in Six Cultures" is supported by grants from the Deutsche Forschungsgemeinschaft (DFG) (Tr 169/4-1,2,3) (Principal investigators: Gisela Trommsdorff, University of Konstanz and Bernhard Nauck, Technical University of Chemnitz). I am grateful to Beate Schwarz, Isabelle Albert, and Boris Mayer (all University of Konstanz) who are collaborating the psychological part of this project.

# REFERENCES

Albert, I., & Trommsdorff, G. (2003, August). *Intergenerational transmission of family values*. Poster presented at the XIth European Conference on Developmental Psychology in Milan, Italy.

Albert, I., & Trommsdorff, G. (2003, September). *Gegenseitige Unterstützung zwischen Müttern und ihren erwachsenen Töchtern im Zusammenhang mit Bindung und Beziehung: Ein deutsch-japanischer Vergleich* [Reciprocal support between mothers and their adult daughters in connection with attachment and relationship: A German-Japanese comparison]. Poster auf der 16. Tagung der Fachgruppe Entwicklungspsychologie der Deutschen Gesellschaft für Psychologie, Mainz, Germany.

Albert, I., & Trommsdorff, G. (2004, July). *Aspects of the relationship quality between adolescents and their maternal grandmothers*. Poster for the 18th Biennial Meeting of the International Society for the Study of Behavioural Development (ISSBD), Ghent, Belgium.

Arnold, F., Bulatao, R. A., Buripakdi, C., Chung, B. J., Fawcett, J. T., Iritani, T., Lee, S. J., & Wu, T. S. (1975). *The value of children: Vol. 1. Introduction and comparative analysis*. Honolulu: East-West Population Institute.

Azuma, H. (1986). Why study child development in Japan? In H. W. Stevenson, H. Azuma, & K. Hakuta (Eds.), *Child development and education in Japan* (pp. 3–12). New York: Freeman.

Baltes, P. B., & Baltes, M. M. (1990). Psychological perspectives on successful aging: The model of selective optimization with compensation. In P. B. Baltes & M. M. Baltes (Eds.), *Successful aging: Perspectives from the behavioral sciences* (pp. 1–34). Cambridge, MA: Cambridge University Press.

Bandura, A. (1986). *Social foundations of thought and action: A social cognitive theory*. Upper Saddle River, NJ: Prentice-Hall.

Barber, B. K. (1996). Parental psychological control: Revisiting a neglected construct. *Child Development, 67*, 3296–3319.

Baumrind, D. (1967). Child care practices anteceding three patterns of preschool behavior. *Genetic Psychology Monographs, 75*, 43–88.

Baumrind, D. (1991). Effective parenting during the early adolescent transition. In P. A. Cowan & E. M. Hetherington (Eds.), *Family transitions: Advances in family research series* (pp. 111–163). Hillsdale, NJ: Erlbaum.

Bell, R. Q. (1979). Parent, child, and reciprocal influences. *American Psychologist, 34*, 821–826.

Bengtson, V. L., Giarrusso, R., Marby, J. B., & Silverstein, M. (2002). Solidarity, conflict, and ambivalence: Complementary or competing perspectives on intergenerational relationships? *Journal of Marriage and Family, 64*, 568–576.

Bengtson, V. L., & Kuypers, J. A. (1971). Generational difference and the developmental stake. *Aging & Human Development, 2*, 249–260.

Bengtson, V. L., & Robertson, J. F. (Eds.). (1985). *Grandparenthood*. Beverly Hills, CA: Sage.

Blenkner, M. (1965). Social work and family relationships in later life with some thoughts on filial maturity. In E. Shanas & G. F. Streib (Eds.), *Social structure and the family: Generational relations* (pp. 46–59). Englewood Cliffs, NJ: Prentice-Hall.

Bornstein, M. H. (Ed.). (1991). *Cultural approaches to parenting*. Hillsdale, NJ: Erlbaum.

Bornstein, M. H. (2001). Some questions for a science of "culture and parenting" (…but certainly not all). *International Society for the Study of Behavioural Development Newsletter, 1*, 1–4.

Bornstein, M. H., Toda, S., Azuma, H., Tamis-LeMonda, C. S., & Ogino, M. (1990). Mother and infant activity and interaction in Japan and in the United States: II. A comparative microanalysis of naturalistic exchanges focused on the organisation of infant attention. *International Journal of Behavioral Development, 13*, 289–308.

Bowlby, J. (1969). *Attachment and loss: Vol. 1. Attachment*. New York: Basic.

Bradley, R. H., & Corwyn, R. F. (1999). Parenting. In L. Balter & C. S. Tamis-LeMonda (Eds.), *Child psychology: A handbook of contemporary issues* (pp. 339–362). Philadelphia: Psychology Press/Taylor & Francis.

Bronfenbrenner, U. (1979). *The ecology of human development: Experiments by nature and design*. Cambridge, MA: Harvard University Press.

Bugental, D. B., & Goodnow, J. J. (2000). Socialization processes. In W. Damon & N. Eisenberg (Eds.), *Handbook of child psychology: Vol. 3. Social, emotional, and personality development* (5th ed., pp. 389–463). New York: Wiley.

Chao, R., & Tseng, V. (2002). Parenting of Asians. In M. H. Bornstein (Ed.), *Handbook of parenting: Vol. 4. Social conditions and applied parenting* (2nd ed., pp. 59–93). Mahwah, NJ: Erlbaum.

Collins, W. A., Maccoby, E. E., Steinberg, L., Hetherington, E. M., & Bornstein, M. H. (2000). Contemporary research on parenting: The case for nature and nurture. *American Psychologist, 55*, 218–232.

Cooney, T. M. (1997). Parent-child relations across adulthood. In S. Duck (Ed.), *Handbook of personal relationships* (2nd ed., pp. 451–468). Chichester, UK: Wiley.

Cooney, T. M., & Uhlenberg, P. (1992). Support from parents over the life course: The adult child's perspective. *Social Forces, 71*, 63–84.

Cooper, C. R., Grotevant, H. D., & Condon, S. M. (1983). Individuality and connectedness in the family as a context for adolescent identity formation and role-taking skill. *New Directions for Child Development, 22*, 43–59.

Doi, T. (1973). *The anatomy of dependence*. Tokyo: Kodansha.

Duck, S. (Ed.). (1997). *Handbook of personal relationships: Theory, research, and interventions* (2nd ed.). Chichester, UK: Wiley.

Dunn, J. (1999). Siblings, friends, and the development of social understanding. In W. A. Collins & B. Laursen (Eds.), *Relationships as developmental contexts. The Minnesota symposia on child psychology* (Vol. 30, pp. 263–279). Mahwah, NJ: Erlbaum.

Elder, G. H., Jr. (1998). The life course as developmental theory. *Child Development, 69*, 1–12.

Erikson, E. H. (1959). *Identity and the life cycle*. New York: International University Press.

Fiske, A. P., Kitayama, S., Markus, H. R., & Nisbett, R. E. (1998). The cultural matrix of social psychology. In D. T. Gilbert, S. T. Fiske, & G. Lindzey (Eds.), *The handbook of social psychology* (4th ed., Vol. 2, pp. 915–981). Boston: McGraw-Hill.

Ford, D. H., & Lerner, R. M. (1992). *Developmental systems theory: An integrative approach*. Thousand Oaks, CA: Sage.

Friedlmeier, W., & Trommsdorff, G. (1998). Japanese and German mother–child interactions in early childhood. In G. Trommsdorff, W. Friedlmeier, & H.-J. Kornadt (Eds.), *Japan in transition. Sociological and psychological aspects* (pp. 217–230). Lengerich, Germany: Pabst Science.

Friedlmeier, W., & Trommsdorff, G. (2004). *Children's negative emotional reactions and maternal sensitivity in Japan and Germany*. Manuscript submitted for publication.

Furman, W., & Buhrmester, D. (1985). Children's perceptions of the personal relationships in their social networks. *Developmental Psychology, 21*, 1016–1024.

Furman, W., & Buhrmester, D. (1992). Age and sex differences in perceptions of networks of personal relationships. *Child Development, 63*, 103–115.

Giarrusso, R., Stallings, M., & Bengtson, V. L. (1995). The "intergenerational stake" hypothesis revisited: Parent–child differences in perceptions of relationships 20 years later. In V. L. Bengtson, W. K. Schaie, & L. M. Burton (Eds.), *Adult intergenerational relations: Effects of societal changes* (pp. 229–296). New York: Springer.

Greenfield, P. M., Keller, H., Fuligni, A. J., & Maynard, A. (2003). Cultural pathways through universal development. *Annual Review of Psychology, 54*, 461–490.

Grotevant, H. D., & Cooper, C. R. (1986). Individuation in family relationships: A perspective on individual differences in the development of identity and role-taking skill in adolescence. *Human Development, 29*, 82–100.

Grusec, J. E. (2002). Parenting and the socialization of values. In M. Bornstein (Ed.), *Handbook of parenting* (pp. 143–168). Mahwah, NJ: Erlbaum.

Grusec, J. E., & Goodnow, J. J. (1994). Impact of parental discipline methods on the child's internalization of values: A reconceptualization of current points of view. *Developmental Psychology, 30*, 4–19.

Hareven, T. K. (1996). *Aging and generational relations over the life course: A historical and cross-cultural perspective*. Berlin, Gemany: Aldine de Gruyter.

Harkness, S., & Super, C. M. (2002). Culture and parenting. In M. H. Bornstein (Ed.), *Handbook of parenting: Vol. 2. Biology and ecology of parenting* (2nd ed., pp. 253–280). Mahwah, NJ: Erlbaum.

Havighurst, R. J. (1972). *Developmental tasks and education*. New York: MacKay.

Hess, R. D., Kashiwagi, K., Azuma, H., Price, G. G., & Dickson, W. P. (1980). Maternal expectations for mastery of developmental tasks in Japan and the United States. *International Journal of Psychology, 15*, 259–271.

Ho, D. Y.-F. (1994). Filial piety, authoritarian moralism, and cognitive conservatism in Chinese societies. *Genetic, Social, & General Psychology Monographs, 120*, 347–365.

Hofstede, G. H. (2001). *Culture's consequences: Comparing values, behaviors, institutions and organizations across nations* (2nd ed.). Thousand Oaks, CA: Sage.

Kagitcibasi, C. (1996). *Family and human development across cultures: A view from the other side*. Mahwah, NJ: Erlbaum.

Kelley, H. H., & Thibaut, J. W. (1978). *Interpersonal relations. A theory of interdependence*. New York: Wiley.

King, V., & Elder, G. H. J. (1997). The legacy of grandparenting: Childhood experiences with grandparents and current involvement with grandchildren. *Journal of Marriage & Family, 59*, 848.

Knafo, A., & Schwartz, S. H. (2003). Parenting and adolescents' accuracy in perceiving parental values. *Child Development, 74*, 595–611.

Kohli, M. (in press). Intergenerational transfers and inheritance: A comparative view. In M. Silverstein, R. Giarrusso, & V. L. Bengtson (Eds.), Intergenerational relations across time and place [Special Issue]. *Annual Review of Gerontology and Geriatrics*.

Kornadt, H.-J., Hayashi, T., Tachibana, Y., Trommsdorff, G., & Yamauchi, H. (1992). Aggressiveness and its developmental conditions in five cultures. In S. Iwawaki, Y. Kashima, & K. Leung (Eds.), *Innovations in cross-cultural psychology* (pp. 250–268). Amsterdam: Swets & Zeitlinger.

Kornadt, H.-J., & Trommsdorff, G. (1990). Naive Erziehungstheorien japanischer Mütter: Deutsch-japanischer Kulturvergleich [Japanese mothers' naive child-rearing theories: A cross-cultural comparison between Japan and Germany]. *Zeitschrift für Sozialisationsforschung und Erziehungssoziologie, 10*, 357–376.

Kuczynski, L. (Ed.). (2003). *Handbook of dynamics in parent-child relations*. London: Sage.

Lang, F. R., & Fingerman, K. L. (Eds.). (2004). *Growing together: Personal relationships across the lifespan*. New York: Cambridge University Press.

Laursen, B., & Bukowski, W. M. (1997). A developmental guide to the organization of close relationships. *International Journal of Behavioral Development, 21*, 747–770.

Lerner, R. M., & Busch-Rossnagel, N. A. (1981). Individuals as producers of their development: Conceptual and empirical bases. In R. M. Lerner & N. A. Busch-Rossnagel (Eds.), *Individuals as producers of their development* (pp. 1–36). New York: Academic.

LeVine, R. A., Dixon, S., LeVine, S., Richman, A., Leiderman, P. H., Keefer, C. H., & Brazelton, T. B. (1994). *Child care and culture: Lessons from Africa*. New York: Cambridge University Press.

Lewin, K. (1951). *Field theory in social science: Selected theoretical papers*. New York: Harper & Row.

Lewis, M. (1997). *Altering fate: Why the past does not predict the future*. New York: Guilford.

Lin, I.-F., Goldman, N., Weinstein, M., Lin, Y.-H., Gorrindo, T., & Seeman, T. (2003). Gender differences in adult children's support of their parents in Taiwan. *Journal of Marriage & Family, 65*, 184–200.

Maccoby, E. E. (1999). The uniqueness of the parent–child relationship. In W. A. Collins & B. Laursen (Eds.), *Relationships as developmental contexts: The Minnesota Symposia on Child Psychology* (pp. 157–175). Mahwah, NJ: Erlbaum.

Maccoby, E. E. (2000). Parenting and its effects on children: On reading and misreading behavior genetics. *Annual Review of Psychology, 51*, 1–27.

Magnis-Suseno, F. (1997). *Javanese ethics and world view. The Javanese idea of the good life*. Jakarta, Indonesia: Gramedia Pustaka Utama.

Makoshi, N., & Trommsdorff, G. (2002). Value of children and mother–child relationships in Japan: Comparison with Germany. In U. Teichler & G. Trommsdorff (Eds.), *Challenges of the 21st century in Japan and Germany* (pp. 109–124). Lengerich, Germany: Pabst Science.

Mannheim, K. (1952 [1928]). *The problem of generations. Essays in the Sociology of Knowledge*. London: Routledge and Kegan Paul.

Marcoen, A. (1995). Filial maturity of middle-aged adult children in the context of parent care: Model and measures. *Journal of Adult Development, 2*, 125–136.

Markus, H. R., & Kitayama, S. (1991). Culture and the self: Implications for cognition, emotion, and motivation. *Psychological Review, 98*, 224–253.

Matsumoto, D. (1999). Culture and self: An empirical assessment of Markus and Kitayama's theory of independent and interdependent self construal. *Asian Journal of Social Psychology, 2*, 289–310.

Mayer, B., & Trommsdorff, G. (2003, July). *Child-related value structures of East- and West-German mothers*. Paper presented at the Sixth European Regional Congress International Association for Cross-Cultural Psychology "Cultures in Interaction," Budapest, Hungary.

Mayer, B., & Trommsdorff, G. (2003, September). *Kindbezogene Wertstrukturen bei tschechischen Müttern und Großmüttern [Child-related value structures of Czech mothers and grandmothers]*. Poster at the 16th Meeting of the Section of Developmental Psychology of the German Psychological Association, Mainz, Germany.

Miller, J. G. (2003). Culture and agency: Implications for psychological theories of motivation and social development. In V. Murphy-Berman & J. Berman (Eds.), *Cross-cultural difference in perspectives on the self* (Vol. 49, pp. 59–99). Lincoln, NE: University of Nebraska Press.

Nauck, B., & Suckow, J. (2003). Social networks and intergenerational relationships in cross-cultural comparisons: Social relationships of mothers and grandmothers in Japan, Korea, China, Indonesia, Israel, Germany and Turkey. In German-Japanese Society for Social Sciences (Ed.), *Environment in natural and socio-cultural context. Proceedings of the 7th Meeting 2002* (pp. 275–297). Inaho Shobo, Tokyo, Japan: Musashi Institute of Technology.

Neugarten, B. L. (1968). *Middle age and aging: A reader in social psychology.* Chicago: University of Chicago Press.

Radcliffe-Brown, A. R. (1940). On joking relationships. *Africa, 13,* 195–210.

Reis, H. T. (1998). Relationship science grows up. *Contemporary Psychology: APA Review of Books, 43,* 393–395.

Richman, A. L., Miller, P. M., & LeVine, R. A. (1992). Cultural and educational variations in maternal responsiveness. *Developmental Psychology, 28,* 614–621.

Rohner, R. P. (1976). *They love me, they love me not.* New Haven, CT: HRAF Press.

Rohner, R. P., & Pettengill, S. M. (1985). Perceived parental acceptance-rejection and parental control among Korean adolescents. *Child Development, 56,* 524–528.

Rossi, A. S., & Rossi, P. H. (1990). *Of human bonding: Parent-child relations across the life course.* Hawthorne, NY: Aldine de Gruyter.

Rothbaum, F., Pott, M., Azuma, H., Miyake, K., & Weisz, J. (2000). The development of close relationships in Japan and the United States: Paths of symbiotic harmony and generative tension. *Child Development, 71,* 1121–1142.

Rothbaum, F., & Trommsdorff, G. (in press). Cultural perspectives on relationships and autonomy-control. In J. E. Grusec & P. Hastings (Eds.), *Handbook of socialization.* New York: Guilford.

Rothbaum, F., Weisz, J., Pott, M., Miyake, K., & Morelli, G. (2000). Attachment and culture: Security in the United States and Japan. *American Psychologist, 55,* 1093–1104.

Rusbult, C. E., & Arriaga, X. B. (1997). Interdependence theory. In S. Duck (Ed.), *Handbook of personal relationships* (2nd ed., pp. 221–250). New York: Wiley.

Schaie, K. W., & Willis, S. L. (1995). Perceived family environments across generations. In V. L. Bengtson, K. W. Schaie, & L. M. Burton (Eds.), *Adult intergenerational relations* (pp. 174–209). New York: Springer.

Schwartz, S. H. (1994). Beyond individualism/collectivism: New cultural dimensions of values. In U. Kim, H. C. Triandis, C. Kagitcibasi, S.-C. Choi, & G. Yoon (Eds.), *Individualism and collectivism: Theory, methods, and applications* (pp. 85–119). Thousand Oaks, CA: Sage.

Schwartz, S. H., & Sagi, G. (2000). Value consensus and importance: A cross-national study. *Journal of Cross Cultural Psychology, 31,* 465–497.

Schwarz, B., Chakkarath, P., Fecher, L., Mayer, B., & Trommsdorff, G. (2001). *Bericht zu ausgewählten Erhebungsinstrumenten der Value of Children Pilotstudie(n): Herkunft, Reliabilität und Verteilung [Report on selected evaluation instruments of the Value of Children pilot study(-ies): Origin, reliability, and distribution].* Unveröffentlichtes Manuskript, Universität Konstanz, Germany.

Schwarz, B., Chakkarath, P., & Trommsdorff, G. (2002). Generationsbeziehungen in Indonesien, der Republik Korea und Deutschland. [Intergenerational relationships in Indonesia, the Republic of Korea, and Germany]. *Zeitschrift für Soziologie der Erziehung und Sozialisation, 22,* 393–407.

Schwarz, B., & Trommsdorff, G. (2004). *Adult daughters' and their mothers' perception of the relationship in different cultures: A study on the "intergenerational stake hypothesis."* In preparation for B. Nauck & C.-C. Yi (Eds.). Intergenerational Relations.

Schwarz, B., Trommsdorff, G., Albert, I., & Mayer, B. (2004). *Adult parent–child relationship: Relationship quality, support, and reciprocity.* Manuscript submitted for publication.

Schwarz, B, Trommsdorff, G., & Chakkarath, P. (in press). Intergenerational relationships in Indonesia, the Republic of Korea, and Germany. In B. N. Setiadi, A. Supratiknya, W. J. Lonner, & Y. H. Poortinga (Eds.), *Proceedings of the XVI Conference of the International Association of Cross-Cultural Psychology.* Yokyakarta, Indonesia: Kanisius.

Schwarz, B., Trommsdorff, G., Kim, U., & Park, Y.-S. (2004). Intergenerational support: A comparison of women from the Republic of Korea and Germany. *Manuscript in preparation for Current Sociology.*

Segall, M. H., Dasen, P. R., Berry, J. W., & Poortinga, Y. H. (1999). *Human behavior in global perspective: An introduction to cross-cultural psychology* (2nd ed.). Boston: Allyn & Bacon.

Sigel, I. E. (Ed.). (1985). *Parental belief systems: The psychological consequences for children.* Hillsdale, NJ: Erlbaum.

Singelis, T. M. (1994). The measurement of independent and interdependent self-construals. *Personality and Social Psychology Bulletin, 20,* 580–591.

Steinberg, L. (1990). Autonomy, conflict, and harmony in the family relationship. In S. S. Feldman & G. R. E. Elliott (Eds.), *At the threshold: The developing adolescent* (pp. 255–276). Cambridge, MA: Harvard University Press.

Stevenson, H. W., Chen, C., & Lee, S. (1992). Chinese families. In J. L. Roopnarine & D. B. Carter (Eds.), *Parent–child socialization in diverse cultures: Advances in applied developmental psychology* (pp. 17–33). Norwood, MA: Ablex.

Stevenson, H. W., & Zusho, A. (2002). Adolescence in China and Japan: Adapting to a changing environment. In B. B. Brown, R. W. Larson, & T. S. Saraswathi (Eds.), *The world's youth: Adolescence in eight regions of the globe* (pp. 141–170). Cambridge, UK: Cambridge University Press.

Szinovacz, M. E. (Ed.). (1998). *Handbook on grandparenthood.* Westport, CT: Greenwood.

The Research Committee on the Study of the Japanese National Character (1997). *Changing Japanese values. Statistical surveys and analyses.* Tokyo: Institute of Statistical Mathematics.

Thompson, R. A. (1999). Early attachment and later development. In J. Cassidy & P. R. Shaver (Eds.), *Handbook of attachment: Theory, research, and clinical applications* (pp. 265–286). New York: Guilford.

Triandis, H. C. (1995). *Individualism & collectivism.* Boulder, CO: Westview.

Trommsdorff, G. (1985). Some comparative aspects of socialization in Japan and Germany. In I. Reyes Lagunes & Y. H. Poortinga (Eds.), *From a different perspective: Studies of behavior across cultures* (pp. 231–240). Amsterdam: Swets & Zeitlinger.

Trommsdorff, G. (1991). Sympathie und Partnerwahl: Enge Beziehungen aus interkultureller Sicht. In M. Amelang, H.-J. Ahrens, & H. W. Bierhoff (Eds.), *Partnerwahl und Partnerschaft: Formen und Grundlagen partnerschaftlicher Beziehungen* (pp. 185–219). Göttingen: Hogrefe.

Trommsdorff, G. (1995). Parent–adolescent relations in changing societies: A cross-cultural study. In P. Noack & M. Hofer (Eds.), *Psychological responses to social change: Human development in changing environments* (pp. 189–218). Berlin: De Gruyter.

Trommsdorff, G. (2000). Subjective experience of social change in individual development. In J. Bynner & R. K. Silbereisen (Eds.), *Adversity and challenge in life in the new Germany and in England* (pp. 87–122). Basingstoke, England: Macmillan.

Trommsdorff, G. (2001a). Eltern-Kind-Beziehungen im interkulturellen Vergleich [Parent–child relations in cross-cultural comparisons]. In S. Walper & R. Pekrun (Hrsg.), *Familie und Entwicklung: Perspektiven der Familienpsychologie* (S. 36–62). Göttingen: Hogrefe.

Trommsdorff, G. (2001b). Value of children and intergenerational relations: A cross-cultural psychological study. Retrieved from http://www.uni-konstanz.de/FuF/SozWiss/fg-psy/ag-entw/.

Trommsdorff, G. (2002). An ecocultural and interpersonal relations approach to development over the lifespan. In W. J. Lonner, D. L. Dinnel, S. A. Hayes, & D. N. Sattler (Eds.), *Online readings in psychology and culture: Unit 15. Culture and human development: Adulthood and old age* (Chapter 1). Center for Cross-Cultural Research, Western Washington University, Bellingham, Washington. Web site: http://www.wwu.edu/~culture.

Trommsdorff, G. (2003). Environment and intergenerational relations. In German-Japanese Society for Social Sciences (Ed.), *Environment in natural and socio-cultural context. Proceedings of the Seventh Meeting 2002* (pp. 257–273). Inaho Shobo, Tokyo: Musashi Institute of Technology.

Trommsdorff, G. (in press). Transmission from the perspective of value of children. In U. Schönpflug (Ed.), *New perspectives on transmission of values*. Oxford, UK: Oxford University Press.

Trommsdorff, G., & Dasen, P. R. (2001). Cross-cultural study of education. In N. J. Smelser & P. B. Baltes (Eds.), *International encyclopedia of the social and behavioral sciences* (pp. 3003–3007). Oxford, UK: Elsevier.

Trommsdorff, G., & Friedlmeier, W. (1993). Control and responsiveness in Japanese and German mother–child interactions. *Early Development and Parenting, 2,* 65–78.

Trommsdorff, G., & Friedlmeier, W. (in press). Zum Verhältnis von Kultur und Individuum aus der Perspektive der kulturvergleichenden Psychologie [The relation between culture and the individual in cross-cultural perspective]. In A. Assmann, U. Gaier, & G. Trommsdorff (Eds.), *Positionen der Kulturanthropologie*. Frankfurt am Main, Germany: Suhrkamp.

Trommsdorff, G., & Kornadt, H.-J. (2003). Parent–child relations in cross-cultural perspective. In L. Kuczynski (Ed.), *Handbook of dynamics in parent-child relations* (pp. 271–306). London: Sage.

Trommsdorff, G., Mayer, B., & Albert, I. (2004). Dimensions of culture in intracultural comparisons: Individualism/collectivism and family-related values in three generations. In H. Vinken, J. Soeters, & P. Ester (Eds.), *Comparing cultures: Dimensions of culture in a comparative perspective* (pp. 157–184). Leiden, The Netherlands: Brill Academic.

Trommsdorff, G., & Nauck, B. (Eds.). (2004). *National reports on the study of value of children and intergenerational relations*. Manuscript in preparation.

Trommsdorff, G., & Schwarz, B. (2003). *Adult daughters' and their mothers' perception of their relationship in different cultures: A study on the "Intergenerational stake hypothesis."* Paper presented at the Institute of Sociology at Academia Sinica and Committee of Family Research (RC06) "Intergenerational Relations in Families' Life Course," Taipei, Taiwan.

Trommsdorff, G., Zheng, G., & Tardif, T. (2002). Value of children and intergenerational relations in cultural context. In P. Boski, F. J. R. Van de Vijver, & A. M. Chodynicka (Eds.), *New directions in cross-cultural psychology. Selected papers from the Fifteenth International Conference of the International Association for Cross-Cultural Psychology* (pp. 581–601). Warszawa, Poland: Polish Psychological Association.

Valsiner, J. (1989). *Human development and culture: The social nature of personality and its study*. Lexington, MA: Lexington.

Van IJzendoorn, M. H., & Sagi, A. (1999). Cross-cultural patterns of attachment: Universal and contextual dimensions. In J. Cassidy & P. R. Shaver (Eds.), *Handbook of attachment: Theory, research, and clinical applications* (pp. 713–734). New York: Guilford.

Whiting, B. B., & Whiting, J. W. (1975). *Children of six cultures: A psycho-cultural analysis.* Cambridge, MA: Harvard University Press.

Yamagishi, T., Cook, K. S., & Watabe, M. (1998). Uncertainty, trust, and commitment formation in the United States and Japan. *American Journal of Sociology, 104,* 165–194.

Yeh, K.-H., & Bedford, O. (2003). A test of the dual filial piety model. *Asian Journal of Social Psychology, 6,* 215–228.

Youniss, J. E., & Smollar, J. (1985). *Adolescent relations with mothers, fathers, and friends.* Chicago: University of Chicago Press.

Zarit, S. H., & Eggebeen, D. J. (2002). Parent–child relationships in adulthood and later years. In M. H. Bornstein (Ed.), *Handbook of parenting: Vol. 5. Practical issues in parenting* (2nd ed., pp. 135–161). Mahwah, NJ: Erlbaum.

# 7

# Cultural Dynamics of Family Relations Among Indian Adolescents in Varied Contexts

## SUMAN VERMA AND DEEPALI SHARMA

## INTRODUCTION

The vastness and richness of India's diversity can best be understood by a passage from Mehta's (1993, pp. 458–459) *Portrait of India*: India teems with languages. There are 14 officially recognized regional languages, 250 major dialects, and thousands of minor languages and dialects. English, which was the official language during the Raj, has never been understood by more than 3 percent of the population. The closest thing to a national language is Hindi, yet it is understood by only 40 percent—or, at most, 50 percent—of the population. Most Indians can understand only one language—that of the place in which they were born. This diversity having been noted, we must ask: what is the unifying factor that binds this diversity? How does one understand Indian society? D'Cruz and Bharat (2001), in a review on family research in the Indological phase, consider the family in India to be one of the three most important social institutions for understanding Indian society. Building upon the theme of the Indian family, in this chapter we address issues related to this aspect from the perspective of the parent–adolescent relationship.

### Historical Background

In order to understand the roots of the modern Indian family, we present a brief historical background that examines the socialization process held sacred in the past centuries for children as they grow up. Some of the traditions have remained the same and some have changed with the ongoing process of social change.

Currently, there is a greater stress than ever before in India on reviving old traditions and family values held sacred by elders. The media is playing a very crucial role in this revival, especially because it has a wide outreach. Recognition by the media of the importance of continuity of family values by the future generation is portrayed through commercial films and popular sitcoms and television networks that reemphasize the importance of carrying out one's expected roles within the integral framework of a united family. The unifying messages that are portrayed through the various forms of media also draw reference from Indian historical texts and epics.

Levels of family authority and care and upbringing of infants and children by the parents find references in ancient Indian texts and epics such as the *Mahabharata, Ramayana,* and *Manu Smriti,* which are replete with values of duty and devotion for the children toward their parents. These epics also highlight the *samskaras* (sacred and ritualistic ceremonies) provided by parents to their growing children during various stages of life. *Samskaras* are visualized to delineate childhood stages and give an indication of the chief characteristic of each stage (Kakar, 1978; Saraswathi & Pai, 1997). *Arthashastra,* the ancient Indian discourse on economics, considers age 16 to be the demarcation between childhood and youth for the boys and age 12 to be the cutoff year for girls. *Bhagvat Purana,* a 10th century essay considers that, "A son should be doted on for the first five years, he should be disciplined for the next ten years, when he is 16 he should be treated like a friend" (Dube, 1981, p. 187).

Ceremonies depicting the transition of children from one stage to another were visualized to provide a sense of identity to the growing children. The major task as visualized by the lawmakers during India's ancient history was the gradual transformation of children into able and contributing youth who show responsibilities toward both family and society (Kakar, 1978). Being an able family person meant being respectful and showing the foremost duty toward the parents. This was encouraged and portrayed through literature (Kumar, 1993). However, an important point to be noted is that in Indian scriptures and ancient literature, mention of a specific role for *girls* other than that of being a subordinate is conspicuous by its absence! Most references to "child" usually meant a male child and therefore had provisions and expectations only for boys (Kakar, 1978).

Returning to the discussion of the modern Indian family, even though socioeconomic and cultural changes have resulted in gradual changes in family lifestyles and life experiences, the essence of the traditional Indian culture remains (Saraswathi, 1999; Verma, 2000). Traditional Indian values stress continuity rather than discontinuity in family ties from childhood to adulthood (Kumar, 1993). These traditions are reflected in religious ceremonies, rituals, and social controls, with interdependent family patterns that give high priority to collectivist values and deference to family hierarchy and power structure (Bharat, 1997; Kakar, 1978; Saraswathi, 1999; Sinha, 1988).

The issues that are deliberated in this chapter reflect the dynamics of relationships that adolescents have with their parents in varied contexts and settings. These variables are then discussed within the broader framework of cultural dynamics.

# VARIED CONTEXTS INFLUENCING
# PARENT–ADOLESCENT RELATIONSHIPS

The first section of this chapter considers gender as a crucial variable that influences the socialization process and experiences that adolescents have while growing up in an Indian family. The next section elaborates on modifications of family dynamics in Indian society that have resulted in structural changes with direct implications for adolescent development. Parent–adolescent relationships in circumstances where the parent is single due to death or divorce is described in the next section. This is followed by a section on children and adolescents and their family relationships under difficult circumstances. In this chapter special mention is also made of children battling abuse within their families and discusses the possible outcomes on parent–adolescent relationships.

Finally, current family trends illustrate that in the face of industrialization, urbanization, migration, and employment of women there are certain evident changes in the roles of mothers and fathers. Although these changes are more apparent in urban rather than rural areas, they demand role adjustment on the part of mothers, fathers, and children. These changing adjustment patterns and the consequent impact on the parent–adolescent relationship are examined.

## Gender Issues in Parent–Adolescent Relationships

**Role Expectations.** In India, across social classes, there is a clear demarcation of the roles expected of boys and girls. These role expectations give boys much greater power, freedom, and authority than girls. This results in females being dependent on their fathers before marriage and their husbands after marriage. This picture is not too different even among the increasing number of career-oriented young women who clearly prioritize family obligations and consider their identity to come from their family rather than from themselves (Dube, 1988; Kakar, 1978; Verma & Saraswathi, 2002). This perception of gender discrimination, which cuts across social classes, is likely to lead to differential child-rearing practices by the parents.

**Challenges for Boys.** Because of the clear-cut role expectations in Indian society, it is likely that boys might face an identity crisis and a role conflict much earlier than girls. Kakar (1978) mentions that boys are likely to undergo what is known as their *second birth*, when they come of age, because their social world suddenly widens from the protective cocoon of maternal protection to an unfamiliar world of the masculine network, "woven by the demands and tensions, the comings and goings, of the men of the family" (p. 126). Thus, the contrast between before-and-after standards of obedience often comes as a shock to boys, along with bewilderment and misunderstanding as they have to learn to be conforming to family values and learn to be like the other men of the family. An almost complete reversal of things that are expected of the boys may result in serious long-term developmental implications for them that continue into adolescence and sometimes into adulthood. However, girls remain in the maternal cocoon for a longer time (until they get married) than boys; this allows them to learn to be like their mothers. The transition process is, thus, slightly easier for the girls when compared with boys (Kakar, 1978).

### Challenges for Girls.

Crisis and conflict in identity due to role transformation is one that boys might face more frequently than girls. Even though there is a much greater move toward equality in gender roles, especially in the urban parts of India, girls still continue to be enveloped in a more protective family web when compared with boys. This protection enhances dependence on the family by girls and limits their opportunities in several spheres such as education, career choices, and choice of marriage partners, friends, and leisure. Parental restrictions that encourage the dependence of their daughters can conflict with the desire for adolescent girls to have more freedom and independence (Verma & Saraswathi, 2002).

### Choice of Educational Courses as Shaped by Parental Expectations.

Data reveal that in both rural and urban areas, the proportion of literate females in the population decreases with age (International Institute for Population Sciences & ORC Macro, 2000). This reflects the low priority that is given to the education of adolescent girls by the family members. Karlekar (2000) reported that in the sphere of higher education, although females make up 24 to 50 percent of those enrolled across different states of India, only one in three students opts for science courses and only seven in every hundred engineering students are female. Education courses are the most popular choices for girls and up to 50 percent of students in education courses are girls. Academic choices for higher education, especially for adolescent girls, also reflect the choices that parents make for them. The popularity of education courses as perceived by the family members for girls is due mainly to the satisfaction that parents derive of having completed their *dharma* of equipping their girls with a basic education. Anything beyond this basic level of education is viewed as conflicting with the primary roles of girls: that of being a wife, a mother, and a daughter/in-law (Saraswathi, 1999). However, with the increasing influence of media and Western ideologies showcasing women in different and challenging occupations, there is an increasing trend among adolescent girls, especially in urban areas, to opt for alternate and nonstereotyped courses that may differ from the choices that parents may make for their daughters (Verma & Saraswathi, 2002).

### Peers and Romantic Relationships.

Adolescent boys are provided with much greater freedom than girls with regard to their involvement in romantic relationships and choice of friends. Although whole-hearted approval is never given even to adolescent boys for a romantic relationship, they are still indulged in and if they are not encouraged, then neither are they discouraged. Similarly, the choice of boys' friends and their curfews are not often commented upon by their parents. Adolescent girls, on the other hand, are fiercely protected by the parents in fear of their being involved in a romantic relationship and having premarital sex (Uplaonkar, 1995). Concern that girls may be involved with someone from a different caste or religion is an even greater stress for the parents (Verma & Saraswathi, 2002).

## Leisure and Free Time Opportunities.

Although adolescent boys and girls have similar amounts of leisure time in middle- and upper-middle-class families, gender socialization for girls leads them to pursue more home-based hobbies and interests such as interior designing, sewing, knitting, and cooking. These hobbies are in stark contrast to the ones pursued by boys who actively take part in more outdoor activities. Thus, the free time activities of boys and girls differ both quantitatively and qualitatively (Verma & Sharma, 2003). Also, female adolescents perceive that parental control is more focused on their home-based and social activities, whereas boys perceive parental control as more focused on matters related to their academic achievement. These perceptions suggest the areas of priority that parents have for their adolescent sons and daughters (Hegde & Gaonkar, 1991). A time-use study on gender differences in home-based versus community-based leisure, employing the *Experience Sampling Method* (Verma & Sharma, 2003) suggested that adolescent boys have more opportunities and parental support than girls to take part in community-based activities. These activities are seen to foster autonomy, creativity, ego-integration, and expansion of interests. Lack of adequate exposure of girls to outdoor activities leads them to be more dependent and tends to reinforce the traditional segregation of boys and girls in Indian society. Verma (1995) has noted that the very fact that girls are more likely to pursue leisure activities in the vicinity of their home, college, or neighborhood is an indicator of parental and social control.

## Conflicts Due to Social Change.

Differentiation and restriction among siblings due to gender is likely to lead to feelings of greater discontentment among adolescent girls (Kanitkar, 1996). This is becoming especially more evident due to the increase in literacy rates and media exposure that has resulted in a far greater awareness than ever before among girls. Although girls may not accept parental restrictions willingly, in the face of parental pressure and childhood socialization to be obedient to parents, they may internalize their conflicts and doubts. These internalizing symptoms are a cause of concern as they may surface later as a more rebellious attitude in adulthood (Verma, 1995).

In summary, gender differences continue to remain a reality within the Indian family system and also dictate, to a large extent, the quality of parent–adolescent relationships. However, with the ongoing and rapid process of social change, girls have greater opportunities in education, vocation, and careers. As noted above, these changes are currently creating conflict among parents and adolescents because of their novelty and an accompanying awareness about egalitarian gender roles in both rural and urban areas of India.

## Type of Family Structure and Adolescent Experiences

**Family Interactions in Nuclear Versus Joint Families.** Changes in the structure and types of Indian families are resulting from processes of industrialization, urbanization, and migration of the population from the villages to the cities. Sinha (1984) has reported that due to the small size and limited number of adults in nuclear families there are closer bonds and intense parent–child relations. Children in nuclear families are likely to enjoy greater autonomy, independence, and initiative when compared with children from joint or extended families. Socialization practices are also more permissive and less harsh for the developing child. Conversely, in a typical extended Indian family, symbiotic relationships are promoted and separation and individuation are inhibited (D'Cruz & Bharat, 2001).

**Parenting Styles by Family Type.** Ojha and Sinha (1982; c.f. D'Cruz & Bharat, 2001) recognize the nuclear and extended family structures in India as being instrumental in giving rise to distinct parental styles. The authoritarian parental style is seen to be more of a trademark within the extended family system because to survive, it needs its members to readily cooperate; in nuclear families, on the other hand, emphasis on individualism leads to democratic parenting styles. Restraints characterizing extended families provide less freedom for children and adolescents to explore their surroundings and function in an independent manner. This often leads to conflict among family members (Sinha, 1981).

**Changing Times.** Despite the apparent negative feelings and conflicted interactions that are generated in the typical extended family, many Indian scholars argue that this family system is still considered the ideal to which many Indians aspire. This is because of the ingrained belief in the Indian psyche that promotes groupism and conformity (Sinha, 1981; Bharat, 1991). Although individual relationships among family members are more formally laid out in a typical extended family these trends are changing. In today's urban Indian family, parents are becoming less authoritarian and more child centered. Yet, despite the relaxation of parenting styles, parents still believe that they are the final authority in all matters related to their children's major decisions in life such as choosing a career or selecting a marriage partner (Verma & Saraswathi, 2002). This cycle of expectations of the parents for their children is very typical of Indian tradition because of the deep-rooted belief that children, especially sons, are an investment for their parents' old age. This belief is ingrained in children and leads to increasing conformity to adult roles with increasing age.

## Single-Parent Families and Parent–Adolescent Relationships

Single-parent families in India are established when one parent dies spouses divorce or separate, one partner migrates for employment, a partner is hospitalized or imprisoned, a marital partner deserts or abandons a spouse, or through unwed motherhood (D'Cruz & Bharat, 2001).

**Death, Divorce, and the Single Mother.** Estimates in India are that about 7 percent of all family units likely to have dependent children are single-parent family units, where one parent is absent due to death, divorce, or separation. In over 80 percent of these cases, death is the cause of single parenthood and more than 70 percent of single parents are women (Census of India, 1991). Several studies in India have documented the impact of single-parent families on children (Chen & Dreze, 1992; Kaushik, 1991). Results indicate that women are more frequently depressed than men and that it makes these women more predisposed to neuroses (Davar, 1999). As a result, their children also report suffering negative psychological and socioeconomic consequences. Also, the helplessness often associated with being single influences not only the single women themselves, but also the health and well-being of their children (Chen & Dreze, 1992). Children are seen to be particularly vulnerable to the effects of divorce and manifest symptoms of emotional insecurity and low well-being (Sundaram, 1993).

**Some Positive Aspects for Adolescents in Single-Parent Families.** Even though single parenthood creates a number of stressors for children and their mothers, it also manifests strengths among family members. A recent study by Sharma (2003) on 185 adolescents and their single mothers (113 widows and 72 divorced mothers) examined the family life experiences and psychosocial well-being of adolescents from single-parent families in the city of Chandigarh, India. Results indicated that although children did experience stress, nowhere did the sample match up with the popular notion that is usually associated with such children. The children from single-parent families were no less well-disciplined, troubled, or engaged in juvenile delinquency than children from married households. The children did not display low self-esteem, and were not at enhanced risk of childhood psychopathology.

**Strengths Displayed in Family Interaction Patterns by Adolescents in Single-Parent Families.** Sharma (2003) has reported that Indian youth growing up in single-parent families recognize the importance of immediate family members as having an important influence in their lives and acknowledge their understanding, the love, affection, and sacrifices made by the single parent during moments of crisis. A young adolescent with a divorced mother in the study pointed out, "I value my mother for her experience, her love, and her boldness. Mummy has not changed at all for us. She is still the same except for the fact that she tries to fulfill the role of a father too. She has changed for our better."

Furthermore, contrary to the popular belief that adolescents will display aggressive behavior and primarily negative personality characteristics after being in a single-parent family, respondents in Sharma's (2003) study reported certain positive aspects such as having the feeling that they had become more mature, responsible, independent, and relaxed. A young boy felt, "I have become much, much more mature as I know I have to support my mom." Another adolescent male with a widowed mother said, "Yes, I have become more mature, sensitive, and emotional after my father passed away." Also, adolescents reported strong sibling relationships and an even greater bonding after being in a single-parent family ("Yes, I feel that my brother has become much more caring"; "We share more things now"; "I have noticed a change as earlier we used to fight a lot but now this has decreased").

However, there are important individual differences in the psychological adjustment of children and their single mothers with gender of the child, marital status of the mothers (widows/divorcees), and family structure (nuclear/joint) playing a crucial role.

### Social Support Available to Single-Parent Families.

A crucial factor that provides immense support to single Indian mothers and their children is the family. Siganporia (1993, p. 357) indicated that "for an Indian, the family and kinship groups are the beginning and end of his/her human universe." Researchers indicate that single parents and their children are most likely to stay with extended families that include parents, in-laws, and other relatives (Leela, 1991; Mehta, 1975; Pothen, 1986) than take support from their peers (Chaudhary, 1988). The Indian family is founded on the belief that the *dharma* or righteousness of the ancestors protects the descendants. This is one of the reasons why India does not have a well-defined social security system; the family is expected to protect and provide support for widowed and divorced women, and also provide support for the aged (Invest in India Report, 2002). Thus, it is expected that the extended family in India will provide social, economic, and emotional support to children as well as to the single parent. In this regard, the family is viewed as promoting mental health and the individual's subjective well-being (Diener , 1985; Sethi & Chaturvedi, 1992; Siganporia, 1993).

### Parent–Child Relationships in the Case of the Single Father.

Thus far, discussion has focused on the case of single mothers. Typically, Indian children are more likely to be with single mothers than single fathers (Patil, 2000). The percentage of single mothers is greater than single fathers due to certain demographic factors such as age difference between husband and wife and occupational hazards resulting in the wife outliving the husband. Also, the social sanction given to remarry in the case of death of the spouse or divorce is far greater for men than for women in India. However, there is a slow trend that suggests that widowers/divorced fathers are taking up the responsibility of rearing their children after the death or divorce of the spouse.

Resulting father–adolescent relationships can be expected to differ from mother–adolescent relationships because, in the case of single fathers, they have to learn new roles. They must learn to be more nurturing and less formal in their relationships with their children than when they had the role of the head of the family and a breadwinner in a two-parent family. Also, single fathers rely heavily on the support of the extended family for being emotional anchors to both the children and themselves. Even though there is very scarce work available that documents the experiences of children growing up in single-father families and of the fathers themselves, research on a limited sample of in-depth case studies suggests that fathers are high in the areas of providing financial support and as acting as disciplinarian (Sharma, 2003). Over time, single fathers may gradually adapt to the role of being an emotional anchor for their children; however, typically, they continue to rely on their extended relatives, especially the women, to provide emotional support for their children. Grandparents are likely to become the sounding boards for the growing adolescents; relationships with grandparents and other extended family members add new dimensions to father–adolescent bonds.

The main theme emerging from the above discussion is that children and their single parents report a variety of psychological symptoms after being in a single-parent family. However, in most circumstances the children and the single parent do adapt to the changed family life situation, showing resilience, and not dysfunction, considering the stressful adjustments that they have to make (Amato, 1993; Emery, 1998; Hetherington & Clingempeel, 1992). Positive aspects in the personality of adolescents and parent–adolescent relationships are also a reflection of the changing time in India that is more accepting of alternate family forms.

## Children and Adolescents in Difficult and Crisis-Prone Circumstances

Crises occur in almost every individual's life in varying degrees at one point or another. However, in many instances the crisis situation gets so magnified that it alters conventional family interaction patterns and relationships between parents and their children. Crises have an impact on the overall well-being of the family members. In this section, we highlight three special crisis situations that make children vulnerable to stress. These crisis contexts include the life and family conditions of (a) working and street children, (b) children affected by terrorism, and (c) children growing up in families in which mothers are sex workers.

### Life and Family Conditions of Working and Street Children.
India has one of the largest concentration of child workers in the world. Rough estimates indicate labor force participation rates vary from 5 percent (10 to 14 years) to 36 percent (15 to 19 years) among the adolescent population (UNFPA, 1998). Children and adolescents who are employed in the small-scale industries are covered to some extent by existing laws and legislation. It is the condition of the children on the streets that gives rise to greater concern because they are outside the purview of legislation (Verma, 1999). Estimates suggest that as many as 11 million Indian children and adolescents fend for themselves on the streets of metropolitan cities or large townships (Phillips, 1992).

Verma and Saraswathi (2002) suggest that child labor is deeply embedded in the Indian tradition of home-based or family work, where there is an unwritten rule that expects boys to follow their father's craft in order to maintain continuity of vocation and girls to assist in household chores and learn family responsibilities as early as possible. This traditional perspective fits within the cultural reality of being born into a role (Dube, 1981). Children and adolescents also join the workforce or live in the streets because of family migration, broken homes, parental abuse, abandonment, family size, low incomes, low literacy, and chronic poverty (Fonseka & Malhotra, 1994).

Verma (1999) has recently suggested that in cases where Indian street children have families to return to, they report frequent disputes with parents because of authoritarian and harsh parental disciplinary practices. These children also get in trouble with their parents because of their low earnings, keeping money for themselves, and using their slim earnings to watch movies. Crises in terms of health, unemployment, and criminality are common in these families with alcoholism being frequently reported among fathers. These crisis situations do not allow for proper parental attention to the developing children or for the strong and positive parent–child or family relationships. In the cases of these families in crisis, parents place an emphasis on the learning of socially prescribed roles and they reinforce learning skills that will allow the children to earn an income on the streets. These family climates are clearly not conducive to normal social, cognitive, and affective development.

### Risks for Street Children Living Without Their Families.

Verma (1999) has reported that the experiences that children have on the streets makes them more resilient, independent, conforming, and self-preserving. Yet Verma (1999) notes also that in the case of adolescents who have no home to return to at night, negative consequences are likely to occur. Life on the streets increases the prospects of antisocial activities and can cause youngsters to leave homes and lead semi-independent lives with minimal parental supervision (Institute of Psychological and Educational Research, 1991; Verma & Bhan, 1996).

Thus, between two groups of children, those who have families to return to and those who do not, the former category seems to be in a better position because street children staying with families feel wanted and loved, enjoy joint recreational activities, reach out to each other in times of crises, and learn socially prescribed roles and skills (Phillips, 1992; Panicker & Nangia, 1992; Verma, 1999). In the case of adolescent girls, they are more likely than boys to be protected by their families; yet when girls break their family bonds they risk getting lured into prostitution and becoming vulnerable to exploitation and abuse.

In summary, in circumstances where street and working children have a family to return to, the demands of everyday living pale slightly in comparison with children who cannot return to their family. Family solidarity and family cohesiveness, despite varied stressors for children, provide an important safety network for these children (Verma, 1999).

**Children Affected by Terrorism.**  Given the increasing incidence of terrorism in many states of India, it becomes a matter of concern to understand the psychological and physical turmoil that families undergo. Of a greater concern is the impact that this crisis has on the minds of young children and adolescents, which is evident from the following quote.

> I have no school
> I was always praying to God
> that somehow I did not have to go to school.
> I longed to play all day
> and wished there was no school.
> One day it really happened
> There was no school
> Someone had burnt it down.
> Thrilled, I enjoyed it for a while.
> Now I am bored
> I wish I had not wished
> that there was no school.

Poem by a 14-year-old in Kashmir (cf. Pushkarana, 1998)

Limited research on this sensitive issue suggests that individual family members suffer emotionally, intellectually, physically, and economically when terrorism exists (Singh, 1991). In India, near-negligible support is offered to families of terrorist victims. Even though the government offers monetary assistance to the families of terrorist victims, power plays between family members sometimes make it difficult for the aid to reach those for whom it was intended. In the case of widows and their children, there are frequent reports of harassment by in-laws.

A study on women and children in Punjab and Kashmir by Pushkarana (1998) portrayed how 200 children, aged 11 to 16, who wrote essays on "the story of my life" and "events that made me happy and sad," gave graphic descriptions of how relatives and neighbors died. They drew pictures of schools and houses reduced to rubble and narrated crackdowns and search operations by security forces and midnight knocks by militants. Few of these children portrayed themes of happiness and family.

Often, the impact of losing a parent through a terrorist attack is not diagnosable immediately after the trauma, but becomes evident months or even years later. In addition, children with existing mental health needs are at an increased risk of long-term psychological effects. When a child loses a parent through a terrorist attack he or she also loses the security of a complete home. Also, children who become victims of violence have a possibility of inflicting violence on others (Ranasinghe, n.d.; Moser & Bronkhorst, 1999; Rodgers, 1999). For children who have lost both parents in terrorist attacks, the repercussions are more adverse inasmuch as the loss involves establishment of new relations in the care of their relatives or foster homes. In such cases, there are often reports of maltreatment that result in such psychological problems as feelings of insecurity, tension, and depression (Singh, 1991). Although the government does extend support to the families of terrorist victims by providing monetary assistance, intervention strategies in terms of family and individual counseling is sadly lacking.

In summary, evidence from the scant research carried out on children and families of terrorist victims shows that the losses are greatest for children who are left alone and have the task of starting afresh and re-establishing trust in the homes of relatives or in foster care. Longitudinal studies that document the long-term impact of terrorism on children is clearly needed.

**Children of Sex Workers.** In India there are approximately 5 million children who are the offspring of sex workers. Sex workers in developing countries rarely use contraceptives, either because they are not easily available or because they cannot afford them. Thus, in many cases, unwanted pregnancies and children derive from unprotected sex of prostitutes (Power, 1997). Given the dearth of substantial research in India on the family relationships of children and their prostitute mothers, it is difficult to provide a conclusive, research-generated profile. Yet, there have been laudable efforts by select nongovernmental organizations that not only document the impact on children where the mothers are sex workers, but also go a step forward and implement rehabilitative measures in order to safeguard the welfare of these children. One such NGO working with children of prostitutes is *Prajawala,* a Hyderabad-based NGO founded in 1996. In the following section, we focus on children of sex workers being raised by *Prajawala* (Narayana, 2003).

The main goal of *Prajawala*, which means an internal flame that cannot be extinguished, remains the social reintegration and rehabilitation of sex workers and their children. Sex workers are considered to be victims of "societal subjugation, deprivation, and compulsion" (Narayana, 2003 , p. 18). But the children are at an even greater risk because they are victimized because of the mothers. These children are exposed, from a young age onward, to very adult experiences. These experiences involve the children being direct witnesses to the buying and selling of the human body; very often these children become involved in illicit drug and liquor trafficking. Young girls are at a high risk of becoming involved in the same trade as that of the mothers. The harsh experiences that children have are instrumental in shaping their perceptions of psychological well-being; often, the children report suffering from a variety of psychosocial disorders with long-term developmental implications.

Rehabilitative measures, currently being followed by *Prajawala,* and other like-minded organizations, involve building up a strong network of agencies and organizations, including the state and central governments. Community-based actions to combat trafficking, programs that empower women to be economically independent, and education and adequate care of children form the core theme of programs working toward the benefit of sex workers and their children. The NGOs have an underlying belief that through an integrated approach, in which the mother is the key, help can be given to the victimized children.

## Harsh Parenting Styles

Another dimension that is of interest in furthering our understanding of parent–child/adolescent relationships in the Indian context is the existence of authoritarian parenting styles. In some cases, the authoritarian parenting style brings with it physical, emotional, and sexual abuse. Physical abuse involves the intentional, nonaccidental use of physical force on the part of the parent or caregiver (Gil, 1970).

**Kinds of Abuse.**   Emotional or psychological abuse occurs when children are hurt emotionally or by withholding love and support (Menon, 1988). Sexual abuse occurs when children are forced into a physical relationship for either pleasure or material gain or for the sexual gratification of an adult (Bajpai, 1996).

**Impact of Abuse on Adolescents.**   Kaur (2003) studied the incidence of abuse among rural adolescents. The results indicated that discipline-related problems of adolescents emerged as the most predominant cause of harsh parenting styles resulting in physical abuse. Furthermore, unhealthy criticisms of ideas, along with authoritarian, reluctant, rejecting, and discouraging attitudes of parents, coupled with demands for higher academic performance from their children, and unhealthy comparisons with their siblings and peers, were reported to result in emotional problems among the children. Also, the authoritarian attitude of elder siblings, conflicts and rivalry between children, and limited communication between the family members all generated feelings of neglect and rejection among children (Kaur, 2003). The impact of authoritarian parenting styles and harsh treatment meted out by the parents is also known to result in poor self-concept among the children, especially among adolescents (Kewalramani, 1996). Girls are especially vulnerable to the impact of abuse (Kaur, 2003).

**Linking Family Background With Abuse.**   Parenting styles in Indian families are likely to vary and be dependent on certain variables such as poverty, lack of education, characteristics of the child and the parents, and the family context (Sharan, 1995). Grewal (1982), Khanna (1987), and Nain (1985) observed that harsh parenting styles and physical abuse are more likely to be prevalent in families with low socioeconomic status. However, parents from higher socioeconomic status also report adopting measures such as frequent punishment to control their children (Anuradha & Rehman, 1991). Although no generalizations can be made, Indian research does suggest that parenting styles are harsher for boys than girls, especially when they reach adolescence. Because the father is considered to be the main disciplinarian, results of these studies indicate that fathers frequently report using techniques such as physical punishment in the cases of adolescent boys who disobey or go out without permission (Kang & Singh, 1994). Therefore, it is not surprising that adolescents perceive their fathers to be always angry and ill-tempered (Paintal & Pandey, 1996). This restrictive and rejecting behavior of parents is likely to lead to the same authoritarian behavior pattern among the children irrespective of gender (Ojha, 1977).

**Summary.** Child abuse due to child characteristics, parental characteristics, or familial and community context, occurs either due to a combination of the above-mentioned four factors or occurs due to one of the four factors, each one in isolation from the other. Whoever or whatever is the motive of the perpetrator, the core issue remains that it is the child who gets traumatized with long-term implications for his or her mental health and well-being. Limited research suggests that the documented incidence of abuse in India is low, especially in the rural areas. However, the strict patriarchal family context, often accompanied by an authoritarian home environment, and especially in the rural areas, suggests that child abuse is likely to be much higher than what is usually reported.

## Changing Parental Roles and Family Relationships

**Changing Role of Mothers.** In traditional Indian families mothers are perceived as the caregivers for children and fathers as the main providers. However, with changing times and women making an increasing presence felt in the workforce the concept of dual-earner families is slowly becoming a reality in the Indian context along with a greater crossover of roles in the parenting dimension.

## Impact of Mother's Employment on Individual Family Members.

The modified family roles of wife/mother from a homemaker to a co-provider have altered the patterns of mother–child interaction, the domestic division of labor, and also the role of husband/father (Kumar, 1994; Ramu, 1987; Rao, 1990; Venugopal and Swaminathan, 1997). Although many mothers perceive that they have become more independent and confident after taking up employment, the mothers' employment is likely to be instrumental in determining the home climate with the impact of their job leading to readjustments in the family's present pattern of living. Although research evidence does indicate that there is no significant difference among members in dual- and single-career families with respect to cohesion and expressiveness, conflict is viewed as being more frequent by husbands and children in dual-earner families than in single-earner families (Rani & Khandewal, 1992). Dixit and Vishnoi (1980) report that mothers who are employed are perceived by their children as more neglecting and rejecting and as less protecting and rewarding compared with children of unemployed mothers.

In a recent study, Sharma, Verma, and Larson (2000) found that the mother's employment was associated with adolescent reports of significantly lower cohesion levels; mothers, fathers, and adolescents reported significantly higher conflict levels in the family environment when the mother was employed. These readjustments in the accustomed patterns of living for the family members in general, and the adolescents in particular, can result in added stress.

D'Cruz and Bharat (2001) indicated that employed mothers have fewer children than nonworking women and that their children are usually cared for by relatives (living usually with or near the family), by husbands in case they are unemployed, by elder siblings, by the mothers themselves, and by servants. Also in many instances, working mothers in India perceive that their employment is the root cause of their children being adversely affected and feel that there are certain personality changes that their children undergo because of their employment. The children also express a preference for the mother's presence at home rather than going outside for employment.

However, the above-mentioned findings on mother's employment and family interaction patterns cannot be generalized because family environment varies from one household to another and is dependent, to a large extent, on the quality of support and understanding by the children and the husbands. Yeole (1993) has noted that Indian adolescents feel very strongly that their mothers should have their own identity (also through employment), be modern, and progressive. With a more proactive attitude at the working place of women and a more supportive attitude of family members regarding the mother's employability, the existing dilemmas and role conflict can be met with more progressively.

**Changing Role of Father.**  Men in Indian society, to a large extent, have been continuing with their traditional roles as the main provider for the wife and children. Consequently, they provide little support in carrying out household chores and the responsibilities of everyday involvement in child-rearing, even when the women are employed. Because of this apparent division of spheres, the role of Indian fathers in daily parenting is ambiguous and peripheral (Kakar, 1978). However, there are certain slow but definite changes visible in the Indian family regarding the role of fathers; parenting roles are changing from exclusivity toward interchangeability, with fathers becoming more involved in childcare (Saraswathi & Pai, 1997; Sriram & Ganapathy, 1997). In this section, findings from two studies are described. The first study deals with the daily life experiences of fathers and the emerging interaction patterns with their children (Larson, Verma, & Dworkin, 2001) and the second study provides a glimpse of the visible changing roles of fathers in child-rearing against a backdrop of continuing traditional roles (Sandhu, 2001).

**Time Spent With Children.**  The time-use study using the *Experience Sampling Method* by Larson, Verma, and Dworkin (2001) was carried out on a sample of 100 fathers of eighth-graders in the city of Chandigarh, India. The fathers provided information on their hour-to-hour time use and subjective states. The 4308 time samples obtained from the fathers revealed that because of their heavy involvement in the job sphere, they were able to spend less time with their children when at home. The time that they spent with their children involved activities related to leisure and relaxation where they reported experiencing favorable emotions when with their children. Fathers in nuclear family households spent more total time with their children ($M = 24.1\%$) in a day when compared with fathers in extended households ($M = 15.7\%$). Also, the fathers and adolescents in the study described their relationships as close and comfortable with a great deal of free exchange. The fathers perceived their relationships with their adolescent children to be much less formal and authoritarian than the relationships that their fathers had had with them.

**Changing Role of Indian Fathers.** The second study carried out by Sandhu (2001) is an interesting reflection on the changing roles of Indian fathers who are trying to maintain a balance between the traditional and modern expectations of parenting. The study carried out on a sample of 45 fathers examined fathering ideologies and variations with ages of children. The results indicated that the fathers of college and school-going children reported more difficulties than those with children of younger ages. The results also show evidence that even though there is continuity from the past to present regarding the fathering beliefs and practices, the fathers are having an increased involvement with children in some aspects. The fathers perceive themselves as more involved in child-rearing such as taking time out to play with the children, discussing different issues with them, planning joint activities with them, listening to children, and giving them timely advice.

An important observation made in Sandhu's (2001) study is that even though fathers have the power of being the final decision makers, there is evidence of more consultation with children and spouse in the process of decision making. This is reflective of a positive change toward the sharing of power, especially when compared with fathers in the past who enjoyed complete authority. Because of these changes, the fathers carry out a "balancing act" where they combine their present-day dual role of provider and nurturer. Indian fathers are more likely to provide the same opportunities to their sons and daughters in their education and career and have an equal set of rules and regulations for them as compared with earlier times when there were definite indications of gender differentiation and clear-cut masculine and feminine roles.

However, returning to the finding that fathers face more problems with their adolescent children than with younger children, it appears as if there are good reasons for this. In keeping with historical roles, Indian fathers are still more likely to emphasize training in household chores for daughters than sons and are likely to treat their daughters with more affection than their sons with whom they prefer to maintain an emotional distance. Furthermore, traditional beliefs of Indian fathers may sometimes act as a hindrance for the nurturance of close bonds with their adolescent children. More now than ever before, adolescent Indian children are independent, having their own sets of beliefs and values that might not necessarily gel with those of their fathers. Therefore, although Indian fathers do realize that they need to be less conforming and more understanding of their adolescent children, they find the kind of authority to which they are accustomed especially difficult to relinquish. Hence, the conflicting experience of accepting changes in the process of fathering raises its own set of dual standards.

The process of social change in India that is reflective of increased participation by women in the workforce and the changing role of fathers to keep pace with the expectations of modernity, is still in its infancy. Therefore, in this transitional period, Indian families are making their own sets of rules and standards to understand what works well and what does not. It appears that over a period of time when more stability sets in, positive changes will be reinforced and negative changes will be discarded in order to have a more fulfilling and invigorating quality of husband–wife, parent–child/adolescent, and overall family relationships.

## CONCLUSION

Is it possible to provide a conclusion on the state of the contemporary Indian family? No. What was once held as sacred and valuable in the area of family solidarity is being questioned today and may be subject to an entirely different set of rules tomorrow. Parenting styles are changing, resulting in strong implications for adolescents. Certain conflicts are evident due to the differences in expectations of parents and their children. So what is constant among all this change? The only thing constant is the fact that families continue to strongly bind individual members in Indian society. The complete support that Indian families provide, even under extremely adverse circumstances to individual family members, continues to shape the socialization experiences of children and young adolescents and maintains the institution of "family" as one of which all Indian individuals aspire to be part.

## REFERENCES

Amato, P. R. (1993). Children's adjustment to divorce: Theories, hypotheses, and empirical support. *Journal of Marriage and the Family, 55*, 23–38.

Anuradha, B. S., & Rehman, L. (1991). *An attitude survey of parents towards child abuse* (pp. 1–18). Bangalore: National Institute of Public Cooperation and Child Development, Southern Regional Centre.

Bajpai, A. (1996). Child sexual abuse: Need for law reforms. *The Indian Journal of Social Work, 57* (4), 630–639.

Bharat, S. (1986). Single-parent families in India: Issues and implications. *The Indian Journal of Social Work, XLVII* (1), 55–65.

Bharat, S. (1991). Research on families with problems in India: Utility, limitations and future directions. In Tata Institute of Social Sciences Unit for Family Studies, *Research on families with problems in India: Issues and implications: Vol. II* (pp. 545–560). Bombay: TISS.

Bharat, S. (1994). Alternate family patterns and policies. In M. Desai (Ed.), *Enhancing the role of the family as an agency for social and economic development* (pp. 72–117). Mumbai: TISS.

Bharat, S. (1997). Family socialization of the Indian child. *Trends in Social Science Research, 4*(1), 201–216.

Census of India (1991). *Census of India, 1991, Series 1—India. Part IV A–C: Vol. 1, Table C-1.* New Delhi: Office of the Registrar General, India.

Chaudhary, J. N. (1988). *Divorce in Indian society.* Jaipur: Rupa.

Chen, M., & Dreze, J. (1992, October 24–31). Widows and health in rural India. *Economic and Political Weekly,* WS 81–92.

Davar, B. V. (Ed.). (1999). *Mental health of Indian women: A feminist agenda.* New Delhi: Sage.

D'Cruz, P., & Bharat, S. (2001). Beyond joint and nuclear: The Indian family revisited. *Journal of Comparative Family Studies,* 167–194.

Devasia, L., & Devasia, V. V. (1991). *Girl child in India.* New Delhi: Ashish.

Diener, E. (1985). Subjective well-being. *Psychological Bulletin, 95*, 542–575.

Dixit, R. C., & Vishnoi, P. L. (1980). Employment of the mothers as a determinant of mother–daughter relationship and the development of masculinity–femininity among young girls. *Psychologia: An International Journal of Psychology in the Orient, 23* (3), 167–172.

Dube, L. (1981). The economic roles of children in India: Methodological issues. In G. Rodgers & G. Standing (Eds.), *Child, work, poverty and underdevelopment* (pp. 179–213). Geneva: IL.

Dube, L. (1988). On the construction of gender: Hindu girls in patrilineal India. *Economic and Political Weekly, 23*(18), WS 11–WS19.

Emery, R. E. (1998). *Marriage, divorce, and children's adjustment.* Newbury Park, CA: Sage.

Fonseka, L., & Malhotra, D. D. (1994). India: Urban poverty, children and participation. In C. S. Blanc (Ed.), *Urban children in distress* (pp. 161–215). Luxembourg: Gordon & Breach.

Gil, D. G. (1970). *Violence against children: Physical abuse in the U.S.* Cambridge, MA: Harvard University Press.

Grewal, B. (1982). *Family violence: A case study of slum dwellers of Chandigarh.* Master of Philosophy thesis. Punjab University, Chandigarh.

Hegde, B., & Gaonkar, V. (1991). Perception of parental control by adolescents. *Indian Psychological Review, 36*(5–6), 19–24.

Hetherington, E. M., & Clingempeel, W. G. (1992). *Coping with marital transitions.* Chicago: University of Chicago Press.

Indian Express (2003, May 19). Father, cousin beat girl to death over intercaste marriage.

Institute of Psychological and Educational Research (1991). *A composite report of situational analysis of urban street children in India: Study reports of six major cities in India.* Calcutta: Author.

International Institute for Population Sciences (IIPS) & ORC Macro (2000). *National Family Health Survey (NFHS-2), 1998–99: India.* Mumbai: Author.

Invest in India Report (2002). Retrieved February 27, 2002, from http://www.invest-india.com/newsite/social/family.htm.

Kakar, S. (1978). *The inner world: A psychoanalytical study of childhood and society in India.* Delhi: Oxford University Press.

Kang, T. K., & Singh, M. B. (1994). Disciplinary techniques used by fathers as perceived by adolescents in rural and urban areas. *Indian Psychological Review, 42* (11–12), 22–27.

Kanitkar, S. D. (1996). Gender discrimination in the family: Views and experiences of teenage girls. *The Journal of Family Welfare, 42*(4), 32–38.

Kapadia, K. M., & Pillai, S. D. (1971). *Young runaways: A study of children who desert home.* Bombay: Popular Parkasan.

Karlekar, M. (2000). Women's studies and women's development. In M. S. Gore (Ed.), *Third survey of research in sociology and anthropology* (pp. 117–120). New Delhi: Indian Council of Social Science Research.

Kaur, S. (2003). *Abuse among rural adolescents: Incidence, causes and practices.* Doctor of Philosophy thesis submitted to Panjab University, Chandigarh.

Kaushik, S. (1991). *Single parent families: Their needs and problems.* New Delhi: Department of Women and Child Development, Government of India.

Kewalramani, G. S. (1996). Child abuse: A system analysis. *Indian Journal of Social Work, 57* (1–4), 396–413.

Khanna, S. (1987). *Social correlates of child battering.* Master of Philosophy thesis. Panjab University, Chandigarh.

Kumar, K. (1993). *Political agenda of education: A study of colonialist and nationalist ideas.* New Delhi: Sage.

Kumar, P. (1994). Gender differences, wife's employment and marital duration as factors in marital adjustment. *Indian Journal of Clinical Psychology, 21*(2), 23–26.

Kumari, R. (1989). *Women-headed households in rural India.* New Delhi: Radiant.

Larson, R., Verma, S., & Dworkin, R. (2001). Men's work and family lives in India: The daily organization of time and emotion. *Journal of Family Psychology, 15*(2), 206–224.

Leela, D. S. (1991). Women-headed families: Problems, coping patterns, support systems and some related policy matters. In Tata Institute of Social Sciences Unit for Family Studies, *Research on families with problems in India: Issues and implication: Vol. I* (pp. 88–102). Bombay: TISS.

Mehta, R. (1975). *Divorced Hindu women.* Delhi: Vikas.

Mehta, V. (1993). *Portrait of India.* New Haven: Yale University Press, pp. 458–459.

Menon, L. (1988). *Understanding child abuse in the Indian context.* Paper presented at the National Seminar on Child Abuse in India. Symposium conducted at the National Institute of Public Cooperation and Child Development, June 22–24.

Moser, C., & Bronkhorst, B. V. (1999). *Youth violence in Latin America and the Caribbean: Costs, causes and interventions.* The World Bank, August, Working Paper No. 3.

Nain, K. (1985). *Child abuse: A case study of Hassangarh village in Haryana.* Master of Philosophy Thesis. Punjab University, Chandigarh.

Narayana, A. V. (2003). Trafficking in women and children. Break the chains. *SPAN,* May/June, 16–19.

Ojha, H. (1977). Parental behaviour as perceived by the authoritarian and nonauthoritarian college students. *Psychologia: An International Journal of Psychology in the Orient, 20* (1), 49–53.

Ojha, H. & Sinha, M. (1982). Family structure and parental behavior. *Psychologia, 25,* 107–114.

Paintal, H. K., & Pandey, N. (1996). A conflict-based study of attitudes of adolescents towards their parents: Implications for parental counseling. *Indian Journal of Clinical Psychology, 23*(1), 4–11.

Panicker, R., & Nangia, P. (1992). *Working and street children of Delhi.* Noida, India: Child Labour Cell, National Labour.

Patil, G. D. (2000). *Hindu widows—A study in deprivation.* New Delhi: Gyan.

Phillips, W. S. K. (1992). *Street children of Indore.* Noida: Child Labour Cell.

Pothen, S. (1986). *Divorce: Its causes and consequences in Hindu society.* Delhi: Shakti.

Power, J. (1997). Paedophilia—What next? Retrieved May 20, 2003, from http://www.transnational.org/forum/power/1997/pow19-2.html.

Pushkarana, V. (1998). Traumatic sequels. The Week. Retrieved May 20, 2003, from http://www.the-week.com/98feb15/events4.htm.

Ramu, G. N. (1987). Indian husbands: Their role perceptions and performance in single and dual earner families. *Journal of Marriage and the Family, 49,* 903–915.

Ranasinghe, I. (n.d.). War and its effect on children. Retrieved May 20, 2003, from http://www.lankaweb.com/news/items/240700-1.html.

Rane, A. J. (1994). Dynamics of child abuse intervention. In M. Desai (Ed.). *Family and intervention: A course compendium* (pp. 161–172). Bombay: Tata Institute of Social Sciences.

Rani, V., and Khandewal, P. (1992). Family environment and interpersonal behaviour: A comparative study of dual career and single career families. *Indian Journal of Social Work, 53*(2), 232–243.

Rao, M. H. (1990). Employment of the wife and husband's participation in house work. *The Indian Journal of Social Work, 51*(3), 447–455.

Rodgers, D. (1999). Youth gangs and violence in Latin America and the Caribbean: A literature survey. The World Bank, August, Working Paper No. 4.

Sandhu, K. (2001). *Demystifying fatherhood: Variation with ages of children.* Master of Philosophy thesis submitted to Maharaja Sayajirao University of Baroda, Baroda.

Saraswathi, T. S. (1999). Adult–child continuity in India: Is adolescence a myth or an emerging reality? In T. S. Saraswathi (Ed.), *Culture, socialization, and human development* (pp. 214–232). New Delhi: Sage.

Saraswathi, T. S., & Pai, S. (1997). Socialization in the Indian context. In H. Kao and D. Sinha (Eds.). *Asian perspectives in psychology* (pp. 74–92). New Delhi: Sage Methodology Series.

Sethi, B. B., & Chaturvedi, P. K. (1992). Family and social support in the care of the mentally ill. In R. S. Murthy and B. J. Burns (Eds.), *Community mental health: Proceeding of the Indo-U.S. Symposium.* Bangalore: NIMHANS.

Sharan, M. B. (1995). *Child abuse and neglect in Indian families.* Kharagpur, India: Department of Humanities and Social Sciences, Indian Institute of Technology.

Sharma, D. (2003). *Family life experiences and psychosocial well-being of adolescents from single parent families.* Doctor of Philosophy thesis submitted to Panjab University, Chandigarh.

Sharma, D., Verma, S., & Larson, R. (2000). *Mother's employment and the daily emotional lives of their families.* Poster presentation at the XVIth Biennial Meeting of the International Society for the Study of Behavioural Development, July 11–14, 2000, Beijing, China.

Siganporia, M. (1993). Indian Muslim women: Post divorce problems and social support. *The Indian Journal of Social Work, LIV* (3), 355–363.

Singh, S. (1991). Problems of the terrorism affected families in Punjab. In Tata Institute of Social Sciences Unit for Family Studies, *Research on families with problems in India: Issues and implications: Vol. I* (pp. 204–211). Bombay: TISS.

Sinha, D. (1984). Some recent changes in the Indian family and their implications for socialization. *The Indian Journal of Social Work, XLV* (3), 271–286.

Sinha, D. (1988). Basic Indian values and behaviour dispositions in the context of national development: An appraisal. In D. Sinha & H. S. R. Kao (Eds.), *Social values and development: Asian perspectives* (pp. 31–55). New Delhi: Sage.

Sinha, D. (Ed.) (1981). *Socialization of the Indian child.* New Delhi: Concept.

Sriram, R., & Ganapathy, H. (1997). The unresolved dilemma: Child care options in agricultural contexts. *Economic and Political Weekly, 32* (43), 64–72.

Sundaram, I. S. (1993). Deleterious dimensions of divorce. *Social Welfare, XL* (5), 24–25.

UNFPA. (1998). *Socioeconomic, demographic, and reproductive health profile of adolescents in SAARC countries.* South Asia Conference on the adolescent, CA3, July 21–23, New Delhi.

Uplaonkar, A. T. (1995). The emerging rural youth: A study of their changing values towards marriage. *The Indian Journal of Social Work, LVI* (4), 415–423.

Venugopal, J. A., and Swaminathan, V. D. (1997). Adjustment patterns of husbands with working and nonworking wives. *Indian Journal of Applied Psychology, 34*(1), 19–21.

Verma, S. (1995). *Expanding time awareness: A longitudinal intervention study on time use sensitization in the Indian youth. A time use analysis.* Chandigarh, India: Government Home Science College.

Verma, S. (1999). Socialization for survival: Developmental issues among working street children in India. In M. Raffaelli & R. W. Larson (Eds.). *Homeless and working youth around the world: Exploring developmental issues* (pp. 5–18), *New Directions for child and adolescent development, 85.* San Francisco: Jossey-Bass.

Verma, S. (2000). The Indian social reality of passage to adulthood. *International Society for the Study of Behavioural Development Newsletter, 2* (37), 6–9.

Verma, S., & Bhan, T. P. (1996). *Daily life activities in the physical and social milieu of Indian street children*. Paper presented at the Fourteenth Biennial Meeting of the International Society for the Study of Behavioral Development, Quebec, Canada, August 12–16.

Verma, S., & Saraswathi, T. S. (2002). Adolescence in India. Street urchins or Silicon Valley millionaires? In B. B. Brown, R. W. Larson, & T. S. Saraswathi (Eds.), *The world's youth. Adolescence in eight regions of the globe* (pp. 105–140). Cambridge, UK: Cambridge University Press.

Verma, S., & Sharma, D. (2003). Cultural continuity amid social change: Adolescents' use of free time in India. In S. Verma and R. Larson (Eds.), *Examining adolescent leisure time across cultures. Developmental opportunities and constraints*, 99 (pp. 37–52). San Francisco: Jossey-Bass.

Yeole, C. M. (1993). A study of the adolescent view of the changing role of the mother. In A. K. Srivastava (Ed.), *Researches in child and adolescent psychology: Seminar readings.* (pp. 117–122). New Delhi: National Council of Educational Research and Training.

# 8

# *Hyo* (효) and Parenting in Korea

## KWANG-WOONG KIM

## INTRODUCTION

The purpose of this chapter is to clarify how *Hyo* (filial piety) has been reflected in Korean parenting. First, I analyze what *Hyo* has meant traditionally to Koreans, and describe how *Hyo* has dominated Korean value-systems and behaviors. Second, I explore, through the review of recent studies, how contemporary parents and children define *Hyo*. The meaning and significance of *Hyo* and the way it is reflected on parenting are explored in order to draw an inference on how *Hyo* influences Korean life patterns.

Traditionally, there are various cultural factors that have permeated Koreans' lives: *Jung* (情 Affection) and *Hahn* (恨 regret/lament/grudge), *Ja* (慈 mercy) and *Hyo* (孝), *Yon* (緣 relationship) and *Up* (業 karma), *Choong* (忠 loyalty) and *Youl* (烈 faithfulness), *Sung* (誠 wholeheartedness/sincerity) and *In* (忍 patience), *Shin* (信 trust) and *Eui* (義, righteousness), *Gyung* (敬 respect) and *Ihn* (仁 humanity), *Mot* (멋 aesthetics), and *Shinmyung* (신명 delightfulness). These traditional factors still have an influence on the way Koreans think and behave, because they have been rooted, as a collective spirit (collective unconscious), in the lives of the Korean people (Kim, 2002). These cultural factors are neither completely independent nor mutually exclusive. Rather, they interactively set the frame for Korean behavior and lifestyles, *Hyo* being the most essential element that shapes parent–child relationships and parenting in Korea.

### Koreans and Their Hyo

The history of *Hyo* goes back more than 1500 years. Stories of *Hyoja* (filial son) and *Hyohang* (filial conduct) took an integral role in *Samguk-sagi* (AD 1145) and *Samguk-yusa* (AD 1281), which are chronicles that were published during the period of the Three States (BC 57 to AD 668). During the Koryo Dynasty in which Buddhism was the national religion of Korea, *Hyo*, based on Buddhistic sutra, was emphasized. And during the Chosun Dynasty, when Confucianism was the dominant religion, *Hyo* was paralleled with *Choong* (忠 loyalty to the king and kingdom), the dominant ideology pervading people's lives. The teaching of *Hyo* (filial piety) was considered a preparation for serving the ruler of the country. Respecting one's elders was considered a preparation for serving all the elders of the country.

*Hyo* in Confucian terms originates from the thought of "father and son keeping closeness" (父子有親). Confucius and Mencius claimed that, "A father must be father like, a son must be son like" (*Analects of Confucius*), and that the "Father must be benevolent, son must be filial" (*The Book of Rites: Yegi*). These writings constitute the origin of filial culture in the Chosun Dynasty. Buddhistic *Hyo* during the Koryo Dynasty (AD 918 to 1392) explicated "the parents' infinite love of their children" and emphasized children's devotion to the parents in return (Wolun, 1995, p. 125). During the Chosun Dynasty (AD 1392 to 1910), although affection was still the basis of *Hyo*, affection and moral duty were distinguished, and mutual responsibilities of parents and offspring were emphasized.

Historical literature provides evidence that *Hyos* remains the essential way of life and culture of the Korean people. *Hyo* continues to govern the behavior of Korean parents and their children, even though 100 years have passed since the end of the Chosun Dynasty.

## The Conceptual Meaning of Hyo

### Hyo, the Relationship of Mutual Responsibility: Father's Benevolence and Son's Filial Piety.
*Hyo* is a bidirectional interpersonal responsibility between parents and children. *Hyo* is not only the concept of children's vertical obligation toward parents but also the mutual responsibility defining the way of love and interpersonal moral ethics between parents and children. The most representative phrase that explains this conception is "a father's benevolence, a son's filial piety" (Han, 1973, p. 87). In other words, *Hyo* means the relationship based on mutual responsibilities, in which "parents love their children" and "children serve and respect their parents with sincerity."

The fact that *Hyo* in the Confucian version defines moral responsibilities between parents and children indicates that parents should be affectionate and children respectful and devoted. In the same vein, *Hyo* in Buddhism defines parents' infinite love and children's payback for the love. Therefore, *Hyo* is completed only when parents and children fulfill their respective roles. It is important to note that parents' benevolence and children's respect comes unconditionally. Therefore, children's filial piety is neither conditioned by a father's benevolence, nor vice versa. The father's benevolence and son's duties are conceived to be God-given ethics that occur simultaneously and spontaneously.

### Hyo, as Social Ethics: Good Standing and the Rule of Behavior.
The ultimate goal of *Hyo*, written in *Hyo-Gyung* (*The Book of Filial Duty*), is "good standing and self-realization" and "realizing the ideal value." "Good standing" means becoming an independent human being who has the

right self-identity. The nature of *Hyo* starts with relationships between parents and their children; this expands to loving neighbors and the love of all human beings in the world (Ryu, 1995). Thus, according to the principles of *Hyo*, a rightly cultivated personal life leads to a properly regulated family life which, in turn, brings an orderly national life, and ultimately leads to peace in this world. In this sense, *Hyo* is viewed as the harmony of the nature and the order of the universe.

### Hyo as an Educational Principle: Stern Fathering and Benevolent Mothering.

Traditionally in Korea, *Hyo* has been the basis of education of children. Filial education is the responsibility of parents. Traditionally, education is carried out in a stern manner. The typical method is called "stern fathering and benevolent mothering." In traditional Korea, fathers are supposed to be stern yet loving. And the appropriate role of the mother was to be benevolent. These different parental roles have been the main pillars of child education in traditional Korean families (Chung et al., 1996a). In traditional Korea, the principle of stern fatherhood and benevolent motherhood means that a father loves the children but should discipline children sternly when they behave inadequately. On the other hand, a mother should nurture children when they do well, and also tolerate them and love them even when they behave inadequately. Therefore, a father's sternness and a mother's love constitute the balanced acts in framing a child's character (Lee, 1995a).

In these regards, sternness has important meaning in *Hyo*, because the essence of *Hyo* is love and respect. Love alone does not actualize *Hyo*. Respect is the combination of "love" and "a feeling of awe" (Lee, 1995a). This feeling of awe constituting *Hyo* is shaped by the principle of stern fatherhood and benevolent motherhood.

## THE PRACTICAL VIRTUES OF *HYO*

To date, the empirical study of *Hyo* has not been extensive. In 1996, however, a small number of scholars interested in the traditional conception of filial piety and parenting in Korea proposed to examine, empirically, the practical virtues of filial piety (Chung et al., 1996a, 1996b, 1997). These scholars established specific guidelines for filial practice and utilized principles of behavioral science research to guide their work (e.g., Kim, Lee, Bang, & Koo, 2000; Kim, Kim, & Chung, 2002, 2003).

The list of practical virtues of *Hyo* proposed by Chung et al. (1996a, 1996b, 1997) especially emphasized the mutual responsibilities and interdependency between parents and children. The list of practical virtues was composed of 12 items of parental mercy and of children's filial piety.

### Twelve Virtues of Parental Mercy

*Soo-shin* (Self Cultivation). In traditional Korean culture, *Hyo* education of children started with the parents' own cultivation. Cultivation of oneself depends on keeping one's heart and mind balanced. This applies not only to educating children, but also to parents' management of public affairs. Parenting and family life begin with self-discipline.

*Mo-bum* (Modeling). Parents are significant models, and parental behavior is significant in setting the value standards for their children. Parents create situations in which the expression of values becomes salient (Kim, 1999).

*Chek-im* (Responsibility). Traditional Korean principles suggest that it is the responsibility of parents to be teachers of their sons and daughters. For example, in the education part of Sa-so-jul it is revealed that "Not teaching your son will ruin your own family. And not teaching your daughter will ruin other families." Consequently, teaching children is a parent's responsibility.

*Jung-sung* (Wholeheartedness/Devotion). Parental devotion to childcare starts from the onset of pregnancy. Lessons in the Yul-nyu-jon (Devoted Wives Stories) became the model of attentive child education. Even after the children are grown up, it was a common practice for Korean parents to pray for the children's health and success at an altar with a bowl of pure water.

*Heui-saeng* (Sacrifice). Korean parents believe that children should be raised without parental sacrifice.

*In-nae* (Patience). Korean ancestors have conceived of patience as a necessary characteristic in the socialization of children.

*Om-chin* (Stern Fatherhood). Stern fatherhood and benevolent motherhood are basic principles of parent–child relationships and child education in Korean homes. Parents try to avoid uncontrolled love; instead, a balance between sternness and benevolence is viewed as the best principle in child-rearing.

*Jon-joong* (Respect for Children). The Korean proverb that "Children grown in respect become respectable adults," is a guideline of child education. In Korea, the thought of child-centered education, that children should be treated with respect, has been transmitted for a long time.

*Guan-sim* (Attention/Concern). Traditionally, Korean parents have paid keen attention to their children. Korean parents' attention to their children has to do with such values as devotion, patience, and respect as mentioned above.

*Ga-reu-chim* (Lesson). Dong-mong-sun-sub (Lessons for the Children) prescribes that "Parents teach children with correct principles to prevent falling into wrongdoing"; And Sa-so-jul (士小節) teaches that "A newborn baby-horse cannot become a good adult-runner if it is not trained in a stern manner. Along the same lines, a young child cannot become a proper adult without proper education." These lessons illuminate how Korean traditions place a strong emphasis of teaching on child education.

*Guan-dae* (Generosity/Tolerance). Generosity is the eleventh value of parenthood. Generosity is also considered to be a basic characteristic trait of teachers in recruiting them. The "Motherhood" chapter of Na-hoon

(Lesson for Women) describes the desirable characteristics of young children's teachers as being generous, benevolent, polite, sincere, and taciturn. This shows the importance of generosity for caretakers of children.

*Mid-um* (Trust). Trust is a basic element of any human relationship. Traditionally, Koreans tended to emphasize trust as a basic foundation of human relationships. When parents do not trust their children, any lessons or expectations for the children are useless.

## Twelve Virtues of Children's Filial Piety

*Gam-sa* (Gratitude/Appreciation). Gratitude to one's parents for one's birth and life is the starting point of filial piety. It is a fundamental and absolute attitude towards the parent.

*Soo-shin* (Self Cultivation). Because parents gave life to the child, the child should preserve the body thoroughly and cultivate the mind clearly for their parents' sake.

*Bong-yang* (Supporting Parents' Sustenance). Supporting parents' sustenance is a basis of Hyo (filial piety). Even though it is considered a minor filial piety, there is no major filial piety without supporting parents' sustenance.

*An-lak* (Comfort). Securing the physical and emotional comfort of the parents is an important part of Hyo.

*Gong-gyung* (Respect of Parents). Respecting one's parents is assumed as the key element of filial piety.

*Choong-gan* (Point Out Parents' Wrongdoing in a Polite Manner). It is not genuine filial piety to obey parents if you permit them to commit wrongdoing. Children are to advise parents politely when they commit such wrongdoings.

*Seung-zee* (Inheriting Parents' Will/Follow Parents' Directions). It is a duty of children to respect their parents' will and teachings.

*Ip-shin* (Good Standing and Success in Life). The essence of Hyo is not confined to the relationship between parents and children. The ultimate goal of Hyo is to cultivate one's personality, study hard, achieve success in life, contribute to society, and polish the reputation of the family name.

*Choo-mo* (Cherishing the Deceased Parents). Remembering and cherishing deceased parents are expected behaviors of Hyo.

*Jull-ze* (Moderation/Controlling of Desire). Hyo is not confined to the human relationship between parents and their children. Hyo also involves abstaining from all kinds of excessive desire and to follow the natural principle by obeying universal harmony and human dignity.

*Ye-eui* (Etiquette). Hyo requires showing appropriate behavior and etiquette to other people as well as to the parents.

*Woo-joo Cho-hwa* (Universal Harmony). Maintaining harmony with the universe is the optimal goal of *Hyo*.

# PRACTICAL GUIDELINES OF *HYO*

The following are practical guidelines of *Hyo*. These guidelines of *Hyo* were made in the context of modern life of Korea (Chung et al., 1997; Kim et al., 2000).

## Practical Guidelines of Parental Mercy

    *Soo-shin* (Parents Self Discipline/Moral Cultivation)
- Demonstrating proper attitude and behavior in front of children and spouse
- Making an effort to maintain a harmonious and peaceful family life
- Making an effort to understand children
- Keeping reasonable expectations of children
- Learning parents' appropriate role according to children's developmental stages

    *Mo-bum* (Modeling)
- Providing adequate financial conditions for the family
- Keeping authority as an elder
- Being the model of honesty and righteousness
- Model loving and respecting grandparents
- Creating a wholesome family culture

    *Chek-im* (Responsibility)
- Making efforts to accomplish the common goal of the family
- Taking responsibility of supporting the family
- Establishing the norms and the values of the family

    *Jung-sung* (Wholeheartedness/Devotion)
- Doing one's best to take care of children
- Paying careful attention to the developmental needs of children
- Making an effort to spend time with children
- Taking conversation with children sincerely

    *In-nae* (Patience/Tolerance)
- Maintain composure when you are angry
- Refrain from too many instructions or excessive praise
- Restrain from proposing a premature solution

    *Om-chin* (Stern Father)
- Giving precise discipline for children's faults
- Interact with children sternly as well as lovingly
- Establish rules and standards for the social order of the family
- Refrain from using degrading or harsh language when scolding children

    *Jon-joong* (Respect)
- Respecting the individuality and independent thinking of children
- Expressing love and concern to your children
- Recognizing children's life goals
- Accepting individual differences among your children
- Taking other's children seriously as much as one's own children
- Not blaming or spanking children easily even when they make mistakes

*Guan-sim* (Attention/Concern)
  -Investing time in making intimate relationships
  -Guiding children's thoughts and behaviors
  -Listening to what children say with an open mind so that children feel free to talk

*Ga-reu-chim* (Lessons)
  -Providing prenatal education
  -Letting children be aware of their thoughts
  -Teaching them correct behavior
  -Disciplining without scolding or put-downs
  -Advising them to clean their body and clothes
  -Teaching adherence to rules and social order
  -Teaching family values
  -Teaching safety
  -Teaching respect for others
  -Teaching protecting the environment
  -Teaching self-confidence and self-control
  -Teaching taking pride in their family
  -Teaching participation in family affairs
  -Teaching loving their neighbors
  -Teaching having harmonious relationships with others
  -Teaching participation in family events
  -Teaching not to intrude on others
  -Concerning and guiding proper friendships
  -Teaching diligence and the worth of labor
  -Teaching adjusting creatively to a changing society

*Guan-dae* (Generosity)
  -Pointing out children's mistakes specifically and giving lessons only with love
  -Being patient and waiting until children are aware of their faults
  -Trying to find children's merits instead of shortcomings
  -Being generous, even when children don't seem to have a talent
  -Tolerating the generational gap

*Mid-um* (Trust)
  -Trusting one's own children
  -Making an effort to help children trust their parents

*Heui-saeng* (Sacrifice)
  -Taking worth of giving birth and nurturing children
  -Admitting that guiding children righteously takes the sacrifice of parents

## Practical Guidelines of Children's Filial Piety

*Gam-sa* (Gratitude/Appreciation)
  -Appreciation for the parents giving birth to and nurturing them
  -Expressing thanks with words or actions

*Soo-shin* (Self Discipline/Cultivation of Oneself)
  -Maintaining health through proper management of the body and spirit
  -Managing self through a regulated life
  -Knowing the skill of controlling anger and not easily getting angry
*Bong-yang* (Supporting Parents' Sustenance)
  -Not treating parents' possessions mindlessly
  -Discussing with parents important affairs and problems
  -Spending more time with parents
  -Taking care of parents' comfort
  -Taking care of parents' health
  -Talking with parents in an open-minded manner
*An-lak* (Physical Comfort)
  -Keeping their parents' minds peaceful
  -Giving priority to parents
  -Making their parents happy, with smiles
  -Refrain from making their parents worry
  -Let parents know about their whereabouts
*Gong-gyung* (Respect of Parents)
  -Behaving politely in front of parents
  -Respecting other's parents politely
  -Not doing what parents forbid
  -Respecting yourself and others politely
*Choong-gan* (Point Out Parents' Wrongdoing With Polite Manner)
  -Not defending yourself prematurely when parents' condemnation
    seems unfair
  -Respecting the desire of parents
  -Suggesting advice politely when parents commit wrongdoings
*Seung-zee* (Inheriting Parents' Will/Following Parents' Directions)
  -Paying attention to parents' will
  -Trying to obey parents' intentions even when personal opinions are
    different
  -Doing one's best to live a fulfilling life in succession of parents' hopes
*Ip-shin* (Good Standing and Success in Life)
  -Accomplishing what you want through fulfilling your tasks
  -Becoming a useful person in society
*Choo-mo* (Cherishing Deceased Parents)
  -Making time to listen to stories about ancestors
  -Appreciating ancestors' favors and accomplishments
  -Serving ancestors attentively
  -Remembering parents' wishes after they die
*Jul-ze* (Moderation/Abstention of Desire)
  -Having the habit of being frugal and economical
  -Controlling own desires and serving others
  -Refraining from buying overly expensive goods
  -Dealing with emotion and behavior properly

*Ye-eui* (Etiquette)
- -Proper greetings
- -Using formal speech
- -Taking polite attitudes toward parents
- -Abiding by social norms and public etiquette
- -Yielding seats to elders on subways and buses
- -Using correct titles and words

*Woo-Joo Cho-hwa* (Universal Harmony)
- -Taking care of public property
- -Acknowledging the value of ancestors' cultural inheritance
- -Recycling materials
- -Loving and preserving the natural environment leaving the same to our descendants

## KOREAN PARENTS' UNDERSTANDING OF *HYO*

Koreans' awareness of *Hyo* has changed with modernization. Awareness and attitudes about *Hyo* have changed from the rigid ideas of the Chosun Dynasty to being in harmony with the modern lifestyle of the Korean populace. This change should be regarded as an inevitable consequence caused by the transition from an agricultural to a modern industrial and technological society. In the sections that follow, I examine Korean parents' and their adolescent children's understanding of Hyo.

### Parents' Understanding of Hyo

In Table 8.1, fathers' opinions of the 12 virtues of *Ja-Hyo* (Children's Filial Piety) are presented. Two hundred and eleven fathers whose children ranged from infants to adolescents participated in the study. They were asked, "Do you think this virtue is *Hyo?*"

Of the 12 virtues, over 90 percent of Korean fathers agreed with *Gam-sa* (Thanks), *An-lak* (Comfort), *Soo-shin* (Self Discipline), *Gong-gyung* (Respect), and *Ip-Shin* (Good Standing and Success in Life). Agreement was highest regarding *Gam-sa* (Thanks), and *Choong-Gan* (Point Out Parents' Wrongdoing With Polite Manner) was the lowest.

Table 8.2 presents the result of mothers' opinions on the 12 Virtues of Children's Filial Piety. The four virtues to which over 90 percent of Korean mothers agreed were *An-lak* (Comfort), *Gong-gyung* (Respect), *Soo-shin* (Self Discipline), and *Gam-sa* (Thanks). Agreement was highest for *An-lak* (Physical Comfort), and lowest for *Choong-gan* (Point Out Parents' Wrongdoing With Polite Manner).

Taken together, the tabulated results indicated only slight, but nonsignificant differences between fathers and mothers. Generally, both mothers and fathers were almost unanimous in approving of *Gam-sa* (Thanks), *Soo-shin* (Self Discipline), *An-lak* (Physical Comfort), *Gong-gyung* (Respect), and *Ip-shin* (Good Standing and Success in Life) as indicators of *Hyo*.

TABLE 8.1   Fathers' Opinions on the 12 Virtues of *Hyo-Hang*

| Virtues of *Hyo-Hang* | Yes (%) | No (%) |
|---|---|---|
| *Gam-sa* (Gratitude/Thanks) | 99.1 | 0.9 |
| *Soo-shin* (Self Discipline) | 96.2 | 3.8 |
| *Bong-yang* (Supporting) | 87.1 | 12.9 |
| *An-lak* (Comfort) | 97.6 | 2.4 |
| *Gong-gyung* (Respect) | 96.9 | 3.1 |
| *Choong-gan* (Point Out . . .) | 69.3 | 30.7 |
| *Seung-zee* (Inheriting Will) | 84.1 | 15.9 |
| *Ip-shin* (Good Standing . . .) | 91.0 | 9.0 |
| *Choo-Mo* (Cherishing . . .) | 86.7 | 13.3 |
| *Jull-ze* (Moderation) | 76.1 | 23.9 |
| *Ye-eui* ( Etiquette) | 77.4 | 22.6 |
| *Woo-joo Cho-hwa* (Harmony . . .) | 69.8 | 30.2 |

*Note:* N = 211.

TABLE 8.2   Mothers' Opinions on the 12 Virtues of *Hyo-Hang*

| Virtues of *Hyo-Hang* | Yes (%) | No (%) |
|---|---|---|
| *Gam-sa* (Gratitude/Thanks) | 94.9 | 5.1 |
| *Soo-shin* (Self Discipline) | 95.7 | 4.3 |
| *Bong-yang* (Supporting) | 78.5 | 22.5 |
| *An-lak* (Comfort) | 99.2 | 0.8 |
| *Gong-gyung* (Respect) | 96.1 | 3.9 |
| *Choong-gan* (Point Out . . .) | 62.6 | 37.4 |
| *Seung-zee* (Inheriting Will) | 77.3 | 22.7 |
| *Ip-shin* (Good Standing . . .) | 89.4 | 10.6 |
| *Choo-Mo* (Cherishing . . .) | 78.8 | 21.2 |
| *Jull-ze* (Moderation) | 76.6 | 23.4 |
| *Ye-eui* ( Etiquette) | 78.8 | 20.8 |
| *Woo-joo Cho-hwa* (Harmony . . .) | 72.4 | 27.6 |

*Note:* N = 371.

The fathers' agreement rates tended to be higher than the mothers for *Bong-yang* (Supporting Parents' Sustenance), *Choong-gan* (Point Out Parents' Wrongdoing with Polite Manner), *Seung-zee* (Inheriting Parents' Will), and *Choo-mo* (Cherishing the Deceased Parents). Perhaps fathers' attitudes regarding *Hyo* are more action-oriented than the mothers'. Clearly, the analyses presented do not allow an understanding of why fathers and mothers may have somewhat different ideas about the defining properties of *Hyo*. This remains a question for further empirical study.

## Children's Understanding of Hyo

The following data present children's agreements or disagreements with the 12 virtues of *Hyo-Hang* (Chung et al., 1993a). Six hundred and forty-eight students (289 boys, 359 girls) from elementary school, middle school, high school, and college were included in this study. Agreement rates of children on the virtues of *Hyo-Hang* (Filial Conduct) are presented by gender in Table 8.3. Sex differences were somewhat apparent in the data. Thus, for example, for the age group of 16 to 20 years, the statistical analysis revealed that there was significant difference on *Seung-zee* (Inheriting Will) between boys and girls ($\chi^2 = 3.92$, $df = 1$, $p < .05$). For the age group of 16 to 20, the statistical analysis revealed that there was a significant difference on *Ip-shin* (Good Standing) between boys and girls ($\chi^2 = 8.79$, $df = 1$, $p < .005$). For the age group of 21 to 26, the statistical analysis revealed that there was a significant difference on *Jull-je* (Moderation) between boys and girls ($\chi^2 = 9.22$, $df = 1$, $p < .005$). For the age group of 10 to 15, the statistical analysis revealed that there was a significant difference on *Ye-eui* (Etiquette) between boys and girls ($\chi^2 = 11.21$, $df = 1$, $p < .005$).

Looking at the agreement rates of the children on traditional virtues of *Hyo-Hang* (Filial Conduct), there were similarities and differences between them and their parents. Their agreement rates on *Gam-sa* (Thanks), *Soo-shin* (Self Discipline),

**TABLE 8.3** Children's Agreement Rates on the Traditional Virtues of *Hyo* by Gender

| Virtues of *Hyo-Hang* | Age 10–15 | | Age 16–20 | | Age 21–26 | |
|---|---|---|---|---|---|---|
| | Boys (N=121) | Girls (N=188) | Boys (N=105) | Girls (N=134) | Boys (N=61) | Girls (N=34) |
| *Gam-sa* (Thanks) | 97.5 | 93.1 | 92.4 | 92.5 | 93.4 | 94.1 |
| *Soo-shin* (Self Discipline) | 95.0 | 91.4 | 93.3 | 95.5 | 96.7 | 97.1 |
| *Bong-yang* (Supporting) | 76.5 | 71.4 | 75.0 | 67.4 | 82.0 | 73.5 |
| *An-lak* (Comfort) | 95.8 | 94.1 | 94.2 | 98.5 | 98.4 | 100.0 |
| *Gong-gyung* (Respect) | 84.5 | 86.9 | 89.4 | 83.7 | 98.4 | 97.1 |
| *Choong-gan* (Point Out . . .) | 72.2 | 68.3 | 61.5 | 58.2 | 54.1 | 52.9 |
| *Seung-zee* (Inheriting Will) | 65.2 | 60.4 | 59.2 | 46.3 | 70.5 | 58.8 |
| *Ip-shin* (Good Standing . . .) | 77.4 | 82.4 | 68.3 | 84.4 | 82.0 | 79.4 |
| *Choo-Mo* (Cherishing . . .) | 78.3 | 78.0 | 70.2 | 70.9 | 65.6 | 67.6 |
| *Jull-ze* (Moderation) | 61.1 | 63.2 | 57.7 | 58.5 | 50.8 | 82.4 |
| *Ye-eui* ( Etiquette) | 60.7 | 78.5 | 56.7 | 53.0 | 67.2 | 79.4 |
| *Woo-joo Cho-hwa* (Harmony . . .) | 58.8 | 63.4 | 43.3 | 51.1 | 49.2 | 52.9 |

*Gong-gyung* (Respect), and *An-lak* (Physical Comfort) were about 90 percent, much like their parents. However, *Ip-shin* (Good Standing and Success in Life) was slightly lower and the agreement rates on *Choong-gan* (Point Out Parents' Wrongdoing With Polite Manner), *Seung-zee* (Inheriting Parents' Will), *Jull-ze* (Moderation), *Ye-eui* (Etiquette), and *Woo-joo Cho-hwa* (Harmony With the Universe) were relatively lower.

One difference between parents and children was that overall the children's agreement rates appeared lower than those of the parents. Thus, it may be that the children were as able to understand *Hyo* as well as their parents. However, given that age differences were not assessed, it may well have been that with age, the children's agreements with statements about *Hyo* became more similar to those of their parents.

## KOREAN PARENTS' PRACTICING DEGREE OF *HYO*

Table 8.4 presents the results of a survey of Korean parents' practicing of *Hyo*. The data were drawn from Chung et al. (1997). The participants consisted of 211 fathers and 371 mothers who had children ranging from infants to adolescents. The practice of *Hyo* was measured on a 5-point scale with a mean of 2.5. According to Table 8.4, the parents' group reported relatively higher levels of practicing *Hyo* in terms of *Gam-sa* (Thanks), *An-lak* (Physical Comfort), *Gong-gyung* (Respect), *Ip-shin* (Good Standing and Success in Life), *Woo-joo Cho-hwa* (Harmony With the Universe), and *Soo-shin* (Self discipline). It is important to note, however, that the practice of these behaviors was in the three- to four-point range, suggesting only moderate support for the

**TABLE 8.4  Korean Parents' Degree of Education About *Hyo***

| Virtues of *Hyo* | Father<br>M (SD) | Mother<br>M (SD) |
| --- | --- | --- |
| *Gam-sa* (Thanks) | 3.55 (.53) | 3.45 (.59) |
| *Soo-shin* (Self Discipline) | 3.25 (.60) | 3.27 (.65) |
| *Bong-yang* (Supporting) | 2.87 (.80) | 2.48 (1.00) |
| *An-lak* (Comfort) | 3.39 (.58) | 3.26 (.69) |
| *Gong-gyung* (Respect) | 3.29 (.55) | 3.19 (.61) |
| *Choong-gan* (Point Out . . .) | 2.78 (.82) | 2.76 (.75) |
| *Seung-zee* (Inheriting Will) | 3.08 (.67) | 2.82 (.71) |
| *Ip-shin* (Good Standing . . .) | 3.28 (.57) | 2.97 (.63) |
| *Choo-Mo* (Cherishing . . .) | 3.12 (.82) | 2.70 (.95) |
| *Jull-ze* (Moderation) | 3.13 (.58) | 3.11 (.61) |
| *Ye-eui* ( Etiquette) | 2.87 (.49) | 3.13 (.58) |
| *Woo-joo Cho-hwa* (Harmony . . .) | 3.28 (.63) | 3.26 (.60) |

socialization of *Hyo*. The practice was relatively low in terms of *Choong-gan* (Point Out Parents' Wrongdoing with Polite Manner) and *Bong-yang* (Supporting the Parents' Sustenance).

It should be noted that the practice of *Bong-yang* (Supporting Parents' Sustenance) was quite low although this virtue is a fundamental characteristic of *Hyo*. This result could be interpreted as Korean parents subjectively regretting their own inadequacies in providing for their parents, even if they were actually supporting their parents well. Partial evidence of this interpretation stems from the finding that Korean people always consider themselves as *Bul-Hyo-Ja* (a person who is lacking *Hyo*: the Impious Son) and are repentant about it.

## KOREAN PARENTS' DEGREE OF EDUCATION REGARDING *HYO* (FILIAL PIETY) TO THEIR CHILDREN

Table 8.5 presents the result of Korean parents' degree of educating their children about *Hyo*. The participants consisted of 211 fathers and 371 mothers who had children ranging from infants to adolescents. The degree of education was measured on a 5-point scale with a mean of 2.5.

According to Table 8.5, Korean parents do emphasize educating their children regarding the virtues of *Hyo*, although the emphasis on *Bong-yang* (Supporting Parents' Sustenance), *Choong-gan* (Point Out Parents' Wrongdoing With Polite Manner), and *Seung-zee* (Inheriting Parents' Will) was relatively lower than the other virtues.

TABLE 8.5   Korean Parents' Practicing Degree of *Hyo*

| Virtues of Filial Piety | Father<br>M (SD) | Mother<br>M (SD) |
|---|---|---|
| *Gam-sa* (Thanks) | 3.39 (.64) | 3.32 (.64) |
| *Soo-shin* (Self Discipline) | 3.53 (.56) | 3.50 (.54) |
| *Bong-yang* (Supporting) | 2.69 (.76) | 2.59 (.95) |
| *An-lak* (Comfort) | 3.22 (.62) | 3.12 (.67) |
| *Gong-gyung* (Respect) | 3.48 (.48) | 3.41 (.58) |
| *Choong-gan* (Point Out . . .) | 2.84 (.84) | 2.75 (.80) |
| *Seung-zee* (Inheriting Will) | 2.91 (.70) | 2.83 (.80) |
| *Ip-shin* (Good Standing . . .) | 3.55 (.58) | 3.52 (.62) |
| *Choo-Mo* (Cherishing . . .) | 3.01 (.89) | 2.72 (.95) |
| *Jull-ze* (Moderation) | 3.38 (.58) | 3.32 (.62) |
| *Ye-eui* ( Etiquette) | 3.52 (.51) | 3.44 (.59) |
| *Woo-joo Cho-hwa* (Harmony . . .) | 3.42 (.64) | 3.47 (.58) |

## KOREAN PARENTS' PRACTICING DEGREE OF PARENTAL MERCY

*Hyo* is completed by balancing *Boo-Ja* (parents' love; parental mercy) and *Ja-Hyo* (son's filial piety). It would be inappropriate to expect that children would learn and practice *Hyo* if their parents did not provide them with loving care. Table 8.6 presents the results of the study on Korean parents' practicing degree of *Boo-Ja* (Parental Mercy). According to Table 8.6, Korean parents' practicing degrees of *Boo-Ja* (Parental Mercy) were reasonably high except for *In-nae* (Patience).

## CONCLUSION

In this chapter, I attempted to illuminate the historical and cultural meaning of Korean *Hyo* ideology. I examined contemporary Korean understanding of the meaning and practice of *Hyo*, and investigated the features that are reflected in the education of children. Empirical support was drawn from the research of Chung et al. (1996, 1997). The data appeared to confirm that *Hyo* still stands firmly in Korean people's lives and that *Hyo* is a cornerstone for the education of children.

*Hyo* is not a way of life only for Korean people. *Hyo* is also an important cultural element not only in China to which Korea owes its origin, but also in Japan and many other countries of Southeast Asia. Recently, scholars in Korea, China, and Japan have examined the nature of the *Hyo* through a modern perspective (Lee, S. S., 1995; Ts'ai, 1995; Yutaka, 1995) and have attempted to integrate *Hyo* with a reorganization of the modern ethic (Cho, 1995; Chen, 1995; Jiao, 1995). In addition, there have been attempts to reinterpret *Hyo* in the context of modern society (Dams, 1995; Lancaster, 1995). Scholars have discovered the

TABLE 8.6 Korean Parents' Degree of Education About *Hyo*

| Virtues of "Parental Mercy" | Father M (SD) | Mother M (SD) |
| --- | --- | --- |
| *Soo-shin* (Self Discipline) | 3.29 (.49) | 3.29 (.56) |
| *Mo-bum* (Role model) | 3.20 (.55) | 3.19 (.67) |
| *Chack-im* (Responsibility) | 3.17 (.59) | 3.15 (.51) |
| *Jung-sung* (Wholeheartedness) | 3.38 (.56) | 3.45 (.47) |
| *In-nae* (Patience) | 2.81 (.70) | 2.91 (.50) |
| *Um-chin* (Stern Fatherhood) | 3.25 (.40) | 3.24 (.39) |
| *Jeon-joong* (Respect for Child) | 3.32 (.46) | 3.38 (.53) |
| *Guan-sim* (Concern/Attention) | 3.20 (.51) | 3.30 (.47) |
| *Gr-re-chim* (Lesson/Instruction) | 3.49 (.63) | 3.50 (.54) |
| *Guan-dai* (Generosity) | 3.19 (.55) | 3.40 (.51) |
| *Mid-um* (Trust) | 3.32 (.53) | 3.19 (.78) |
| *Heui-saeng* (Sacrifice) | 3.25 (.66) | 3.09 (.44) |

meaning of *Hyo* in Western and African cultural cultures (Bahemuka, 1995; Helmy, 1995). As such, selected aspects of *Hyo* appear to be universal.

In summary, from the research of Korean scholars, *Hyo* is a principal element driving the lives of Korean parents and their children (Kim, Kim, & Chung, 2002, 2003). The spirit of *Hyo* will be held in an important position in the minds of Koreans even though times may change. Korean children are affected by *Hyo* ideology in their socialization to become Koreans.

## REFERENCES

Bahemuka, J. M. (1995). *The impact of social change on filial piety within the African family.* Paper presented at the International Conference of "Hyo" Philosophy, May 15–17, Sungnam, Korea (Organized by The Academy of Korean Studies).

Chen, S. F. (1995). *Confucian methodology of filial piety education and its application in contemporary society.* Paper presented at the International Conference of "Hyo" Philosophy, May 15–17, Sungnam, Korea (Organized by The Academy of Korean Studies).

Cho, N. K. (1995). *The essence of filial piety and its method of application in society.* Paper presented at the International Conference of "Hyo" Philosophy, May 15–17, Sungnam Korea (Organized by The Academy of Korean Studies).

Chung, O. K., Kim, K. W., Yoon, C. H., Yoo, G. H., Choi, Y. H., Choi, K. S., Kim, D. C., & Jeong, H. H. (1996a). Perceptions and practices of Korean's filial piety "Hyo". *Korean Journal of Home Economics, 34*(6), 387–403.

Chung, O. K., Kim, K. W., Yoon, C. H., Yoo, G. H., Choi, Y. H., Choi, K. S., Kim, D. C., & Jeong, H. H. (1996b). Parenting and socialization of Korean traditional society. *Korean Journal of Family Welfare, 1,* 46–66.

Chung, O. K., Kim, K. W., Yoon, C. H., Yoo, G. H., Choi, Y. H., Choi, K. S., Kim, D. C., & Jeong, H. H. (1997). Perception of parental filial piety and child-rearing behavior. *Korean Journal of Child Studies, 18*(1), 81–107.

Dams, T. (1995). *The doctrine and practices of filial piety in the framework of socio-economic order.* Paper presented at the International Conference of "Hyo" Philosophy, May 15–17, Sungnam, Korea (Organized by The Academy of Korean Studies).

Han, G. O. (1973). "Hyo-Do" (孝道) and education. In S. B. Yoon (Ed.), "*Hyo*" (pp. 45–82). Seoul: Seoul-Munhwasa.

Han, J. S. (1998). A study on the educational growth motives of Korean women. *Journal of Asian Women, 37,* 67–99.

Helmy, E. I. (1995). *Filial piety's development in Egypt.* Paper presented at the International Conference of "Hyo" Philosophy, May 15–17, Sungnam, Korea (Organized by The Academy of Korean Studies).

Jiao, G. C. (1995). *Filial piety and Chinese society.* Paper presented at the International Conference of "Hyo" Philosophy, May 15–17, Sungnam, Korea (Organized by The Academy of Korean Studies).

Kim, J. H., Kim, K. W., & Chung, O. B. (2002). *Investigation of Korean parents' understanding of filial piety: Is it still working as an educational objectives?* Paper presented at the annual meeting of the Association for Childhood Education International. April 3–6, 2002, San Diego.

Kim, J. H., Kim, K. W., & Chung, O. B. (2003). *Korean children's understanding of filial piety: Challenges and implications for childhood education.* Paper presented at the annual meeting of the Association for Childhood Education International. April 13–16, Phoenix, AZ.

Kim, K. W. (1999). Principles of Korean traditional home education. *The Journal of Humanities*, 8, Kangnam University, 237–262.

Kim, K. W. (2002). *Child: From home to society*. Paper presented at the Symposium on Ecological Perspectives in Home Economics. Ewha University, Seoul, Korea.

Kim, K. W., Lee, S. H., Bang, E. R., & Koo, B. Y. (2000). *A model of Korean home education*. National Committee of Youth Protection, Korea.

Kim, Y. H., Lee, I. H., & Park, H. J. (1993). *Educational enthusiasm of Korean people*. Seoul: Korean Educational Development Institute.

Lancaster, L. (1995). *The role of filial piety in Buddhism: A study of religious spread and adaptation*. Paper presented at the International Conference of "Hyo" Philosophy, May 15–17, Sungnam, Korea (Organized by The Academy of Korean Studies).

Lee, K. H., Yoo, H. R., Sohn, J. S., & Lee, H. W. (1993). Thoughts of traditional home education in Korea. Collection of Treatises 93–18, Sungnam, Korea: The Academy of Korean Studies.

Lee, K. H. (1995a). *Formation of personality and education: An investigation of filial piety focusing on education what should be*. Seoul: Wonmisa.

Lee, K. H. (1995b). Filial piety as an educational method. Paper presented at the International Conference of "Hyo" Philosophy, May 15–17, Sungnam, Korea (Organized by The Academy of Korean Studies).

Lee, K. H., K, J. E., Kim, K. W., Yoo, G. H., & Choi, K. S. (1997). *An exploratory study of new family education*. Sungnam, Korea: The Academy of Korean Studies.

Lee, S. S. (1995). The essence of the doctrine of filial piety and modern society. Paper presented at the International Conference of "Hyo" Philosophy, May 15–17, Sungnam, Korea (Organized by The Academy of Korean Studies).

Ryu, J. S.(1995). "Hyo" education for children in Chosun Dynasty. Paper presented at the Symposium in 1995 Spring Semester, Korean Association of Child Studies.

Sung, G. T. (1995). *"Hyo" for New Age*. Seoul: Yonsei University Press.

Ts'ai, M. S. (1995). The essence of filial piety and its modern significance. Paper presented at the International Conference of "Hyo" Philosophy, May 15–17, Sungnam, Korea (Organized by The Academy of Korean Studies).

Wolun (月雲). (2000). *The story of "Hyo" in Buddhism*. Seoul: Chogyejeong.

Yoon, S. B. (1975). *Contemporary Society and "Hyo-Do" (孝道)*. Seoul: Eulyou-munhwasa.

Yutaka, Y. (1995). Filial obligations and justice. Paper presented at the International Conference of "Hyo" Philosophy, May 15–17, Sungnam, Korea (Organized by The Academy of Korean Studies).

# Index

Lightning Source UK Ltd.
Milton Keynes UK
UKOW05f1812281013

219961UK00009B/185/P